# REALITY
# AND EMPATHY

# REALITY
# AND EMPATHY

## Physics, Mind, and Science in the 21st Century

# ALEX COMFORT

*Neuropsychiatric Institute, UCLA*

**State University of New York Press**   Albany

Published by
State University of New York Press, Albany

© 1984 by Books & Broadcasts Inc.

For information, address State University of New York
Press, State University Plaza, Albany, N.Y., 12246

Library of Congress Cataloging in Publication Data

Comfort, Alex, 1920-
  Reality and empathy.

  Bibliography: p.
  Includes index.
  1. Metaphysics.  2. Science—Philosophy.  3. Intui-
tion.  I. Title.  II. Title: World models.
BD111.C624  1983        110        83-9318
ISBN 0-87395-762-8
ISBN 0-87395-763-6 (pbk.)


10 9 8 7 6 5 4 3 2 1

*It is the duty of the author of a scientific paper to make the subject matter clear to at least two people, one of whom may be the author.*

Freeman Dyson

For my wife Jane

# CONTENTS

## List of Illustrations

# THE STUDY
# OF WORLD MODELS

Worlds are created by brains. At a simple level, bees, migratory birds, dogs and even limpets, which return to a particular spot after feeding, contain internal maps of their surroundings. Humans, who think abstractly, create more complicated inferential maps going beyond their known surroundings, to include the world, celestial objects, real and hypothetical beings, and the past and future as well as the present.

Making world models is a familiar human activity. In our culture they are made on the basis of what we call science, meaning the testing of intuitive or imaginative hypotheses by observation and experiment, conducted upon something which we call "objective reality." Both primitive and scientific world models have, of course, to include the observer, the I who is doing the imagining, observing or experimenting, and the objective world, which appears and presents consistency of behavior to that observing I.

I originally wrote these notes to order my ideas for discussion with one particular group of people, psychiatric residents. These are some of the brightest students one encounters in medicine—bright, perhaps, in a slightly different way from young physicists. They are grounded in science, a fair number of them have read some philosophy, and they are occupationally concerned with people, in the case of my group, with old people. Now old age and terminal illness are two conditions which render the significance of world models urgent. The models we make represent not so much human intellectual curiosity as human response to anxiety, and a great many apparently unrelated anxieties boil down, if we examine them, to the arch-source of human insecurity, the individual's discovery of death (Yalom 1980).

Psychiatrists encounter the world models by which people live, ranging in California from hard-line scientific mechanism to Fundamentalist Christianity, from modern Judaism to exotic and theosophical constructions; but all of these appeal wherever possible to science as arbiter, if only to assert that it does not disprove the Noachic Flood. At the intersection of death anxiety and science stands the physician. If he is a hard-line physician, his own world model is likely to be that of Newton and Helmholtz in which the body is a classical order system, and mind its epiphenomenon. Or he may have a religious or humanistic position of his own, which he is (properly) unwilling to press on patients. Psychiatrists, however, are more open to the generality of world models; they see how these models affect their patients' sense of the significance or absurdity of their lives, and how some patients adopt soft models for reassurance, while others adopt hard-line scientism as a refuge from unwelcome feelings and as a source of personal certainty. Moreover, it is to his colleague the psychiatric physician that the hard-liner in other disciplines confides his problems.

Since the advent of Christianity, Western society has been addicted to certainty. Until the seventeenth century, certainty was expounded by the Church. There followed a longish interval of struggle, and by the end of the nineteenth century, certainty was being expounded by science, in the works of great rationalist educators such as T.H. Huxley. *What* was expounded was a vigorous, austere, coherent reductionism which saw cosmology, biology and human experience as a self-running machine, offering no sentimental consolations and no second chances. After the supernatural world of Christian belief, this no-nonsense model called for a high degree of stoicism— life was real, earnest and short (it was up to our ethical sense whether it would also be nasty and brutish). Remarkably little has been said or written about the psychiatric effects of this very athletic super-Puritan model, which called on whole publics to renounce their defense mechanisms, burn their intellectual teddy bears, and accept their status as mortal and contingent parts of a non-noetic but potentially fully-comprehensible universe. There were compensations, of course: getting rid of the stranglehold of religious dogma, which oppressed nineteenth century believers very much as the Party Line now oppresses intelligent Marxists—relief from the weird sexual and intellectual prescriptions of Nobodaddy. The new religion had prescriptions

of its own, mostly good ones, such as openminded respect for experimental evidence, fearlessness, and the rejection of wishful thinking.
The environment was undoubtedly healthy, but a little chilly for most
people to inhabit. Moreover—because the reductionist shirt really
looked seamless when placed on the Newtonian-Darwinian-Helm-
holtzian universe—"science" unwittingly ran the risk of doing what
Christianity had done before it and pulling the wagons around a group
of core teachings (causality, mechanism, stochastic-genetic evolution,
the equation between mental and neural activity): in defending these
one was defending not hypotheses but Science itself—re-examination
was on the point of becoming "unscientific."

The great achievement of rationalist science, however, has been
its capacity to stay loyal to its original rubric. About the turn of the
century, the seamless shirt began to unravel where it covered, not the
"soft" disciplines like discursive psychology or speculative evolutionary genetics, but the "hardest" of scientific subjects, namely physics.

This is where we came in. For most of the nonscientist public (our
patients) and for all the middle order disciplines (biology, medicine,
psychology and so on), the Huxleyan-Newtonian world effectively
still stands. Meanwhile physics, on which all the others, in a reductionist model, depend, is back wrestling with the problems which
exercised the Eleatic Greeks before "certainty" crystallized as a feature
of civilizations.

Psychiatry is not greatly concerned with what people are, which
might be unknowable. It is greatly concerned, since it addresses patients, with what they feel or experience themselves to be. In a militantly scientific culture, however, these two are inseparable. World
models are the paradigm and reflection of what people "feel themselves to be," as well as the source of information or folklore on which
that self-experience is based, and through which it is interpreted.
Moreover, anxieties arising from the awareness of death, insignificance, "absurdity", and the human predicament generally interact
with, and can be set off or allayed by our world models. These concerns underlie all human anxiety—sexual, personal or free-floating.
Noise from this source feeds into science (one need only recall the
uproar over Darwin or Freud). The Newtonian model, helped out as it
was by supernaturalism, tended to reassurance; the positivistic model
ditched supernatural consolations and tended to realistic stoicism.
Post-Einsteinian models and the rapid rate of advance in physical and
cosmological research, which feeds straight down in garbled form to
nonscientific people, tend to confusion. They are fluid and hard to
understand, unless one has recourse to higher mathematics, and they
are a wellspring of science fiction. Many educated people have given
up on science as a source of any reasonably invariant world model,

and may regress to cargo cults, as the Papuans did when confronted with a chaos of innovation during World War II. If one talks about extraterrestrial visitors or the reality of witchcraft, some of them mumble "nihil obstat." Now a comprehensible world view is hard work, and must indeed be provisional, because its experimental bases are provisional, but psychiatrists must devoutly wish that their patients had one.

Psychiatric residents have the inheritance of science and so they know about physics, about statistics, about drug trials. They have also an occupational experience in reading back the logics and imageries of the mind. They ask penetrating questions about the status of psychoanalytic ideas as science, about the relation of mind and experience to reality, about belief systems and about parapsychology. They then, as they are taught to do if they have been properly taught, make up their minds on these matters by reference to their own clinical experience. They read Karl Popper on scientific logic, and criticize his critique of historicism. It requires agility to be on the receiving end of such seminars. But one does not have to prove to such an audience that world models affect the self-assessment and self-experience of patients. In a society whose world models are confused, self-made or optional, with the support of older consensus models withdrawn, "How do you see yourself?" becomes a key diagnostic question.

Obviously not everyone who reads this book (I hope) will be in the business of medicine. Nor is the idea to give insight to other professionals concerning the motives which influence their choice of models, for interpretation which is unsought is at best impertinent and at worst actually harmful. Nor do any of us really need a world model, however reassuring, which is superstitious, arbitrary, pseudoscientific, or in flat contradiction of observable fact. But since making world models is one of the most critical activities for the actual business of living, and since in doing it we now appeal to science as gatekeeper, there is something to be said for talking about it at length, even if without firm conclusions, and even if the object of the study is to establish the extreme difficulty of reaching conclusions as firm as those which many hard-science colleagues feel they have reached.

Any book which tackles world models has to be able to move fairly freely among three kinds of intellectual objects:

(1) *Facts*, which are limited statements that agree with the results of experiment or observation

(2) *Theories or hypotheses*, which are specific models in the form "If A is true, it implies a, b, c, d" with the aim of going on to ascertain, if possible, whether any of a, b, c, d are demonstrably *un*true. In that case, A is either false or in need of substantial revision

(3) *Intuitions* or *guesses* concerning overall pattern, which serve effectively, if one really wants to know whether a model has substance or not, as an agenda for forming theories.

World models, whether we got them from our culture or thought them up for ourselves, commonly contain all three of the above. Theories (hypotheses) are a special invention of the scientific method. The formalism is that they cannot be confirmed, only refuted. This is, in fact, a little too rigid, because the definition of clear cases can be a problem. It is not a hypothesis to assert that your next child will be a boy, but simply a prediction, which can obviously be falsified or confirmed by inspection of the baby in due course. It is a hypothesis arising from some reflections of mine on genetic mechanisms, that persons over six feet tall with hairy ears should father more boys than girls, and this can be refuted. If its prediction is found accurate, however, the theory on which I made the count could still be wrong, and in any event it will not be the whole truth and nothing but the truth about genetics. Some hypotheses can come close to confirmation. The guess that there is a genetic code composed of words, which is represented chemically in a particular way, may not be "confirmed" in Karl Popper's sense (Popper 1935, 1959) when I find that by writing the language chemically I can code the substances which I expected. It is confirmed to the extent that I can now make insulin or interferon and, in fact, go on writing the language until I hit snags and have to broaden the model. A Martian can confirm his hypothesis that there is a language called Chinese, and that he has learned it by listening to the radio, when he gives a lecture in Shanghai and is manifestly understood. Popper's point is really that true means heuristically useful. No theory is true in any wider sense, simply because its limits cannot be defined in advance, i.e., one cannot now predict what future findings in other areas will require of it. Some early theories in physics which looked, when constructed, like footbridges, have since become thoro-fares for ten-ton trucks. Bad theories collapse early. Good theories have a long run before encountering a system break.

But most world models of the empathic kind (those which coincide with feelings) are not theories. They are semi-intuitive pictures of reality, of Wittgenstein's "everything which is the case," to which we certainly can apply reason or logic (they feel best to us if there are no glaring inconsistencies), but which we cannot test as wholes, except perhaps in the way we can test our supposed knowledge of Chinese by seeing whether we can conduct business in Shanghai. On the other hand there are some critical points in most world models at which they depend on one effective theory which is refutable by a single observation. This, moreover, may be some observation already made and reported, but ignored at the time, because it was not critical at that time.

By empathy I mean incorporation going beyond intellectual assent. We know the earth is spherical, and many actually have flown around it, but not until astronauts saw it *ab extra* can its roundness be said to have been empathized. Even short of this experience, people have long since ceased to be afraid of falling off the edges of a flat Earth. With much modern work in physics, partial empathy is probably the most we can hope for, though if we are mathematicians we have a special kind of incorporation which is all our own. Nor is it new for humans to take the invisible on trust. For the purposes of this book, empathy has two overlapping aspects: how we feel about the world, as a result of incorporating particular knowledge, and how the process of making knowledge incorporable affects the content we give to what is incorporated.

In my view the proper purpose of metaphysics is the study of world models. This has become a scare-word through misuse and through the bad behaviour of metaphysicians. It involves the making of new, and the description of old, world models, and the study of the way such models are formed, with the considerations, mental mechanisms, and other matters which enter into them.

Anyone who requires a non-popular but readable version of the relation between science and metaphysics should read the essay by Agassi (1964). All I am trying to do at this juncture, since we are about to jump into this expanse of water, is to provide lifebelts for readers and malpractice insurance for myself. Reasonably effective but not foolproof lifebelts can be provided by making clear the following points:

(1) *World models are not hypotheses. They are agendas for research* if one is seriously interested in checking them against "what is the case;" they are matters of uncheckable personal conviction if they are not accessible to research. Darwinism or the quantum logic models are agendas for research. Christian world models are matters of personal conviction. Psychoanalysis is a hybrid: it is an agenda for research, in that some of its practitioners' statements are refutable hypotheses (which few psychoanalytic writers have had the scientific good manners to test), but it also deals with the structure of unconscious logics, which comment on the way in which formation of world models is patterned by mentation.

There is also a class of world models, similarly hybrid, which depend on introspective research, and take the form "If you perform certain introspective exercises, you will consistently have the following experiences, which suggest a world model." These are something alien to our cultural experience for which we have not developed a serious technique of philosophical analysis, but we shall have to deal with them since, for example, some people in our culture now practice Buddhism or meditative yoga.

(2) *Pseudoscience* is not world model formation, but an attempt to justify a world model, or a part of one, en bloc by collecting anecdotal instances without the formation and testing of critical theories. In other words, it mistakes an agenda for a theory and then attempts to justify the theory by instances, rather than perform critical experiments. Instances, the equivalent of testimonials at a medicine show, are justified in model-formation, i.e., in drawing up agendas, but they are not answers to the matters on those agendas. The *reductio ad absurdum* in mathematics consists in denying what one sets out to prove, and showing that the denial leads to irrational results. Pseudoscience consists in assuming what one would like to prove and then using the assumption to show that all other assumptions lead to paradox. Psychoanalysis, Darwinism, field theory, or behaviorism are pseudoscience when they do this and a legitimate agenda when they behave themselves.

(3) *Natural history* is a model of its own. It is the detailed description of observation with little or no experiment or interpretation—neither a model/agenda nor a theory/experiment system. Its forte is the detailed compilation of instances which can subsequently lead to model-formation and experiment. Large areas of medicine concern human natural history, some of which is transferred little by little into discursive science. Over a large area—since doctors are obliged to act by using their best judgment ahead of hard science—it provides not theories but best-fit guidelines, for use as tents until permanent buildings can be constructed. Much intuitive psychodynamics, much empirical expertise, and holding operations like the "Copenhagen solution" in physics, are natural-history-type operations.

Popper's distinction between science and metaphysics omits natural history (probably correctly, since it is more lore than science and is not really concerned with testing models by the standard of facts.) By the same token, he downplays historical models, where experimentation is impossible but confirmatory or refutatory evidence may be found. One could agree that in general Darwinism is a research agenda and still be fully entitled to argue that some of its sub-sets, such as the development of mammals from reptiles, are a source of theories which can be refuted by fossil evidence. Popper's dislike of this type of model is personal, and springs from an early brush with Marxism (see Popper, 1974, Halstead 1980) which, in its political aspect, is a refutable theory because it offers social predictions, but this encounter left him disillusioned with all interpretations based on historicism.

The other type of model-hypothesis-reality testing which is left out of the Popperian canon is what might be called the Rosetta Stone Effect. It applies to languages or to models closely similar to language, such as the DNA code, in which interpretation can be considered to be verified if it produces comprehension. The decipherment of hieroglyphs makes sense of all hieroglyphs: the reading of DNA codes makes possible the synthesis of predetermined substances agreeing with our reading. This is an important case in learning to distinguish fanciful from testable constructions, because it is two-edged: a decoding can be verified if the test system is truly objective; it cannot be verified if the supposed code or language is self-sustaining and checked only against instances. This fallacy is a favorite of enthusiasts. It generates specious constructions of which the Shakespeare cyphers, many psychodynamic interpretations, and some of the more numerological excesses of Biblical prophetics are examples. The making of a world model produces others, particularly when some regularity in our heads is projected as fundamental to the universe and then (rather naturally) comes back at us as an echo.

*Consumer advisory.* If you do not clearly comprehend these distinctions, the contents of this book may be hazardous to your intellectual health and my reputation for rationality, since we are about to look at models, feelings, speculations, possibilities, and other potentially toxic material. Anyone who, after reading it, asserts that "Comfort believes in a microcosm-macrocosm model, in parapsychology, in Buddhism, in a recursive universe, etc. etc." had better read the book and especially the preceding few pages, over again.

There is an institution somewhere in Europe which offers doctorates of metaphysics (conveniently bearing on the diploma the initials M.D., and a logo including snakes and a staff) by postal tuition. I thought of including such a document in this book, to be reached and torn out only when you have got through it. Lovers of *The Magic Flute* will recall that Sarastro starts, as Masons do, by asking the initiates if they realize quite what they are getting into, and whether they intend to risk it. There will be a certain amount of cruel and unusual punishment. Instead of girls and a marching band during the intervals, I have rented from Douglas Hofstadter (Hofstadter 1980) some of the discursive animals which *he* rented from Lewis Carroll, to provide a few breaks. The sensible thing might be for those who are interested in world models, but who can't follow the *Scientific*

*American* section on recreational mathematics, to skim chapter II, 1 and 3 and chapter IV, 1 and 3, or read them with a dictionary of science. There is a first-aid station in the glossary. Thereafter, personal involvement will be greater.

# INTRODUCTION: THE CARTESIAN HOMUNCULUS REVISITED

Traditional Western makers of world models have tended to alternate their approaches between introspection and extrospection, looking in and looking out. Although, due to the invention of science, neither in nor out will ever look quite the same again, we appear today to be at a point of change. Post-Newtonian physics has been firmly committed to looking *out*. Modern physics also looks out, in that it conducts experiments on matter and energy, but these results are far less apparently autonomous. The hard-hat model of an objective reality, on which Mind has in some way become fortuitously imposed, has had to yield to a growing perception that the objective is, in form at least, a construct: what we appear to see is a function of the manner of seeing (hardly a new idea to Greek philosophy), but with the awkward complication that the cogitating I arises from the structures which it sees and orders.

Most of us, either in reaching practical decisions or in writing papers on science, take this I as given. It is part of the way we think, though we endeavour to take it out of the printed result by describing phenomena as if no individuals were there as the spectators to whom the phenomena appear. It is good manners, in fact, to write, "Six rats were sacrificed and homogenized," not "I knocked six rats on the head and reduced the bodies to a pulp," rather as an officer-sahib would say "One has to take risks for one's country," not "I take risks etc." The underlying assumption is that there was an I around to kill rats, count particles, and record the result, but we are interested in the objective and prefer to play down the observer.

Joe Blow's drama called "reality" (and for this purpose the scientist is a Joe Blow too, until he starts to ask questions) has a cast of two—I, who am doing the observing, and That, the totality which I observe. The nature of mind and the nature of observation are gnarled philosophical questions. Joe Blow can give us a more instructive picture of I, because he describes what he feels.

He experiences himself as being a black-box sitting on the surface of the planet Earth, equipped with sensors. Unlike a planetary lander, however, the output from these sensors is not telemetered to a remote observation post. Instead it is relayed directly, as experience, to Joe Blow, for Joe Blow—whatever he may be—is inside the box. If we press him for his exact station, and if he is a sighted individual, he will usually experience himself as being just posterior to his own two most-used sensors, the eyes. Other parts of the Box have a special relation to him, because he can control them without external manipulation, and his I has a constant instrument display of their status, called the body-image.

Another feature of Joe is unremarkable to us, because we are like him, but it would probably excite comment from an extraterrestrial: he has a definite location which can be described by reference to three axes, up-down, forward-backward, and left-right, and which he refers to as Here. He also has a location in another axis which is more difficult to explain, but along which he seems to be moving invisibly in a single direction at a steady rate. He describes his approximate location on this axis as Now, though, since movement is continuous, Now is a constantly-moving display. The apparent motion involves changes in Joe and in his surroundings, and since this subjective motion is constant, changes of real location affecting Here also require changes in Now. A more technical way of putting this is that Joe experiences his I as existing in a 4-space with three real dimensions, and one imaginary dimension, time.

In other words the observing I, whatever it is, experiences itself as being located at a definite point in space and time. Before we react to this by saying "Well, so is everything else which is real" it is worth looking at the bald exposition as if it were wholly new. It was Kant's most fruitful contribution to science (he was originally a physicist before taking up philosophy) that he did precisely this. His conclusion was that since whatever the behaviour and structure of That, every human interaction with it is obligatorily funnelled through an I like Joe Blow's, the constraints we impose on the term "real" are direct consequences of the imaging system in I. Kant did not put it quite like that, but in effect the solid framework of Euclidean space and ever-elapsing Time are givens which, in his view, cannot be transcended. He called them a-prioris.

Physicists have to be concerned with the kind of coordinates which govern Joe Blow's world. Philosophers, neurophysiologists and psychologists have been rather more preoccupied with another oddity of the I-experience, namely homuncularity, our conviction that there is a little man or woman inside us doing the observing, willing, thinking, and feeling.

Homuncularity is one of the givens for the hard-hat view of science. Wherever it has spread, this tradition is based on the idea of an objective external universe, displaying regularity, which can be studied by observation and experiment. Its claim to objectivity is that it is 'not-I', and has to be physically manipulated. Mind alone cannot modify it, which is why magic does not work. This definition runs into trouble in disciplines like psychiatry and neurology when it addresses brain processes: Are these part of the I or part of the environment? But for all ordinary purposes the model causes no problems, at least until we reach the particle level, and there only recently. That was why Descartes, in attempting to prove that *something* has to be real, started with the proposition "I have to be real, for I am doing the thinking."

Technology has a way of turning such philosophical conundrums into practical issues. With the growth of computer science, the problem of I-ness has proved no exception. The question has been asked, both by science fiction writers and by engineers, whether, if a mechanical thinking system were to approach the complexity of a human brain, it too would develop self-awareness—a test case for the mind-as-neurological-chip model. Our sense of I, which is basically a sense of ourselves as a focus distinct from everything else, which we call "the objective world," is not present in early childhood: a small baby appears to have difficulty in distinguishing his body at least, and quite possibly his I-ness, from external objects. Accordingly, it appears to be in part a learned mode of experiencing, and to acquire it a computer might have to have the equivalent of a human infancy, childhood, and individuation. More to the point, existing computers have no need of individual identity because they are programmed to extend, and report to, the I of the programmer. For example, they are programmed to do mathematics intelligible to an abstracting mathematician and act as if they were mathematicians; we make them share our intuitive vision. But a computer designed to explore alternatives and objectify when appropriate might quite possibly develop an internal device very like our sense of abstracted viewpoint. Whether that would be a mind or not depends rather obviously on what we mean by the word mind. We will go into distinctions between mind, consciousness and brain later on. At this point in the argument, mind can be taken to cover both consciousness and ratiocination. Clearly the edges of the concept of mind will always be definition-dependent and fuzzy.

Unlike Western philosophy, the Vedic tradition has always tended to treat I-ness as an illusory, or at least an optional, way of viewing self and not-self. Western psychologists and systems theorists coming fresh to the problem are beginning to find that there is a long-standing Sanskrit vocabulary to cover most of the matters under discussion: *ahamkara* for homuncular I-ness and *tat*, THAT, for 'not-I.' By developing a very sophisticated technology of introspection, much Indian philosophy long ago arrived at the conviction that both the experienced I *and* the picture which I have of the objective world are virtual or illusory. This conviction is based on the fact that there are states of mind—inducible by practice, occurring spontaneously, or, both in Vedic times and more recently in the West, facilitated by the use of drugs—in which I-ness is suppressed without the cessation of perception, and perceiver and perceived are experienced as non-different. These so-called oceanic experiences (studied and, indeed, experienced by William James) have been an important source of religious and philosophical insight precisely because they demonstrate experimentally that the objective-subjective distinction is an optional way of experiencing reality. Empirical science is committed to the distinction, because of its practical convenience, but it is not the only justifiable way.

In the oceanic experience, not only does the subject cease to experience the objective self as distinct from what is not-self, but the experience is accompanied by powerful sensations of nondiscursive knowledge, wholeness, rightness, and identity with the entire structure of the world. This might mean simply that the verbalising limb of the 'bridge' has been silenced, so the pattern alone is perceived, or that a time lag has somehow been removed (*samādhi* could be translated not only as 'oceanic experience', but also as 'making equal').

A recent model may throw more light on this question. Karl Pribram at Stanford first suggested (1974, 1979) that the brain functions not as a computer but as a hologram. A hologram is a photorecord of the interference fringes produced by wave fronts reflected at a given wavelength from an array of objects. When viewed in ordinary light it appears as a blur, but when scanned with the coherent beam of a laser, solid objects appear, and can be made to rotate or to move relative to each other by tilting the hologram. Another property of a hologram is that if it is cut up and a small portion is scanned, the whole scene appears, though at a decreasing level of definition; in other words, all parts of the hologram contain all of the information contained in the whole.

On this model, what we normally experience could be the scanned state of the interference pattern generated in the brain by sensory inputs and by its own activity. In an oceanic or I-less mode of perception, the scan would be shut off, and what is intuited would then be the interference pattern itself. Conventional attempts to represent the oceanic vision as "music of the spheres," a many-petalled lotus, or a receding structure of superimposed triangles, bear some resemblance to, or analogy with, interference patterns. All such subjective records stress the continuation and heightening of perception, but with the sense of external viewpoint suppressed.

Our only contact with a real world is by way of the sensory inputs we receive from it, and the conceptual classifying processes which go on in the brain. If both of these are expressed in some form of interference pattern, oceanic states may represent a trick by which this pattern is monitored without being interpreted. In this case, the process connected with our sense of the objective would be of a piece with the rest of the hologram, and the positional I would in fact be seen as containing the information of the whole, like any other subdivided hologram. Switch on the scan again and separate objects and concepts would once more be seen as separate.

Before we commit ourselves to a holographic model for the brain, there are some awkward questions to ask, not least, the nature of the waves of electrical activity which produce the hypothetical interference pattern. Presumably they represent the sum and difference of phase relations between the activity of different synapses. Since it is now possible, using the circuitry developed for side-looking radar, to record brain activity, not as waves, but as a power spectrum which can be scanned like a hologram, Pribram's model is investigable and refutable.

This is now proving to be the case. Pribram (1974, 1979) cites a whole range of neuropsychological studies on image formation to support the active role played by brain mechanisms in putting together wholes out of sensory inputs through a combination of computational and optical-type information processes. The momentary states set up in the course of this processing activity closely resemble those of image constructing devices, i.e., they are holographic. The same applies to memory: rules are stored as in a computer, but images are retrieved from a holographic "deep structure." We need something of the kind to explain the fact that individual "memories" are not localized in the brain. One cannot expunge one memory without expunging the ability to remember at all. Pribram's own work has shown that the anatomic localisation of motor functions in the cortex functions as an array on which environmental invariances are displayed. One interesting confirmation of this comes from the discrepancy between two experiments in which kittens were raised in a striped environment. In one, conducted by Blakemore in 1974, the stripes were painted on the walls of the cylinder in which the animals were raised. These kittens were thereafter unable to follow the movement of a bar traveling at right angles to the direction of the stripes. In Pribram's laboratory, Hirsch and Spinelli raised kittens in striped goggles and found no change in their behavior as a result. It follows from this that to affect behavior, the constant input had to remain invariant across transformations produced by head and eye movements—which is what one would expect, mathematically, of a holographic rather than a perceptual mode of processing.

The holographic model of brain is still speculative, but it looks promising. What started as a powerful metaphor to account for the mathematics of perception has been plausibly shown to be a mechanism which may operate in fact—at least concerning the area of image encoding in the cortex. It should be pointed out to nonbiological as well as philosophical readers that nobody has proposed that *all* brain systems are holographic. Beside the apparatus of imaging, the spatial representation of inputs and their processing in memory and recognition, there must also be readout systems congruent with the creation of conventional or object-centered perception, including language, which is largely the process of giving names to the objects so created. Brain holography is best seen as a department of brain function, like the memory bank in a computer, but more versatile and fundamental. A dichotomy between encoding as image and readout as object or verbalisation aptly fits our subjective experience of identity processes. Identity operates in the focused or object-forming mode present in the sense organs and quintessentially in the eye, where an optical image is formed as in a camera. The two realities, which one might call optical and holographic realities, require different time constants because one is synoptic while the other involves reduction into bits. The identification of I-ness with the predominance of optical reality in everyday experience is practical. It is not confined to philosophical argument as to how far the whole idea of transcendental identity in objects is a positional artefact arising from the human experience of personal identity.

Even more important than the model, however, is the refocusing of our attention on just how far positional identity as a normal mode of experience biases our conception of the world. Science always had a hard time transcending common sense intuitions, and this one must be by far the most compelling. It is far less accessible to correction or additional intuition than the flat earth. The more we think about and investigate neuropsychological processes, the more evident it becomes that the kind of structure which we see as being objective depends on the system which is doing the seeing as much as on what is there to be seen. The real might be grossly counterintuitive—in collapsing time, for example, or not containing cause-effect—and if it were counterintuitive, the 'real' could not be experienced with conventional human intellectual equipment, though it could be and is being inferred. At the intuitive level, in spite of particle physics, our intuitive vision still has to work in terms of discrete objects. Mathematics is a partial recourse, because we can appeal to our holographic equipment to identify an esthetic rightness, but the actual pattern, like the answer to a *koan*, can only be apprehended in an oblique, and hence traditionally unsatisfactory, way.

The holographic model of the world in the brain is, of course, a reconstruction: it has been through an optical system. Images are formed on the retina exactly as in a camera, and are then decomposed for processing. A holographic system is capable of receiving and representing wave functions directly—whether it does so in practice will depend on the position of the object-generating filter. As the Greek philosophers realized, however, the objects which compose our conventional reality are not out there as objects, though the phenomena which generate them are; the primal object which we perceive is a camera-type image on the retina. From what is out there—which includes probabilistic and indeterminate phenomena, superpositions, and a flux of emitted and reflected photons of different energies—our computing system produces a highly eclectic and primarily optical world, on which our other, secondary, sense impressions are hung. Around this, we structure a coordinate framework of three spatial dimensions plus sequence or seriality. All our formulations originate in this experiential world, unless and until we start to run into anomalies—chiefly in recondite and inferential areas such as particle behavior, which stretch the system to the point of breakdown and call for a different, nonintuitive language to integrate them.

The actual material of scientific discourse, we realize, represents a selective mode of seeing, but the teaching of science is that investigation can inherently dissolve fundamental illusions. This was true enough of the flat earth, but we still do not empathise with the inverted posture of Australians. In spite of Heisenberg and his own laboratory findings, the most sophisticated physicist, while knowing that my table and my typewriter are not things but repercussions of local accumulations of energy, is in no better posture than a savage to *see* them in that light. The dissolution of self-evident parts of experience, such as time and causality, cannot be directly empathised in a mode compatible with daily activity, though in doing science it may have, like the square root of minus one, to be taken as given. Mathematics has been the life preserver of physics in this area because creative mathematicians are accustomed to this situation. They have found a mode in the equipment which makes it possible to visualise, say, Lobachevskian space, which does not follow Euclidean rules, without trying to render it into conventional experience, except by way of rough diagrams, rather as a mediaeval artist indicates that a person is a saint by depicting him with light coming out of his head.

None of the above difficulties related to scientific discourse is a problem in interpreting a holographic brain model. The mathematics are conventional, and the brain is a physical object from which electrical and other measurements can be taken. This model becomes relevant because of the sharp reminder it gives us of the artefactual character of most of our habitual modes of thinking: we see things as things, but our brain, for its own purposes, may not.

The uncertainty principle originally set forth the incompatibility between measurements which fundamentally interfere with one another. The existence of a heavily programmed, adaptive, and prosaic sense of reality and of I-ness presents a second, Goedelian type of uncertainty principle. This second type is connected with the problem of using one and the same brain to generate the motivated, investigating I, to criticize the intuitive, and to puzzle out its own manner of working.

For a large part of practical science, the intuitive model has worked and continues to work. For these purposes argument as to how far our perceptions of, say, fossils, influenza viruses, or comets are real is merely diversionary, like a denial that terrestrial surfaces are flat when one is laying tiles. The area of physics, in which the intuitive model has run out the soonest, is to some extent buffered by being able to rely on mathematics to make counterintuitive thinking possible. But even here, mathematical treatment only postpones a philosophical crunch. We are running the human ideational system, if not close to its limits, at least in a highly unusual mode. The method of processing in the system we are using becomes increasingly important, and one part of that system is the intuitive Cartesian I which cogitates and therefore is.

We have, accordingly, a brain (holographic or not) which puts together images out of inputs, and then operates on them by its own internal rules. Both the imaging system and the rules are quite clearly interposed between the observing I (whatever that is) and unprocessed That (whatever that is). The name of the game, if we want to get more information, is using the brain's own resources and circuitry to get around itself and monitor what is going on. Science, accordingly (and there are no exceptions) studies the imagery generated in brains with the circuitry present in brains, aided by the self-monitoring ingenuity of brains. Physics is therefore the prisoner, willy nilly, of neurology: not only does it have to use the resources and avoid the preconceptions of minds—at some point its findings have to be transmitted between minds which treat a 4-space display preferentially as "real." Minds have extraordinary reserve capacity if we use computertime to set up loops in the circuitry of the brain and run them for recreation. This facility for cerebral doodling has given us mathematics, and mathematics not only provides counterintuitive models for application to the study of That: it also sheds light on the circuitry involved. By the help of these time-out uses of brain we can become quite familiar with spaces of more than three or more than four dimensions, and find them applicable to the description of portions of That which we had previously not been able to handle. But the brain is like a circus pony—it may be persuaded to walk on its hind legs and carry a parasol, but that is not its preferred mode of progression. To achieve acceptance as "real," phenomena or models must be reducible graphically, intuitively, or in some other way to optical, 4-space models. That reduction is what I mean here by *empathy*. Mathematicians, with a lot of hard work, or through the possession of overengineered brains, may have empathy for the rightness of even a very abstract model, but it requires training. So at the point where the findings of physics take leave of the world of "middle order experience" and cannot be shown in pictures, science inevitably bifurcates, and the theorists lose their audience and many of their nonphysicist colleagues.

There is even an older technique of creative modelling for the counterintuitive which was formerly a great resource in conveying non-middle-order ideas: not math, but myth. Myth, however, has been marked down as an enemy of science. It works by vague outlines only—mathematics has a logic of demonstration.

Pribram's model of brain process as hologram might suggest other holographic-type structures: what about objective reality itself? This model has moved from hard objects to aggregations of hard atoms, then to aggregations of energy, and finally to the behavior of loci in space-time. This kind of speculation well illustrates the neurological bind. It might be that the brain is holographic. It might be that the mathematics of holograms have heuristic value when applied, for example, to particle physics. Suppose that they do—Does that mean that the universe is a hologram in some fundamental sense? Or simply that if one projects a different neural model involved in the sorting processes in our own heads, one gets a different paradigm for what is real?

Science has advanced as a practical activity by sensibly ignoring this kind of speculation for as long as possible; its potential as a philosophical quagmire leading to mystification is enormous. But with continued technical successes, the hard ground seems to be running out, as it did in physics some time ago. In Heisenberg's words: "The conception of objective reality has evaporated into a mathematics that no longer represents the behavior of elementary particles, but rather our knowledge of this behavior." In Mach we find: "There is no cause or effect in nature. . . . Nature simply *is*: recurrence of like cases exists but in the abstraction we perform for the purpose of mentally reproducing facts." In this new scientific world, nature consists of arrays—which may for all we know be infinite in number—and from this interference pattern our sensorium pulls out structures to fit itself. Phenomena, our only mode of contact with this multifarious nature, are exactly what the name says, namely appearings, to which structure has been selectively added. Moreover, in some cases (time and space are probable instances) what look like phenomena turn out to be structures connected with our conviction of positional identity and the fact that time processes cannot be run backwards if they depend for operation on a delay network. They are programs, not objects of knowledge.

This generates yet another problem: holographic models are recursive, that is to say, if they were visually displayed, each cell or unit of structure would repeat the structure of the whole, whether we viewed the pattern with a telescope or with a microscope. An extraordinary number of possible and even probable models in physics, biology, logic, and human mentation are of this recursive type. One would initially be thrilled to find that the pattern in each was identical, but if one of the hierarchies involved is the mind—and human mind-generated mathematics has long had intuitions about, and ways of handling, recursions, Chinese box systems, and endlessly repetitious fractions—the suspicion arises that we are *not* looking at irreducible reality, but at an artefact of our processing system. What looks, therefore, like the grain of the ultimate is actually something completely tautological or vacuous. Even if we did the computations, plotted points that could be checked by experiment, and found them confirmed, the suspicion would remain. We might simply have fed the computing system a no-exit loop. Nor *is* there any exit from it, except by converting the recursion into an expression which does not contain infinities. This formulation would then be just as artefactual as optical reality, though probably harder to take in. Evidence of holographic representation in the physical brain would arouse suspicion in this case rather than provide reassurance. In spite of this possible and disappointing outcome, we still have to look at recursive models, because, the suspicion fully allowed, there is an intuitive sense in which, if there is universal structure, it would be likely to be of this kind.

Since it is so far from the prosaic, we have difficulty accepting the idea that matter is an optical construction made up from the centroids of virtual subatomic particles whose velocity and position (if we treat them as mini-objects) cannot be simultaneously established. After all, the virtual or probabilistic character of the hundred dollar bill in our pay envelope, the car we are driving, or the beloved with whom we propose to have intercourse, makes precious little practical difference: these things *mutatis mutandis* work just as well as they did before anyone started to poke around. Even for the career scientist, his own findings are interesting or remarkable rather than disconcerting. They have no effect on the immediacy of experience. There was once a convict who, at Christmas, obtained colored chalks and decorated his cell with festive designs and the motto "Stone walls do not a prison make." "Maybe not" said his cellmate "but it's a bloody good imitation." In fact, the virtual character of middle-order reality only becomes bothersome if and when it occurs to us that the I-perceiving and object-creating brain, which is experiencing the imitation, is itself made up of the virtual phenomena which it processes. At that point the sufficiency of the prosaic begins to run out. One can see why physicists avoid it: the immediate response is to ask "Say again?" and retire to meditate on the implications of virtual matter which, by its apparent interactions, becomes able to think itself.

Spencer Brown, who is both a psychologist and a logician of physics, puts the epistemological dilemma in a nutshell. His comment is worth quoting at full length, since it constitutes the subject of this book.

Now the physicist himself, who describes all this, is, in his own account, himself constructed of it. He is, in short, made of a conglomeration of the very particulars he describes, no more, no less, bound together by and obeying such general laws as he himself managed to find and record.

Thus we cannot escape the fact that the world we know is constructed in order (and thus in such a way as to be able) to see itself.

This is indeed amazing.

Not so much in view of what it sees, although this may appear fantastic enough, but in respect of the fact that it *can* see *at all*.

But *in order* to do so, evidently it must first cut itself up into at least one state which sees, and at least one other state which is seen.

In this severed and mutilated condition, whatever it sees is *only partially* itself. We may take it that the world undoubtedly is itself (i.e, is not distinct from itself), but, in any attempt to see itself as an object, it must, equally undoubtedly, act so as to make itself distinct from, and therefore false to, itself. In this condition it will always partially elude itself.

It seems hard to find an acceptable answer to the question of how or why the world conceives a desire, and discovers an ability, to see itself, and appears to suffer the process. That it does so is sometimes called the original mystery. Perhaps, in view of *the form* in which *we* presently *take* ourselves *to exist*, the mystery *arises from* our insistence on *framing* a question where there is, in reality, *nothing* to question.

(Spencer Brown 1972)

# Chapter 1

# *PHYSICS, BRAINS AND WORLD MODELS*

# The Needle, The Haystack, and the Holomovement

Einstein was suspicious of quantum theory, and found it rather disturbing—the universe couldn't be like that. Quantum theory also appeared to have some irrational conclusions, rather like those which attend the idea of time travel. One of them—the Einstein-Rosen-Podolsky paradox—stated that if quantum models were correct, altering the spin of one member of a particle pair should alter the spin of the other. This was clearly impossible, since the hypothetical objects involved are travelling apart at the velocity of light, and no signal could pass between them unless it were in some way "transluminal." The mathematics of the model appeared to postulate a magic trick: the illusionist takes off his left glove and gives it to a member of the audience; he then removes his right glove and turns it inside out. He should now have two left gloves—but, presto, the glove in the audience has mysteriously turned itself inside out to conserve parity, and they remain an enantiomorphic pair. Unfortunately for Einstein, however, repeated experiment tends so far to vinicate the quantum model. The most refined recent experiment on this weird effect, done by Aspect in France, indicates that polarization reversal is propagated from one member of the pair to the other. A number of interpretations of this result have been offered, and it does accord with the prediction of an important mathematical statement, Bell's theorem. Perhaps the simplest interpretation is that the particles which we have treated, almost unaware, as things similar to billiard balls, are neither things nor in fact separate, but phenomena displaying nonlocality and interconnectedness. This is the most widely quoted, but by no means the only, example of the factitious or 'unthinglike' character of subatomic particles.

Having descended a Democritean scale from molecules to atoms and thence to smaller structures, the model of smaller and smaller things, like the flat-earth model, proves to be contraband from middle-order experience. Chemistry books and atomic energy logos may show electrons as miniature planets in orbit round a nucleus, but no physicist now sees them in that light, any more than electronics is serious about an electrical fluid flowing from positive to negative. The convention is imaginary, and as soon as tubes or semiconductors are involved we have to think of negatively charged electrons moving from minus to plus. The frankly erroneous fluid model, however, can still be handy, for example, to simplify a circuit (if only to remind novice radio hams to keep their fingers off the high voltage, positive connections).

It has been remarked that anyone who isn't shocked by quantum mechanics doesn't understand it. Why should a mathematical description of particle events be shocking? First, because it exposes a sharp contrast between the properties of macroscopic "things" and the units or processes of which they are composed: in other words, it is non-Democritean. Secondly, because its basic approach is that all fundamental descriptions concern probabilities: which probable outcome we observe is taken as random so far as causes within space-time are concerned. This was the point of Einstein's objection that God doesn't roll dice. Third, because in contrast to local causes, its mathematics postulates interconnectedness: what is observed at point A affects what can be observed at Point B, and this effect is instantaneous: it does not depend on information transmitted at the finite speed of light. This phenomenon of nonlocality and interconnectedness is a mathematical consequence of quantum wave-mechanics. The formal algebraic proof is Bell's theorem: either quantum wave mechanics, which has an unblemished heuristic record, is erroneous, or "particles" are not separate things. In view of the finite velocity of light, interconnectedness cannot exist within 4-space. The three legs of a stool standing on a piece of paper are not connected in the plane of the paper, which is a 3-space (x,y: t) but they form parts of one object in solid 4-space (x,y,z: t). What appears separate in a 4-space might be hyperspace-connected. Presumably these are very much the attributes we would expect particles to have if they were not "things" but simply a display. Moreover the only new feature of quantum mechanics as against a long history of philosophical models in almost exactly this form (Leibniz' model is a Western example) is that the model works out experimentally. We use it to build devices, and the devices work. What is slightly shocking to a nonphysicist physician is that physicists, bothered by counterintuitive conclusions, go to immense mathematical effort to find a grand unified theory to schematize all this (good) but without reference to the peculiarities of the system to which both ordinary and counterintuitive phenomena appear, namely the brain (extraordinary).

"Quantum logic," used to elucidate these data, is not funny-money logic, simply the consequence of the fact that some quantum-related observables, unlike "ordinary" states, do not follow distributive rules: A and B or C is not, in this system, the same as A and B or A and C. Mathematicians are quite unbothered by special algebras which are non-distributive, non-commutative, and otherwise different from real number logic: logicians, for historical reasons, find them very hard to swallow, especially when the states observed are not submicroscopic but easily seen in a hands-on experiment: the non-distributive character of polarization can be seen by anyone who possesses three small sheets of Polaroid.

I think the shock—which is another word for existential discomfort—sets in with the beginning of empathy. It is not shocking to be told that the "real" world is a largely artefactual display with no separate parts: it is shocking, if one is heavily invested in the solidity of the ordinary, to understand just how artefactual the display is, or to see a phenomenon which appears to violate the ordinary rules of Boolean logic. Try to psych out Bell's theorem, and even worse results follow: if there is no transfer of information into the space-time display from some extradimensional "second layer," then either the entire course of the Universe is fixed in its minutest detail, including the experiment we just performed ("freewill fails"), or at every experimental choice, time bifurcates ("contrafactual definiteness fails"). The second of these is quite possibly, as we shall see, a real comment on the way in which brains carve out a track through spacetime: the first is superdeterminism—and also probably irrefutable, like the hypothesis that the Devil did it. It is not really very shocking, however, if one recognizes the remit of science: if apparently separated parts of the conventional universe are interconnected, and we carefully observe effects where this interconnection is manifest, then we might start looking into them as a faster-than-light signal channel. The interesting thing will be to see if the conventional middle-order "censors" this possibility in some way.

Most of the speculation we shall have to discuss here is really two-aimed—to mathematize observation, and to provide a world model which somebody, even if only a skilled mathematician, can address. In doing this, the gut feeling that I am realistic and commonsensible, but what is Out There is just crazy, has to give place to the awareness that what is Out There, is, and any anomalies arise in the way my brain, with its attendant linguistic imagery and a-prioris, slices the material. Behind this, however, lies the really alarming possibility that not only the fine structure of reality is counterintuitive; the gross, everyday, structure may be so too—only we had not noticed it.

It is a fair generalization that whenever a model produces a gross paradox, it does so because we are using an exhausted analogy which has been overextended and has snapped. The trouble is that we tend to think and to classify by analogy. The thing model, dictated by everyday experience, had serious snags, one of them being the irrefutable ability of postulated things to influence one another at a distance, via gravitation or magnetism. Oddly enough, because these are familiar effects, they were never seen as irrational or threatening, though Newton saw the difficulty they pose—the model was adjusted by adding first "forces" and later the deformation of space-time by mass, or the exchange of vector particles. At some point, however, the model comes to resemble the last elaborations of a species or a group approaching extinction. When ammonites or dinosaurs become completely covered with knobs and appendages, a new deal is imminent. The crypto-Democritean model is approaching the point where, even with unified chromodynamics, it cannot support many more types of particle and in that case what creaks is not Nature but the going model.

What is the world model which we are trying to apprehend? At first flush there are several candidates: not surprising, since it is harder to examine a baby passing through the birth canal than a corpse laid out in the necropsy room. We can see the whole of last century's reductionist model, and perform a necropsy on it; the new model is *in articulo partus* and might even prove to be twins. In fact, by picking any of the emergent models one runs the risk that they may have been dismantled before one can finish writing a book.

There is a basic unity, however, in most of the going models; they differ largely in the mathematics which are being tried for fit. Some are still reductionist (in terms of Grand Unified Theory), but even these are not trying to revive the Democritean corpse with CPR. Others are explicitly speculative and make assumptions outside the idea of a unified state function ("hidden parameter" theories). What both trends have in common is a world in which both familiar objects and the subatomic structure of which they are composed, together with space-time itself, are precisely what the name *phenomena* implies, namely appearings. Far from being a thing, or even a virtual object like a ripple, an electron is conceived as a display. The display may have virtual properties such as location or momentum, but essentially it is like the successive frames of a film, or the successively lit bulbs in a running sky sign. An entity like this can go from one state to another without going through the states in between, and can behave in other unthinglike ways—indeterminate, probabilistic, or nonlocal.

I will touch on several competing models based on this consensus, but concentrate on one, namely Bohm's suggestion that our world model can be seen as an "implicate order" based on total interaction, of which electrons and other phenomena are "explicates." An analogy would be the hologram, where all parts of the pattern contain a microcosmic restatement of the whole pattern, rather as Leibniz's monads reflected all other monads. The diagrammatic picture of this situation is the jewelled net of Indra in Hindu and Buddhist mythology, which was covered with crystals like large Christmas tree ornaments, every one of which contained the reflection of every other. Such a system has an unusual symmetrical algebra, rather like that proposed by Blanco (1975) for images in the unconscious where every element contains the whole. All conventional experience, whether of stars, cats, or particles is a construction—a thread pulled out from, or a section taken through, this hypothetical "holomovement." Looking at a television raster through a very narrow slit at right angles to the lines would be an analogy, in that the forms appearing in the slit would be built up by intermittent flashes in the phosphor which were actually patterned by far larger forms in the entire, but to us, invisible picture. This is a bad analogy, however, because the implicate structure itself is not postulated to be within space-time. If we were to doctor the mental processes which are pulling manifestations out of it and the apparatus we use to manipulate the appearings, the implicate structure might be quite capable of producing wormholes, loops, time reversals and other apparent paradoxes, such as nonlocality, which are paradoxical only because of the way our heads are programmed.

This kind of world model can be described mathematically (Frescura and Hiley 1980) and it has been elegantly presented by Bohm (1980) who devised it. It is also, one must hasten to repeat, not the only going model. Oddly enough, the best description of how it might be apprehended comes not from a physicist but from the amateur yogi and occult philosopher P.D. Ouspensky, describing a vision he experienced during an altered state of mind.

> In trying to describe this strange world in which I saw myself, I must say that it resembled more than anything a world of very complicated mathematical relations . . . in which everything is connected, in which nothing exists separately, and in which at the same time the relations between things have a real existence apart from the things themselves; or possibly "things" do not exist, and only "relations" exist.
>
> (1930)

Ouspensky was a very odd fish, and certainly, from the remainder of his book, no great scientific thinker, but here for once his language is strikingly clearer than that of the physicists. He is coy about the means used to obtain this vision (they appear to have included smoking pot). Whether he contrived to see this natural implicate or was simply guessing, is a matter of some interest, as we shall see later, but his image, like that of Leibniz, accurately describes the model which one trend in mathematical physics is attempting to convey.

Bohm himself uses the following analogy (1973, 1980) to illustrate the idea of implicate and explicate in physics. Consider a tall cylinder filled with a viscous, transparent fluid such as glycerin or oil, and containing a loosely fitting roller-shaped glass core which extends from top to bottom, leaving a thickish layer of fluid between its surface and the cylinder wall. If we place in the fluid a drop of the same fluid loaded with carbon particles, it will appear as a discrete object. If the roller is turned, the drop will elongate, and after a sufficient number of turns it will become a thinner and thinner thread and disappear. Say that this has occurred after $n$ clockwise turns. If we now rotate the roller $n$ turns counterclockwise, the drop will be reconstituted. After a further $n$ counterclockwise turns it will again disappear, but $n$ clockwise turns will reconstitute it once more. Obviously, if during the process of attenuating the first drop, we stop every $m$ turns and insert a new drop, drops may be made to appear sequentially when the roller is then turned backwards. After sufficient turns all will disappear as drops, though all will be present at all times as carbon particles. The drops are implicated in the fluid, but they cannot all be rendered explicate simultaneously. If we stagger successive drops and time their insertion correctly against the rotation of the roller, a single apparent object can be revealed, and it will appear to move. What we shall be seeing, however, is not a moving object but the successive explication of virtual objects from an implicate in which all exist, but only one at a time can be manifested.

Bohm points out that our observation of a moving particle is equally virtual—the particle's momentum and velocity cannot be known simultaneously, nor is it an object. Mathematically it behaves far more like a sequential explication in a total field of which all parts are at all times interdependent. If we treat it in terms of a wave function, other states of the particle may well be explicated outside the time slot, or in other time lines, but the apparent moving object is a confection of our mode of seeing, rather as the successive frames of a film are run together by the persistence of vision to create the illusion of movement. As Frescura and Hiley put it (1980)—rather heavily, but intelligibly:

> the Ding-an-sich is no longer taken as a primitive form. Any object will arise as an abstraction from quasistable, relatively invariant features of the basic underlying activity. For example, in the glycerol experiment the regular appearance of spots of dye could lead to the abstraction of a particle, while its inertial properties are inferred from the regularity of

the sequence of spots. This example shows clearly why a physical process need not be understood solely in terms of an array of locally interacting particles. Indeed, such a restriction could prevent a clear understanding of the phenomena. Nor should we use local fields, because, for example, in the glycerol experiment the appearance of the spot of dye depends on a relatively large volume of the glycerol, suggesting the importance of a nonlocal form. It is this kind of form that is suggested by the quantum interconnectedness. Hence, if we are right to regard what we call the electron as an unfolding process which depends on the total order, then it would be no surprise if when we place two slits in the path of such a process it will respond to the presence of *both* slits.

They go on to suggest that this type of model gives rise to an algebra, based on that of Grassmann, in which space is not given a priori, but each point is a distinctive form in a continuous process which we read as becoming, and apparent motion is the generation of one form by another. Moreover, as a constituent of four dimensional space (4-space), time is treatable on the basis that "Śiva destroys each moment to create the next."

There is actually a still better model of explication than Bohm's ink drops, one which we can see nowadays in any amusement arcade. Consider a computer game consisting of a black box (B) with controls for two players, which generates a VDT display on a television screen. The display consists of a field (x,y : t) representing a three dimensional space (3-space); with additional circuitry it could equally well depict a 4-space, like an ordinary in-depth television picture. Objects—asteroids and space ships—travel across this screen in a randomized manner. If two objects collide, there is a simulated explosion and the objects disappear. A space ship can also fire at an asteroid, and, if it scores a hit, destroy it. The controls alter the speed and coordinates of the imaginary objects and the firing of missiles; the aim of the player is to prevent or cause collisions respectively.

Now the plane of the screen can be treated as a real world, subject to cause-effect: collisions cause explosions. It is, of course, nothing of the kind. What appear as causes and effects are actually numerical correlations, hard wired in B. The entire game would operate as well with the display turned off—its sole object is to exhibit correlations to the players, so that they can aim. B's output is a series of modulated pulses which are not isomorphic with the screen display and are nonlocal with respect to the symbols appearing there. Further, the symbols are not objects and both their continuity and their interaction are entirely virtual. There are no things there.

This is an electronic version, with differences, of the inkdrop model. The world implicated in the circuitry of B is explicated on the screen and can be manipulated, but the wiring of B is invariant. The function of the display is to generate a *manifest* world, something like a real billiard table, on which collisions can be produced. A manifest world is a hands-on model in which organisms can operate without performing cumbersome calculations before doing so. For the relatively slow neurochemical mode used in brains, the algebra necessary to play without the screen would be transcomputable. This is precisely what Kant meant by a prioris—we are hard-wired to see a hands-on world composed of centroids and yes-no approximations. The receptor system centered in optical images is the algorithm evolved by organisms to deal with the regularities existing in *B*, the black box. One set of algorithms generates a 4-space. From the spectrum of hydrogen, one can show that the rotations involved correspond to $(x, y, z, :t)$ and not a higher order, but a hydrogen atom is itself a conceptual object, an algorithm, like an explicated droplet. The overwhelming conclusion is that time represents another such algorithm, that the subjective model has fundamental validity different from that of $t$ in the Minkowski figure (see p. 104) and only partly coincides with it, while in the implicate "All is always Now." How about the final algorithm, positional self? Very probably that too is a priori, even if it is partly learned, and temporarily suppressible during certain unusual states of mind.

Suppose further that the screen display is not of game pieces but of evolution, or the development of an organism. On the screen it looks like a causal sequence—forms or cells appear to compete, to be induced, to die out, but the regularities and cause-effect sequences are transductions of some correlations hard-wired in *B*, the historical flow is an illusion. A nonlocal demon, seeing the equations expressed in *B*, would see a simultaneity, exactly as a model like toroidal hyperspace with closed time represents a simultaneity, not a time-and-motion graphic. *Explication postulates an audience.* In that case, since human brains are themselves material objects, who precisely are the players in the game of asteroids and spaceships? More asteroids and spaceships, symbols on the same screen? Who or what is doing the thinking?

If we combine our two models, the complication strikes home. It never has been really clearly addressed in terms of experimentally verifiable models, only in terms of idealist-realist speculation. What Bohm does is to bring this difficulty to a sharp point. As he himself said in a Berkeley lecture:

> the ultimate perception does not originate in the brain or any material structure, although a material structure is necessary to manifest it. The subtle mechanism of knowing the truth does not originate in the brain.
>
> (Zukav 1979).

Take Bohm's model, and Helmholtz bites the dust.

Whether or not we go along with Bohm's model, this is the type of discussion current in physics, with some workers hoping to get more mileage out of the Democritean model by reducing the "particle zoo" to combinations of still smaller units, and others ready to drop Democritean in favor of Pythagorean or field models. Neither school, however, is under any illusion about the limitation of the thing-particle analogy, which has long been superseded by mathematical expressions. The debate is over which mathematical treatment is most effective as a predictive tool.

The lid is irrevocably off the Cartesian-Newtonian world model. One might have apprehensions about this, especially in dealing with those who do not understand precisely in what way it is off. In the present state of Californianism, a misunderstanding of the state-of-the-art is already a hunting license for every kind of crack-pottery. What is actually needed is something very different, an empathic perception of the new world model, one that, if it cannot be seen, can be, as it were, incorporated. This particular possibility not only opens interest in ongoing non-Western philosophical traditions based on guided forms of introspection, it also makes us look back at Greek philosophy. Often-quoted formulae, such as "all things flow," Zeno's denial of motion, or the Pythagorean notion of structure as music, start to look less like sophistical generalizations and more like good guesses or the description of real mental experiences. In all ages the writings of the sizeable number of dissenters from the Democritean, thing-based, universe begin to merit reinspection. Much of the apparent nonsense written by, say, Pico or Michael Maier, looks less like nonsense and more like premature insight confounded by contemporary misinformation. The Rosicrucian alchemists of the sixteenth century started with an inkling of the model we now derive from quantum logic—sometimes via visionary introspection, sometimes via mathematics, or a combination of the two—but they tried to apply it to what we now know to be a classical system (elements and molecules) for which the Democritean view of discrete objects works very much better. The alchemical speculators produced an awkward hybrid: hard chemistry on the one hand and what we would now call Jungian psychology on the other. Chemistry went from strength to strength; Jung had to wait four hundred years, and was still premature, so far as linkage with physics and neuropsychology was concerned. We shall have to deal with Jung later. What we are now looking at is the prospect of Jungian physics: a physics model compatible with observation which also addressed the image-forming mechanism, and possibly even the nonlocality, of the mind.

Every age has its half-baked theorists. Viewing the Aquarian Revolution one can well understand the irritation of some serious mathematical physicists at the activities of a new brood of Rosicrucians coming out of the woodwork. Was it for this that Science has labored? "In the quantum theory of observation" writes Wheeler,

> my own present field of endeavour, I find honest work absolutely overwhelmed by the buzz of absolutely crazy ideas put forth with the aim of establishing a link between quantum mechanics and parapsychology—as if there were any such thing as "parapsychology." . . . Where there is meat, there are flies. No subject more attracts the devotees of the 'paranormal' than the quantum theory of measurement.
>
> (Gardner 1979)

There is no scientific obligation to suffer fools gladly, especially when science, from Comte down, has worked hard to establish an area of reasonable empirical integrity. Wheeler, who has made some revolutionary suggestions, is not the first to feel like this. Galileo wrote of Kepler (Galileo 1632):

> Everything that has been said before and imagined by other people [concerning the origin of tides] is in my opinion complete nonsense. Among authorities who have theorized about this remarkable set of phenomena, I am most shocked by Kepler. He was a man of exceptional genius, he was sharp, he had a grasp of terrestrial movement, but he went on to take the bit between his teeth and get interested in a supposed action of the moon on water, and other 'paranormal' phenomena—a lot of childish nonsense.

In one sense Wheeler is absolutely right—much 'parapsychology' is not only improbable but scientifically incompetent, and no element in quantum logic demonstrates the validity of any 'paranormal' observation. What has changed is that we can no longer exclude *ex hypothesi* the existence of singularities which the Newtonian-Helmholtzian view excluded. Black Holes are singularities, but they are not paranormal. A little skeptical calmness is in order.

We have fortunately profited from a stiff period in the Cartesian and positivist boot camp. Speculative flights of fancy are no new thing, but in the task of reshaping the world model of scientists and others, only commitment to the discipline of science will do. It can be combined with enough controlled lunacy to bring conventionally self-evident ideas of reality into question (in mathematics this has always been a winning mixture), but it has to produce testable predictions. Luckily, particle physics is well placed to do this. If field-theory models had grown primarily in biology (where several originals, notably Bergson, tried to market them), the credo of hard-hattery and the availability of a classical process model would have been able to fight them off. Quantum mechanics is another matter. Having earned their stripes finding algorithms which work where classical theory does not, quantum theorists have acquired the right to think the unthinkable without upsetting traditionalists.

Now in our culture we do not have direct experiential access to a quantum logical world view (with exceptions which we will come to later, and which may explain the prevalence and accuracy of some of the premature intuitions). The parts of our brains on which we rely most heavily appear to be programmed specifically to avoid it. We do, however, have introspective access to our own brains; whether or not we can be said to be our brains cannot yet be answered with certainty, but it is certain that introspection requires no apparatus beyond those brains, and the same brains are very good at mathematics.

For the scientist who hopes to produce not only a mathematical model of a world view, but a world view which can, as it were, be taken home with us, the place to start now is with the instrument which is doing the seeing and inferring, not with the structures which are seen and inferred, however real and objective these may appear. As Descartes pointed out, nothing seems more real to us than the I which is doing the thinking.

The leading exercise in criticizing conventional world models is to see how a world view would look if it were not based on conceptualizations which inhere in positional I-ness. Most of the conventions involved in Einsteinian space-time are complex attempts to square observation with the shape given to phenomena by a localized Cartesian I who is doing the observing, and to whom phenomena appear. Two interesting psychiatric points arise from this. One is that because visualized models *have* to be identity-regarding (translated, that is, into formalisms which a time-and-space-positional I can visualize), the revolution involved in quantum physics has had absolutely no impact on the day-to-day world view even of people who work with it. Unlike the discoverers of the Copernican and Newtonian world these people experience no reordering of consciousness: they say, "How intensely interesting," and go home to dinner. Aside from occultists who rub their hands at the idea that there may be other worlds, fourth dimensions, and so on to vindicate their preconceptions, modern physics has had no religious and rather little philosophical impact. If, when it has "set," modern physics could somehow be popularly empathized, it would be a blockbuster. The second point is that if there are available states of mind in which such complex models, instead of being computed, are directly perceived as we normally perceive in terms of conventional space and conventional time they might "do the trick"—not only in providing a new mathematical and scientific resource, but in altering their possessors' world view as well. Now this is what mystics and other cultivators of oceanic states

have always claimed. So far they have been uninterested in the physical universe and given to making the religious noises required by
their particular tradition. Most have been far more moved by the
components in the experiences they sought which led to feelings of
oneness (with God, with the Brahman), and which probably owe their
attraction to emotions connected with the psychoanalytic stock-in-
trade of human individuation. It would take a tough, rather than an
analyzed, yogi to set these intoxicant psychedelia aside, and set about
making the ineffable effable in terms of world models. Westernized
yogis, when genuine and tough, still point out the difficulties of thinking about physics while in a state of *samādhi* and most bring back
only a salutary experience of the conditionality of conventional perception. A computer, with no Kleinian backlog from childhood experience, might do better—present computers neither do, nor are likely
to, exhibit human I-ness because at present they are programmed to
act like, and report to, a homuncularly oriented mathematician, who
*provides* the Cartesian observer.

This need not be so. If we could infer how things would look to
an intelligence not burdened by our preconceptions, we could program a system, holographic or otherwise, to think in nonhomuncular
terms—to treat alternative events, for example, as both/and rather
then either/or and handle divergent time streams, rather as a chess
computer rehearses all possible moves. Although all our chips are
on-off Boolean, dealing in "and," "or" and similar one-valued logics, a
computer could think like this if so instructed. If it could choose all
of the alternatives rather than the most probable, it would see the
matrix of all chess games and not play a particular game.

Nonhomuncular, non-Democritean models of the world—David
Bohm's holomovement, for example—become much easier to comprehend if we recognize that any such nonpositional observer model
basically differs from ours, or can be brought into line with ours,
by the intervention of what amounts to a Fourier transformation,
the conversion of quantities to a sum of frequencies. This involves
the invention of an observer who perceives, by our standards, holographically. Our sensorium receives frequency encoded input and, on
Pribram's model, stores it by frequency-encoded engrams, but between
the two, focusing intervenes, and it is the focused or de-transformed
image which figures as our conventional or intuitive reality, complete
with a representation in space-time and the visualization of discrete
objects. This raises the interesting and, for some, disturbing probability that in giving philosophic definitions of what is real and what
is phenomenal, an imaginary nonlocal observer, who is not bugged in
his perceptions by a positional I and who treats Fourier transforms
as primary, is quite likely to be right.

All western, non-Pythagorean scientific thought prior to Heisen-berg has tended to regard the conventional or intuitive focused version (middle-order reality) as in some way primary, even if it required relativistic correction, and its Fourier derivates as convenient math-ematical transformations. It is just as possible, however, to regard Fourier patterns as the primary objective reality and the conventional world as derived by a transformation, produced by evolution because of the great convenience of space-time and causality in dealing prac-tically with middle-order living, and therefore adaptive. One thing which it generates is the convenient congruence of sensory impres-sions. By transforming to generate objects, we can usually be assured that what we see, we can also touch, if it is in the category of objects.

In support of this idea that our mode of seeing is a special case, adaptive to things which we might normally expect to see in un-sophisticated conditions, one can point out that this mode works so well, covering the range from a grain of sand to a distant star, that it produces no awkwardness: these arise only at the cosmic and the subatomic levels, when we are trying to make consistent sense not of direct perceptions but of inferences. It is in these areas, outside the range for which our particular sensorium was "made a-purpose," that paradoxes start to multiply. One advantage of a holographic or Fourier model for primary reality is that it does deal with sev-eral troublesome paradoxes—ranging from the double-take between particle and wave-mechanical models to some of the deficiencies of classical molecular biology and genetics in fully explaining morpho-genesis which drove biologists like Driesch into neovitalism. Good-win (1976) is indeed already looking at morphogenesis in terms of Laplacian transformations over a field.

This is not a new idea: for Hindu philosophy, field-type or impli-cate reality is Brahman, and the intuitive or focused transform is māya (measurement or division) which is the type of perception gen-erating space-time and discrete objects. The idea, however, is new as a heuristic hypothesis, at least since Pythagoras generalized that real-ity was analogous to music in its structure. In the flush of enthusiasm it has, of course, to be pointed out that holographic models for brain imaging, morphogenesis, and particle physics resemble the near simi-larity of the curves for the growth of pumpkins, bacterial populations, and the gross national product of Ruritania. These similarities may represent either analogy or homology, or (in the case of holographic representations) the direct effects of brain mechanisms on human con-ceptualization. This is a difficult one. Pribram's holographic brain model, despite some vigorous dissent from reputable physiologists, looks from the evidence quite plausible. We have no mechanism of any description, even among computers, which can address reality, whatever that is, without the intervention along the line of a human brain—in fact, *without* a human brain there are philosophical problems in giving a meaning to the word *reality* and even to the word *meaning*. There are the beginnings here of a Catch 22 situation. However, the assignment of experimental science is basically to get around and behind this dependence of concepts on the apparatus which does the conceptualizing, and the same brain has proved a versatile instrument for this kind of low cunning. It should be possible to aim experiments to pick up the counterintuitive in this area as in others. Particle physics, where middle-order reality simply falls apart, is a good place to start. In conventional reality, transfer of properties from one apparent entity to another is usually prohibited; action at a distance is worrying, as it was to both Newton and Einstein, and calls for a cumbersome construction, which then remains around as a challenge to produce mathematical syntheses between postulated forces. In the transform, it presents no problems. By translational invariance, any change is represented in all parts of the field, and vehicular particles—gluons, gravitons, and so on—may not be required (Capra 1978). Nobody is bothered if virtual particles behave as if they were real particles, since in this view all particles are virtual.

This is neither the time nor the place to expound the steady growth of field theories in the area of quantum physics; they were surveyed by Nash (1978), and the state-of-the-art is a moving object. The point is that even strictly mathematical models like the Weinberg-Salam unified field theory (which aims at a reductionist model for the observed forces) are in a covert sense as much concerned with brain physiology as with attributes of nature. Whether a theory is unified or includes systems breaks and multiplication of entities depends on properties of the processing system. Middle-order reality is a most practical device for unification—it involves the generation of conceptual objects relevant to ordinary living, on which the senses can, as it were, converge operationally. It therefore defines *a* reality, the object of which is practical. Pre-Einsteinian physics did the same, but now our practicalities are changing; there is nothing unpractical about quarks or tachyons, since our comprehension of them may very well have practical spin-offs. This is the difference between our scientific pragmatism and the popular (though not the sophisticated) interpretations placed on Hindu and Buddhist nonobjectifying philosophy, which aims at a spiritual quality of comprehension and is not specially interested in the regularities of *māya* or middle-order reality: if it is virtual or illusory, why bother about it? Physicists, however, seem to be discovering these models, aimed in a very different direction, with glee. Starting from the work of Chew at the Lawrence Berkeley Laboratory on S-matrix theory, Capra (1975) has pointed out the likeness between such concepts of "boot-strapping" and the Taoist intuition of a "grain" in nature.

Grassmann algebra (concerned with transitions not quantities), or what has been jocularly called "topsicology" (for structures which are field-determined and accordingly appear to "just grow"), has a further use as a heuristic tool not in physics but in biology. Organisms are real-time and middle-order-reality substrates, but both their phylogeny and their epigenetic development were constantly fought over by philosophically inclined biologists from Cuvier on. Most of the energy of modern hard-nosed science has had to be devoted successively to fighting off naive creationism and neovitalism. Neither is dead, but molecular genetics did at one time appear to have done the reductionist trick, both in evolutionary theory and in embryology.

This is no longer strictly true. For a start, in embryogenesis, genes appear to be far more the providers of available materials than the generators of developmental fields, leaving the $64,000 question: What exactly determines that, of cells having identical genetic structure, some produce an eye and others a toenail? In speciation, Darwinian selectionist models are the models of choice, but they present some awkward problems calling for acts of faith, recourse to indirect selection and the like, which we dutifully make (so as not to give comfort to people who want to fell us with Genesis 1), but which do creak. Maynard Smith's acrostic paradox—how to effect by selection the transition from one encoded character to another without going through a disadaptive or nonsense combination—is the least of these.

Positivism performed an inestimable service by interring chairborn philosophy as a source of knowledge—which it never was. The decent occupation of philosophy is as a source of intuitive models (which can then be used heuristically) and as a critique of existing models—the way in which Kant or Hume used it. The only respectable source of knowledge is observation combined with the inference of relationship. Intuition plays a large part in the detection of relationship ahead of detailed observation, if only because the brain can apprehend pattern both in phenomena and in abstractions before it analyzes detail. Thomist logic, of the kind which set off the endless sterile argument over first causes, is heuristically quite ineffective: it assumes that the logic of reality is the same as our logic, which it almost certainly isn't.

The only specific addition we need to make to the hard-line scientific canon is that introspection is as valid a source of knowledge as extrospection, provided it is done properly. The fact that we may have a vision or experience of a field-determined world does not prove that the real world is field-determined. But it is also true that without critical introspection (of the way the brain forms optical models), we cannot now interpret extrospection. Quantum theory does *not* reverse the hard-line model—all it does is to substitute an unconventional for a conventional algebra in the description of certain events: the old algorithm implied one world model, the new algorithm implies a different world model. Quantum theory is also a critique of our conventional mode of synthesizing an optical world. Endless idealist-realist disputation never really got to this question, except in extremely unpractical terms, derived by pushing ideas about. One cannot now take, or learn much from, say, Fichte or Schelling because their intuitions resemble double garden hybrids incapable of setting heuristic seed.

The "perennial philosophy"—a favorite with those inclined to vagueness—is actually a name for the recurrent intuition of a field-type reality, supported by the use of introspective experiment. It is perennial because, like the optical mode which generates realisms (including, as a historical specimen, Thomas Reid's commonsensism, which is realism in caricature), it represents an experienceable cerebral mode, which tends to surface in successive philosophical systems. Those who have experienced it, like those who experience middle-order, optical reality, comprehend one another because the perceptions involved are roughly the same for all. There is nothing supernatural about it; it is simply one way of perceiving structure—inclusively. It could very well be simply an exaggeration of ordinary Gestalt perception induced by turning off linguistic logic. The perennial philosophy has a discrete logic which contradicts that of ordinary, everyday experience, and is extraordinarily difficult to set out, either mathematically or in plain. But it can be perceived rather easily by empathy and in this it resembles the skill one acquires in reading primary-process thinking in psychiatry. This is comprehensible enough, but will not really do for science; one can read and understand Joyce's *Finnegan* without working out every oblique allusion, but if one wants a world model or a brain process model, one has to buckle down and reduce patterned intuition to words or to mathematics, so that it can be checked. An unconventional vision, however compelling, is no better evidence than common optical perception. Sometimes this can be short-circuited when unformulated intuition leads directly to experiment; otherwise, hard work is required. One can form an intuitive world view by floating about on empathy, but the result is going to be solipsistic and—to maintain the metaphor—wet. So the acausal, inclusivist logic of oceanic modes has to be reduced to mathematical form, simply to see if it makes heuristic sense, and what kind of sense it does make.

One need no more be a Hindu to treat objects as events or loci in an interdependent field than one needs to be Jewish to like rye bread. Interestingly enough, Indian physicists have been too close to their tradition to draw directly on it as a source of ideas in this area. The germs of field theory in Western thought may well have arrived by way of Buddhist influences on Stoicism (Comfort 1979A), but Indian scientists are probably just as scared as most Westerners of the influence of religion on science. However, if a religion is a world view defining the relations of the experience of I-ness to a hypothetical That, then scientific objectivism qualifies as religion no less than Hinduism or Buddhism.

We do not accordingly start from, or need, any soft generalizations about brain-as-microcosm; the brain-as-perceiving system model will do nicely and is more in line with critical analysis. Our brain need not be universe-shaped (though it may be) because our universe is bound to be brain-shaped. At the same time, once we start looking critically at the preconceptions generated by our experience of positional identity, we have to re-examine the instrument we are using. In the case of particles, we have had to stop attributing transcendental identity to these hypothetical objects (Post 1963). There is no way around the closed loop implicit in the *cogito*, awkward as it is—slap-happy excursions into pure mentalism which take the line that "mind is the only reality" will always run into the fact that if we are using a nervous system to think, that too is part of middle-order reality; they also risk the conventional fate of objects which fly in ever decreasing circles. There is still going to be a system break at the point where we have to explain how matter sets about thinking itself if it is in fact virtual and a construct of our (material) sensorium.

This is something on which people like Śankara and Nāgārjuna (the first Hindu, the second Buddhist) are either deliberately obscure, or led to take refuge in a kind of cosmic engram which stands behind illusory I-ness and is the true "dwarf in the middle" (Hindu), or the reflection of Buddha-nature (Mahayana Buddhist). Labelling this as Brahman, for example, and then translating Brahman and māya as God and illusion rather than as field and phenomenal reality add further to the confusion, and fuel edifying rather than illuminating interpretations based on what *we* have traditionally attributed to God. Spinoza brought a similar problem down on himself by doing this, and had to do penance for it; I risk doing so by treating objective science as a religion, which anthropologically it is. Nor are naive Hindus and Buddhists necessarily more consistent than we are if they talk traditionally about reincarnation (in linear time) and the unreality of time and self in the same doctrinal breath, though philosophers like Nāgārjuna saw the point. Such traditions might help us not in being harder-nosed, but in acquiring direct experience of the observerless world, simply to see what such a counterintuitive model would look and feel like. For this reason it is a perfectly serious comment that a systematic pursuit of oceanic perception, starting with traditional methods, might help us in intuiting how a thingless or holographic universe might look, never mind the materiality, middle-order-reality style, of our cortex.

For some time now visualisations have not been much help in modern physics; it was far simpler, in Newtonian days, when they were. Unfortunately, the simple methods of producing I-less modes of perception are unreliable, but if physicists were able to take advantage of a Western, neurology-assisted version of more traditional yogas, they might find them an invaluable aid to empathic comprehension (Le Shan 1969) even if they have no heuristic value. It is one thing to dream up a holographic universe in terms of higher mathematics, and quite another to experience the conditionality of commonsense perceptions such as causality or the linearity of time. One can imagine this kind of exercise going into the mathematics course for astrophysicists much as marine biologists now routinely learn scuba diving. The results would be novel, however traditional the methods, because the cultures which developed them for religious purposes did not have the motivation to apply them, in the crass Western manner, to practical issues like atomic structure, or to test them by experiment.

This kind of argument used to enrage traditional Hindus, rather as J.B.S. Haldane enraged biblical Christians by trying to compute how thick a breastbone an angel would need to support his wing muscles. As a matter of fact Haldane, an entrenched rationalist and a Marxist to boot, was one of the first Western biologists to listen attentively to what Hindu philosophers were saying. The practical implication of adopting their viewpoint and devoting serious attention to the experience of I-ness is that not only neurology but physics will turn its attention to our chief and our only indispensable scientific instrument, the human brain, and its odd assumption of observerhood. At this point Indian philosophers from Śankara on could be pardoned for saying to the West "So what else is new?" Western science in the objectifying tradition has plugged away at its own *sādhana* (or practice, which is really the only basis on which it can be expected to listen to other people's insights) until it has reached the point at which it is obliged to devise techniques of analytic introspection directed at the human way of seeing. Indian philosophers have started with the human way of seeing and developed a sophisticated technology of introspective experiment using the computer to monitor itself. In other words, each tradition got to the same concerns in its own way. I can imagine that just as some hard-line Western scientists will go on regarding Indian philosophers as poetic but unregenerate mystics, some Indian philosophers will see a neurology of I and That as one more Western attempt to de-sacralise experience and get everything down to a derivate of matter. If so, the progress of physics and of neurology will quite simply knock our heads together to our mutual benefit; heuristic science is a brisk purge for the sloppy and theosophically-inclined, and the technology of introspection a sedative for simplistic bumptiousness. It is this, rather than chatter about Western materialism and Eastern spirituality, which is next on the agenda. Western physics might benefit from a direct contact with traditional Hindu philosophy and empiricism derived by reading the Sanskrit literature, but not by way of itinerant swamis who preach in mottos out of fortune cookies. A very interesting shift in our world view might result.

There are in fact neurological grounds for thinking that the brain is an ideal instrument for seeing models like those of Bohm if we can remove the filter which determines normal, or middle-order, experience. If yogis really contrive to remove the filter, we might want to learn from them.

Scientific innovation starts, as Whewell (1840) originally realized, with imaginative vision and proceeds by mathematical or experimental checking: the imaginative phase is the source of ideas and the checking is the source of knowledge. In this regard, Comte and Popper are perfectly right. If it were irrefutable Bohm's model would have interest as a construction, but no merit as physics. Positivism rules out gnosis in its vague sense, but it has not really addressed the experimental validity of introspection.

Comte—and the rest of us—have been heavily biassed by contact with a predominant religion which was wholly and primarily supernaturalist. Christians have not been without introspective or personal experience, but although they would say that such experiences are repeatable by others, and to that extent empirical, they set the experiences in a world which has two levels; Positivism asserts that the phenomenal world cannot be interpreted in this way, and all but uneasy Christians would logically agree. This leaves us, however, with no good standards for dealing with intuitions which are not supernatural, but specifically concern the mind as a natural object, and partake of the nature of empirical observations. Buddhism, for example, which is a religion in the sense that it generates a world model, does not assume a two-level, a priori system. In its most sophisticated form, it examines or discovers a world model, not by looking at objects, but by experimenting on the experience of consciousness and intellection—an enterprise for which it has developed a detailed traditional technology of "skilful means." Is this positive knowledge in

Comte's sense, or not? Consider the following remarks about mind and reality made, according to a Western disciple-rapporteur, by a Tibetan philosopher (David-Neel 1971):

> All our perceptions are nothing but interpretations of a fugitive contact by one of our senses with a stimulus. Thus we are led to contemplate the existence of two worlds: that of pure contact not colored by the screen of "memories"; and that created by the interpretation. The first of these of worlds represents Reality and is indescribable. [The second] consists purely of movement. There are no objects "in movement"; the objects consist of movement.

> This movement is a continued and infinitely rapid succession of flashes of energy. These rapid flashes of energy are sufficiently like one another to remain imperceptible to us. Then suddenly occurs, in this series of moments, a different moment which catches our attention and makes us think a new object has appeared. This process is often explained by comparing it with a grain which remains apparently inert, then one day shows a germ, that is different from the grain. However, the inertness of the grain was only in appearance.

> There are two theories and both consider the world as movement. One states that the course of this movement (which creates phenomena) is continuous. The other declares that the movement advances by separate flashes of energy which follow each other at such small intervals that these intervals are almost nonexistent.

The difference from Christian, supernaturalist experience is immediately obvious. One can forthwith reach for mathematics and put the yogi's opinions into a less exotic form. One can then begin to look for implications in physical, canonical experiment of his idea of the quantal character of perceived time. His model is not unlike Bohr's or Bohm's—the difference being that physicists' models are presented as the result of reflection on experimental results, and the yogi's as the result of reflection on experimentation with states of mind. Outside creative mathematics, which disguises the nature of the operation, this form of experimentation was simply not familiar to Comte's tradition. One can treat it as assisted creative imagination, but in fact—since one can use a technology to repeat the observations—it is actually parasitic analysis of the thinking system by the thinking system, something of which Comte had no field experience in European culture.

Meanwhile, anyone who wants an example of something perfectly intelligible and mathematically prosaic which *cannot* be visualized should read Rucker's (1977) amusing account of the mathematics of hypersolids and four plus dimensional spaces. We can easily compute the volume of hyperspace in a hypersphere (it comes to

$$v = \frac{1}{2}\pi^2 r^4$$

with $v$ expressed in $cm^4$, not $cm^3$ as for an ordinary sphere), but the nearest we can come to seeing a hypersphere is to shuffle the geographer's technique for drawing a round Earth on a flat sheet of paper. Moreover if there were hyperspheres, they would appear to us to be playing what amount to magic tricks. Now it might be possible experimentally to determine whether reality exists in 4-space or in some higher space. The trouble here is that spaces of this kind are confections used, as Einstein did in inferring that space-time is a hypersurface, to model out a particular algebra which yields a best fit to observation. Modern physics formalizes particle behaviors as representable in a higher order space with $3n$ linear dimensions per particle, but this convenient algebra is not the same as asserting that reality exists in a Hilbert space: it is a useful algorithm for some observed particle phenomena, and no more.

Mathematicians are used to this kind of exercise, and in any case they often have peculiar, and peculiarly humorous, minds. There is, however, nothing at all funny about the idea that all objective reality is simply the displayed algorithm by which our brains handle a field-determined reality. For example, when we extrapolate backwards, whether to the cosmological Big Bang or to a landscape inhabited by saber-toothed tigers, our assumption is that things (these things) were there before we were. If we express it in space-time, reality "was there before" we were, and fossil and extinct organisms may have been observed as such by other animals having comparable ways of abstracting reality to ours, but the human type of reality is contingent on the presence of humans to observe it. It is arguable that in the absence of human brains, these things "were not there" though the materials for their construction were inferentially there if such brains had been represented at that point in space-time. This bit of hair-splitting is important, because it bears heavily on some of our formalisms for evolution, organic or cosmological, in which linear historicity is tacitly assumed.

# 1.2

# *World Models: Some Eastern Melodies*

Science begins to take interest in other and previous world models when they begin to make sense, or when, through having seen the same possibility itself, it appreciates what problems the alien world view was addressing: one point of Zeno's paradox of the race between Achilles and the tortoise was largely missed until the advent of set theory. In his denial of motion Zeno comes even closer to the idea of Bohm's implicate-explicate model, but he lacked any algebra to develop it. The interest of such *déjà pensé* examples in past world-modelling is heightened when one reads the comments of later writers on philosophy who *missed* the point. Sometimes what appears naiveté or nonsense to observers from a later world view, who were satisfied they knew the answers, is actually failure to find a common ground of communication.

Pre-eighteenth century philosophers in the European tradition, who were roughly handled by the Enlightenment, have suffered from this failure. Having read Hume, Locke, and Comte, we tend to treat their predecessors, and even some of their successors, as antiques, and occasionally as freaks. The major non-Hellenic traditions—Hinduism and Buddhism in particular—incur a different risk. Positivists never argued with them because they knew nothing about them, except for the tenuous influences on such traditions as Stoicism. The educated European read Greek and Latin, but not Sanskrit or Pali, and in any case the texts were unavailable, while Christians and deists agreed *ex ignorantia* that they were "pagan" and reprehensible superstitions.

At this point we have to stop and look at some of these models, before getting on with science and with our own modelling, because while they are interesting sources of unconventional ideas, they are also being adopted on a basis of minimal exact knowledge by people who have derived their ideas of Oriental philosophy from popularizers; they neither read the languages in which the ideas were presented, nor understand the cultural backgrounds in which they grew. As an example of a different kind, one is constantly inundated with books describing the use of sexuality as a source of insight and of oceanic experience in Tantric yoga (true) combined with the assertion that this *sādhana* is typical of Vedic philosophies (false—during most recent history they have been prudish and celibatistic to a degree). The same thing is occurring in the kidnapping of Oriental models for adaptation to nonlocality, cerebral symmetry, and all manner of other subjects. True, those very varied and sophisticated models have been neglected, and contact with unfamiliar models can be stimulating. It can also, like the abuse of psychedelics, produce "heads" as uncritical as the Victorians who, knowing all the answers, dismissed Hindu and Buddhist philosophy as pagan persiflage.

During the 1900's, when the boycott was lifted and garbled versions of Oriental texts became available, an outburst of Blavatskian enthusiasm resulted, which turned off most scientific thinkers. European disciples, who concentrated on entertaining exotica, and itinerant swamis, who enjoyed access to uncritical disciples they could never have recruited at home, caused intellectual havoc and generated the equivalent of Papuan cargo-cults. Scholars with a better perception of the philosophies, and of the vigor of introspective investigation which went with them, made very little attempt to address for example, physicists. With the exhaustion of old style positivism we are seeing a second wave of uncritical enthusiasm, this time including physicists and neurologists (particularly the popular-book-writing variety) as well as Aquarians, acid-heads, and amateur mystics.

Hinduism and Buddhism—certainly Tantric and Mahayana Buddhism—come to us resembling objects dredged up from a wreck— they are heavily encrusted with local growths. Prying Hinduism apart from the structure, folk beliefs and literary tradition of India is like digging such an object out of a coral reef. Even the manners of Sanskrit post-Vedic and post Upaniṣadic scholarship provide further incrustation—the literature resembles a course in pedagogics produced by the Department of Tiresome Lists in an inferior American university, for the use of termites. The central, and interesting, feature of the conclusions when we actually get to them is that they are the result of direct introspective experimentation. The instructions for this in both traditions, however, are personally imparted by a teacher, not by a book, and the teacher, not surprisingly, incorporates traditional and locally familiar materials. If one wanted to repeat the observations, one is confronted with envisaging the Goddess in her ten manifestations as the Objects of Transcendent Knowledge, or trying to familiarize oneself with an iconography, in the case of Tibetan Buddhism, drawn from a fusion of Bon animism and ikons transmuted from Hinduism. One has to read texts whose style is quite as exasperating as that of some Church Fathers: and even important meditative techniques, like the use of *mantra*, are sufficiently alien to make us self-conscious, unless, of course, we are either serious devotees, or mere cultists. In the second case we shall practice hatha yoga (looked down on by most serious Hindu contemplatives as having more to do with becoming a wizard than with attaining intellectual or spiritual gnosis) and combine it with yoga-babble, to the annoyance of the serious, both scholarly and devout.

There are now readable and adequately scholarly works which enable us to get an accurate perception of the world models postulated by these traditions, devoid of background noise from an alien style, and with minimal cross-cultural problems. Approached in this way they can be seen to be both original and stimulating, because they address traditional Western scientific and philosophical preoccupations from a totally different, and, at their best, a strictly empirical angle. One value of studying them is that the study reveals how strongly scientific conceptualization since Hume has been influenced offstage by the prevailing direction of Western nonscientific philosophy. We should not be put off, accordingly, either by a dismal tradition of orientalizing theosophy, or by uninformed, premature Buddhists or premature Taoists who write popular books on physics. Provided we are decently hard-headed and open-minded about it, the discipline of Western positivism is a salutary advantage.

I started this book by talking, not about philosophy, but about the practical and emotional effects of world views. Christians reading the exposition of modern physics and neurology may quite reasonably tune them out, because the insights imparted by Christianity belong to a different order of discourse. Nothing in modern quantum physics really comments on any of their major beliefs. In this it is unlike hard-hat positivism, which was militantly secularist. Arguments over object-formation have no more relevance to dogmatic Christianity than they have to music or poetry (rather less, in fact, because of the metalanguage implied in the arts, and the relation of music to mathematics and brain structure). The only believers likely to be bothered by quantum physics are the minority who insist on treating Bronze Age myths more literally than the people who wrote them. True, Gnostic and other speculative religious believers who asserted the virtual nature of middle-order experience were drummed out long ago as heretics, and oceanic Christians—like St. John of Avila, Meister Eckhart, or the anonymous parson who wrote "The Cloud of Unknowing"—who were mixing their Christianity with introspective investigation of I-ness—were unpopular with the literal-minded. But it was an error of Victorian rationalism and of Paleyite "natural religion" that one can use physics or biology to confute or prove thoroughgoing supernaturalism. Supernaturalism is a point of view and the intellectual price is a two-level world model, with one level accessible only to revelation or personal experience. It is not a controvertible position, and Christians were probably unwise to get involved in attempting to kidnap science into forced marriage.

Rationalist Christianity foundered in improbability not by being superstitious, but by trying to beat rational positivism at its own game. Judging from the Rosicrucian spirit at large, we are likely to see attempts to orientalize Christianity by a revival of oceanics if these become pseudintellectually fashionable. Christianity's problems as a source of existential anxiety through appearing to be talking nonsense actually spring from the fact that it *was* orientalized, by Hellenists who had absorbed idealism from the Oriental mystery religions, and substituted an immortal soul for belief in resurrection. In spite of medieval graphics which showed bones scrambling out of their graves, the argumentative Christian might now find the idea of a reconstitution from spiritual DNA less silly than it sounded to the Enlightenment; after all, in Christian teaching God made up the prescription once before, and He has the blueprints.

I am not here to argue supernaturalism—supernaturalists can do that for themselves. One properly scans world models both natural and supernatural to see if there are any areas in which they make sense. In counseling patients who are by conviction Christian, physicians who were not supernaturalists have sometimes felt obliged to leave them to the priest (which is reasonable) or to argue from scientific positivism (which is not, especially since the kind of world model they wanted to impose was itself vulnerable). This second response is unanalyzed counter-transference: the hard-liners envied Christians a source of reassurance which they themselves had forgone as intellectually and rationally too expensive. Supernaturalism is not a hypothesis, because it cannot be disproved, unless we adopt the logic that "no man has a right to vote until he has died for Ireland."

Buddhism is a totally different matter: first, because it reached experientially a great many of the conclusions about the virtual nature of I-ness and of objective reality which seem to flow from modern physics and neuropsychology; and second, because it took its origin in "existential anxiety." Prince Gautama was a sheltered aristocrat and a grown man when he first went for a walk incognito and encountered a beggar, a sick man, a corpse, an old man, and a renounced mendicant, the symbol of dedication to meditative philosophy. This paradigm of the human condition made him abandon his home and family to seek enlightenment by meditation. The model developed by his followers is not a two-level model—what looks like supernaturalism is virtual or figurative, and is known to be so. In Buddhist meditative exercises, first middle-order, linear experience, then positional I-ness, then logic, and finally the Cartesian focus of I-ness (ātman in Buddhism), which is doing the thinking or the seeking after comprehension, are experienced to be illusory and suppressed, leaving no thinker or thought, but a ground, no-thing, which is inclusive and contains no categories. This is the completion of enlightenment, described metaphorically in terms very like those of Christian cataphatic mysticism as "pure light." The significant thing about Buddhist philosophy is that it does not originate in hypothesis or in mathematics but in empathic experience, and Buddhist education aims to facilitate the experience, not expound a theoretical basis for it.

Science, of course, is committed to structure and its analysis and while it might value the earlier stages of this process of introspection, which appear to describe an empathic view of the implicate, science would regard the nairātmya (no ratiocination) stage with the ardor of a ski-maker for the forecast of perpetual hot weather, and ask questions about the popular description of this condition as bliss (ānaṇḍa), which seems to imply affect. On the other hand, while earlier stages of the meditative process involve seeing the implicate, the nairātmya mode seems to imply empathic fusion with the holomovement itself, involving the stopping or dissolution of all virtual processes which are generated like secondary ripples by the activity of the homuncular, cogitating and observing I. This dissolution includes both matter and I and consequently science.

Christians generally agree that salvation and being in the presence of God are desirable; whether dissolution in the holomovement is desirable or not would depend, for non-Christians, on one's attitude. Avoidance of middle-order reality altogether because it involves dukha (suffering) might strike us as nihilistic. Dedicated scientists, adhering to the religion of science, might be more willing to abandon ratiocination because it involves illusion, but such dedication is probably rare, for it leaves one no substrate for further activity. Buddhists would argue that one can only know the underlying reality by becoming part of the holomovement, rather than holding out as a virtual construction from it. Buddhist yoga, therefore, contains a clear implication of what amounts to discarnate or noncerebral knowing.

Buddhist psychology regards I-ness as a direct object-formation from the holomovement, and individual I-ness as a kind of pseudopodium or droplet extruded from it, with the brain as transducer, not generator. This is implicit in the idea of reincarnation: the same virtual droplet, complete, in some cases, with at least some memory traces, can continue to be transduced several times before being re-absorbed into the general substrate.

The popular Buddhist model of this process is somewhat confused, however, partly as a result of the conviction, from *nairātmya* experience that I-ness is illusory. This is not so in the sophisticated teaching, which states that there is no "thing" which preserves an identity between successive lives, as in the explication model there is no necessary continuity between successive manifestations of an electron. The relation between manifestations is that of a flame lit from one candle to the next. The continued or re-explication is attributed to *karma* (action or actions), meaning that it is due to some of the behaviors and thought-forms which the virtual identity displayed in middle-order reality. Both Buddhism and Hinduism locate the memory-store at least partly in the *ātman* rather than in brain circuitry, as evidenced by their belief in *jatismaras* (persons who spontaneously recall previous lives). Gautama himself taught that this could be achieved prospectively by willpower, in keeping with the idea that what is vividly in the mind will be expressed as a virtual reality. Buddhaghosa, a fifth-century Indian, elaborates on the technique in the *Vissudhi Magga*.

Rather than becoming argumentative about the demographics of such a view—which the Buddhists, like the Pythagoreans, trace back into phylogeny—it is wiser, from the point of world-model formation, to concentrate on the fact that for Buddhist philosophy I-ness, re-explication and time itself are all wholly virtual displays, and our experience of them is dictated by Kantian a-prioris. On this basis physicists might be readier than biopsychologists to agree with Voltaire that being apparently born twice is not much odder than having been born once.

The Buddhist model is interesting, not only because it is based on very intensive introspection directed at I-ness and the world model, but also because it suggests questions to Western scientific philosophy which are unfamiliar and therefore novel. Buddhism regards some mental processes, including memory, as potentially discarnate but not supernatural nor the expression of some kind of objectively existing spirit or ghost. I-ness is just as epiphenomenal as in the Western positivist model, but it is an epiphenomenon of the implicate, not a spin-off from brain chemistry.

In treating mind, though virtual, as a separate explicate, Buddhist and many Hindu philosophers tend to share a radical view of reality which asserts that since all conventional phenomena are illusory, anyone who adequately masters his own illusion of the phenomenal can manipulate it and other peoples' experience practically at will. One might have thought that so impressive a demonstration of the virtual nature of the real would have had great didactic value, but serious empirics in both traditions are remarkably sheepish about it, not on the ground that an evil and adulterous generation seeks for a sign, but rather that interest in manipulating the illusory indicates continued attachment to it. Questions concerning the reality of *siddhī* (Skt. success, the Hindu term for the ability to induce singularities) tend to be fended off, and disciples are instructed that their only value is as indicators that the process of meditative education is proceeding correctly. One experienced Buddhist instructor remarked "If I showed you some genuine *siddhī*, you wouldn't recognize them." Occasional sages with a sense of humor, like Ramana Maharshi, are said to have used control over singularities to play instructive jokes on overzealous disciples. The *siddhī* of popular tradition include singularities such as mind reading, bilocation, mystical progression, levitation and so on, which are, oddly enough, the canonical manifestations of exceptional virtue accorded to Catholic saints (Farges 1926), all except stigmatization. One would be inclined to question whether that noted Catholic yogi and thaumaturgist St. Joseph of Cupertino, for example, was much exercised by discursive interest in the virtual character of reality. When Buddhism or Hinduism is treated as a model for physics, it is proper to point out that physicists are going to ask some questions.

If we turn to Nāgasena, who is probably the closest expositor of Buddhist world models to our own tradition, some perfectly clear and highly relevant concepts emerge. The most important is that there are no entities. Neither self nor things are continuously existent, as asserted by Democritean physics, commonsense, and teachings concerning immortal souls. All of them resemble the successively lit bulbs in the skysign or the successively explicated states we interpret as particles, and require for their description an algebra of transitions without quantities—one in which all the terms are operators. Nāgasena points out that entities like chariot or person are irreducible, i.e., different qualitatively from the sum of their parts, but at the same time aggregates of this kind have no transcendental identity because of the virtual character of time. This is about as close as any theory prior to that of quantum based space-time has come to putting the problem of time as we experience it in a condition for mathematical treatment. Nāgasena is, in fact, only reiterating a model of long standing: his discussions with King Menander probably took place in ca. 150 B.C., long after Zeno, and the Buddhist disinterest in the structure of the phenomenal (apart from dissolving it) makes him less explicit than Tantric Hindu philosophers who talk specifically of "seeing Time end-on" as a superposition. Over the entrance of several of the fine Orissan temples built under Tantrik influence is a gargoyle spouting the "stream of time" from his jaws—so that the entering worshipper does in fact view it in a complex dimension, with effects similar to those of rotating an iterant to form a superposition. The Vaishnava *Rās Maṇḍala* (alternate dancing Krishnas and milkmaids, with Radha and Krishna intertwined in the middle) actually models a circular iterant with a superposition at its center.

We shall have more to say about the interchangeability of myth and math. If anyone finds it infuriating, on the basis that myths are disreputable while math is the handmaid of science, he or she should rethink the use of schematics in conveying ideas. While naive people in Vedic traditions think of gods and the like as persons, naive people in our own tradition think of *2 + 2 = 4* as a Law of Nature, so the scoring is about even. Buddhists and Hindus who use a complex iconography do not differ much from mathematicians in the way they use it, except that it is solidly analog and concerned with complex forms rather than based in vectors or scalars; the iconographic personages, like algorithms, are thought forms and recognized as such. Moreover Buddhist philosophers have had just as much trouble as physicists in expounding counterintuitive ideas to a not very imaginative audience: their response has been to encourage direct mental experience.

One consequence of modern physics which has not been stressed enough is that it introduces a certain democratic equality among thought forms. If hydrogen atoms, organisms, neurones and the Nonconformist Conscience are all thought forms (algorithms), it is rather hard to assert that some are more real than others, and that there is a category called "real" which is wholly uncompromised by the observing mind. Reification is not an occasional fallacy, but rather the basis of the entire phenomenal world. If one likes one can think of iconographies as putting different game cartridges into the machine, so that one can see the equations, or play Dungeons and Dragons based on the same algorithms, according to taste. Left-hemispheric Englishmen devoted to physics and brought up Episcopalian may find the Jungian undergrowth of older iconographies supererogatory and confusing. Mathematics has its own iconography and we as a culture may be closer to the Islamic contemplatives who reject iconography altogether. There is something to be said for a metalanguage which bans graven images root and branch—nobody, unfortunately, has devised one which is communicative.

Since all world models ultimately comment on existential anxiety, Buddhism incurs the psychological comment that it is itself a denial mythology. Whereas in the eyes of non-Christians Christianity accounts for the human condition but basically denies mortality, Buddhism, in the eyes of some non-Buddhists, accounts differently for the human condition but denies conventional Reality, or at least I-ness.

*Dukha* (existential suffering) cannot be escaped so long as middle-order reality is treated as real. Middle-order reality itself is mere peregrination (*saṃsara*) from which one may be liberated, and which may itself be transformed, first by perceiving it to be self-generated by conventional perception, and then by perceiving identity itself to be equally illusory. In a Freudian view, dissociative bliss (*ānaṇda*) could simply be a reminiscence of pre-individuative stages in infancy when I-ness was not fully developed and embarrassing psychosexual events had not yet occurred. In an existential model, such as that of Yalom (1980), bliss is rather a reminiscence of that stage in childhood when the nature of human mortality and finitude was still unknown and unappreciated. This is very probably correct (Blanco 1975).

At the same time, many ecstatic experiences turn not so much on relief from I-ness as on the intuitive perception of form (Comfort 1969), a far more conscious concern of the scientist as well as the artist. One common existential anxiety is that the events of daily experience, including birth and death, are seen as formless or, in Sartre's phrase, absurd. Absurdity is the post-positivist world model, and a source of much of the concern expressed by patients. Now living in middle-order reality is not dependent upon having a world model, but one needs a world model in order to perform it securely and without an exacerbation of *dukha* through feelings of insignificance and subjugation to the Juggernaut-like character of events.

We have some empirical check on this anxiety in precisely the same area which prompted Yalom's (1980) psychiatric recognition of the primacy of death anxieties, namely the counseling of terminal patients. These have been reported to be greatly alleviated (Pahnke 1969, Grof 1970) by oceanic experiences induced under supervision by the use of psychedelics. Although one can think of a great many other dynamics involved in so spectacular and magical a regression which might alter mood, one component has been reported to be related to world view—namely, that linear experience is factitious, and the world is not like that. Not like what? Not like the existential flat earth of conventional rationalism as popularized by science. Whether what it appears to be like, under such influences, is a rational source of reassurance may prove unimportant if the reassurance is real. What seems to happen is that the disquieting, *unheimlich* (uncanny) quality of processes orthogonal to ordinary experience becomes transmuted by introjection; the heavily fortified I which death anxieties defend is experienced to be arbitrary, and not so much denied as renounced. Grof complicates his interpretation by theorizing that the source of death anxieties lies in unpleasant prenatal experiences. Buddhist tradition would agree, but the prenatal experiences Grof has in mind are prosaic (confinement in the womb, birth-stress), not metempsychotic.

One could accordingly use Grof to explain Buddhist imagery, or Buddhist experience to explain away Grof, according to taste and inclination. Fortunately, no such wild-goose chase is necessary to establish that oceanic experience tends to a more syntonic world view—which tells us something about its clinical utility, though nothing about its validity as a source of heuristic world models.

At this point, simply to avoid disappointment, it is necessary to make clear that neither empiricism nor existential anxiety are about to make our culture into spontaneous Buddhists. Our cultural anxiety is not Gautama's. Given our religious tradition, it would be dissipated quite simply and finally by even the crudest and most *saṁsaric* interpretation of metempsychosis without any further consideration of I-ness, the factitious nature of time, or the desirability of enlightenment. If this is not the only chess game, we need have no existential anxiety about chess. As to *dukha*, one can be baffled, angry, disappointed, or cheated in playing chess, and one may lose, but there will be another game. If there is to be more pie, not in the sky, but in an extension of identity, whether amnesic or not, we can expect statistically to get a slice of it. The seriousness of life, whether one ends in hospital or in a concentration camp, is that it is the only one we shall ever have.

If metempsychosis were to become scientifically credible, the Western response would be great relief (for laymen), re-evaluation of the nature of mind (for systems theorists and psychologists), grave confusion and head shaking (for scientific hard-line positivists, who would take some convincing), and a tendency, if this chess game is going badly, to resign and set up the board again. Reincarnation for us would take the place of the alchemical immortality obtained by that engaging figure in Joseph Needham's account of Chinese philosophy, Mr White-Stone, who, once relieved of anxiety about death, saw no special reason to go further and attain the equivalent of Buddha-hood. What, after all, would be the fun of becoming merged in the holomovement, blissful or not?

> Mr White-Stone was a disciple of Chung-Huang-Jen. In the time of Pheng Tsu he was already over 2000 years old. He was not willing to cultivate the Tao of rising into the heavens (as an immortal) but he just wanted to be an immortal as such. He did not intend to do away with the joys and happinesses of life among men, so the course of action he adopted was to practice the arts of the bedchamber as the main thing, and to emphasize the taking of the medicine of potable gold.
>
> Pheng Tsu once asked him why he did not take the chemical which can make one rise into the heavens, to which he replied: 'Can the joys of the heavens really compare with those that are found among men? If one can go on living here below without getting old and dying, one will be

treated with the greatest respect; would one be treated any better in the heavens?' So the people said: 'Mr White-Stone is a *hsien* [immortal] who wants to avoid becoming a *hsien*.' It was because he did not seek to rise to the heavens and take a place among the celestial bureaucracy. Nor did he have any desire for fame and renown in this present world.

(Needham 1956)

At the other extreme, a medieval Japanese knight who considered himself insulted would resign from the ongoing chess game by disembowelling himself, knowing that if he behaved honorably he would move up a table in the *next* game, and be reincarnated as a samurai, rather than a woman or a dogsbody. In such ways do existential considerations shape our behaviors.

Living in a Hindu culture, Gautama took reincarnation for granted, as a folk belief. Our patients aren't *bodhisattvas*. Aside from genuine contemplatives, the nearest thing we have in the Western tradition are scientists, who may or may not be motivated by compassion, but certainly are motivated by intellectual curiosity. If reincarnation looked likely, they would want to understand it. If an alien technology seemed relevant, they would be quite willing to study it, persevere, acquire techniques, and try to empathize unconventional models of reality or of a non-Cartesian order, which they would then translate into mathematics. People who have no trouble with the stacked planiverses which we will encounter presently would have no trouble with the algebra of serial, nonlocal or simultaneous experience. Given our present understanding of the material universe, the odd and the unconventional can always be made mathematically prosaic—or understood with traditional Buddhist models of "dharmas to be destroyed." In spite of the egotism involved in wanting-to-know and in being-the-first-to-formulate, they might be able to address nonpersonal knowing, existential anxieties or not. (After all, they now live with the epiphenomenal mind; honest pursuit of the evidence and acceptance of the most likely demonstrable explanation are real scientific virtues, as against wishful thinking.) It would be really interesting to see if, by going that far, their interest was transmuted into something quite different, or whether they would become, in effect, wizards in the Buddhist estimation—more interested in manipulating *saṃsara* than in getting beyond it for spiritual reasons. *Saṃsara* is their element; it would take fish a while to grow legs and walk on dry land.

Tradition has it that when an intellectually curious monk called Mālunkyāputta started asking Gautama to elucidate questions of science: "That the world is eternal or not eternal, that it is finite or not finite, that the saint exists, or does not exist, or neither exists nor does not exist after death" and so on, he got an extended rebuke to the effect that if stuck with a poisoned arrow, one does not postpone surgery until one has asked who shot it and what sort of wood it is made of. The poisoned arrow of ordinary human experience is the pressing problem for this philosophy, not speculation about the structure of the phenomenal world (*Majjhimanikāya*, sutra 63). Phenomenal reality is a bonfire which roasts us alive—small wonder if the recognition that it is contingent and that reality is "not like that" is experienced as bliss (*Milindapanha*). Unlike the Hindu play of the Goddess, which involves both rewards and atrocities, traditional Buddhism has at times viewed the phenomenal world as unrelievedly atrocious—not because of human barbarity but quite simply because of transience. In fairness to Gautama, it could be that the author of the sutra missed the point, and that what he was actually saying to Mālunkyāputta was "Stop model-hunting! You will only generate more misinformation." This premise (basic to Zen), however, is not what the sutra says. In the *Milindapanha*, where Nāgasena holds a Platonic dialogue with the Greek trained King Menander, we do, however, get some discursive modelling, largely concerned with the nature of time and the absence of transcendental identity, which cries out for some Bohmian mathematics. One has to agree with Christmas Humphreys that "the West will never be Buddhist," but if it takes Buddhist philosophy as seriously as it has taken Hellenistic, it will generate a Navayana—a new vehicle.

I have gone into this at some length, not out of misplaced zeal for Oriental Studies as a branch of the humanities, nor even to demonstrate that other people were mulling field-type models before they became respectable in physics; the idea was to set an exercise. While seekers read philosophic or religious preachments like singles joining an introduction service, i.e., with a view to matrimony, scientists, who are occupational eclectics, read them with an eye to what the convinced of those traditions will interpret as rape. They gut philosophies, traditions, and belief systems for useful ideas, and their devotional practice for repeatable observations.

The exercise is to take, for example, Buddhist world-modelling *tel quel*, at its face value, as if it had just appeared in mathematical form in *Nuovo Cimento* or some other journal, and look at the scientific implications. One might start with Nāgasena who asserts: (1) that self has no transcendental identity; (2) that a recognizable self is re-explicated (like the propagation of a flame from candle to candle) at numerous points in phenomenal time; and (3) that the flow of time is actually a position artefact. Rather than saying "Pointless exercise—no evidence," or simply, as most hard-nosed psychologists would probably say, "Bosh!!" the answer which goes to the top of the class will be: "If (3), then the apparent iteration postulated in (2) is actually a simultaneity, or more correctly a superposition." And likewise for other fragments of the alien model. One has to explain to students that this exercise does not involve the assumption that Nāgasena, or whoever, is right, or that these are the facts. They are performing a trial run in a discipline, namely demonics, which we shall deal with after a break for recreation.

# Interval:
# Meet the Metaphysical
# Fauna

"Do you think we could put this shield down now, Lion?"

"We should give them another five minutes. In case one of them were to come back."

"You're overconscientious, Lion. I don't believe in overtime."

"Anything one does, one should do properly. That's how we got where we are. Royal Supporters can't behave like members of some damn union. Well, at least put it down carefully. Can't deny it's welcome, to get this crown off."

"I never end the day, Lion, but I blame the College of Arms. They could have made us sejant, not rampant and rampant guardant respectively. Then we could have done the job sitting down."

"Nice that would have looked. Hang that collar up properly, Unicorn. And coil up that chain. That's better. What the devil are those?"

"Cards."

"Pretty funny cards. What are you going to do? Play patience?"

"No: they're my art collection."

"Then hang them up."

"Nowhere to hang them. And these pictures aren't intended to be hung up. I regard them as more analogous to a map."

"Of what? Britain?"

"Not exactly. Of Albion, possibly. A map of the mind."

"What? Whose mind? What's this, anyway? Seems to be a picture of the devil."

"It is. Here are the King, the Lovers and the Fool."

"Give me strength!"

"And Strength."

"Well, there's a lion on it, as you'd expect, but somebody seems to be giving him some medicine. What *is* this damn nonsense, Unicorn?"

"It's called the Tarot. Gypsies use it for telling fortunes."

"Well, Unicorns aren't going to use it for telling *my* fortune. Never held with that sort of superstition. You don't believe that stuff, do you?"

"Not if you mean it literally, Lion, and treat it as science. These images are the material of poetry, which is really where we both come from."

"Poetry my claws. We are heraldic symbols."

"Which is precisely what these are. You're the Solar Beast, even if you don't know it, and I'm the Lunar horse. Obviously you have an extremely short memory and haven't read the literature. I've always been interested in my ancestry. Some of my manifestations are the Night Mare and the Mari Llwyd."

"And one of my manifestations is Nellie of Mullingar. Go on."

"No, seriously, it gives me great satisfaction, holding up that coat of arms, and looking down at all those Nobel prize physicists at the high Table . . ."

"Of whom this college has more, I might add, than any other institution of learning."

". . . to realize that we have played, and still play, an important role in the creation of world models."

"I was brought up to believe, and I still do . . ."

"Naturally!"

"that we're perfectly straightforward symbols. I stand for Strength, and you stand for . . . er . . ."

"Purity, actually."

"A horny horse with a taste for virgins? Come off it."

"Well, we're both overdetermined. You stand for strength, reality, duty, ethics, courage, and no nonsense, the commonsense light of day in which things are what they seem. I represent something a great deal more complex, in this case the creative imagination. You believe what you were brought up to believe, until somebody proves it isn't so. I don't *believe* anything. To believe things one has to say

$$\text{either } a \text{ or } not \text{ } a.$$

That isn't my mode. I always end up thinking

$$\forall a \, \exists b : b \supset a \wedge \sim a$$

Then everyone, lions in particular, say "Shame on you—you can't!!" You're a real animal. I'm imaginary: A wondrous creature of no kind. . . . A coherent superposition on four legs."

"In other words a fraud. Somebody saw an antelope sideways on and made you up. Came home and passed off a narwhal horn as unicorn ivory. You call that science?"

"No, poetic imagination. You're content to exist. I might exist. I'm potentiality—you're a thick-skulled zoological fact. I wouldn't change places for all the tea in China, I assure you. I only stick around here out of a sense of duty. This College needs me."

"Like a hole in the head—horny enough already, and talks far too much. And is full, like every College, of might-have-beens."

"It also knocks down Nobel Prizes like bloody ninepins. Thanks in part to keeping me around."

"As usual, you're forgetting one thing, Unicorn."

"Meaning?"

"That fight we had. I won, remember. *I* got the crown. And you had to leave Cambridge in a hurry, with a thick ear. Round about the end of the seventeenth century when poetical mish-mash was moved out of science."

"When they founded the Royal Society?"

"Precisely."

"Well, if it's the *Royal* Society, we're both still there. Holding up the shield, and all that. They asked me back. They didn't choose two lions!"

"You want another round? All right, sharpen up your horn!"

"We can't now, Lion. Another time. Pax. No referee."

"Very well then. Put those ridiculous things away."

"Frankly, Lion, I'm surprised they bother you so much. Nobody pretends they tell fortunes. All that these cards are is a set of crude oversimplications of some preferred bits of mental imagery. If I lay them out in a row, and you have a problem, *they* don't correlate with your problem, *you* correlate with them. They set you talking, and you tell your own fortune, or give yourself advice, or whatever. Wouldn't matter which cards came up, they'd always fit. Rohrschach used blots of colored ink, so that the patient makes his own cards."

"Which is how all pseudoscience works, by selection of instances."

"Whereas genuine science . . . ?"

"Proceeds by observation and deduction. You look, think, understand, and then test your understanding."

"Codswallop."

"*What?*"

"I said codswallop! What happens is that you look, and think, and put the whole thing out of the front of your mind. Then, over a period of time, a model pops out, like a slice of bread from a toaster. You look at it, think what it means, and test that to see if there's anything which doesn't fit it. If not, you're in business."

"And what, may I ask, pops it out?"

"I do. You pass it down to me. I look through my art collection, find some patterns which fit, and pass them up to you. No, of course you don't notice. A lot of the time I work at night, when you're asleep. I'm a nocturnal beast. Actually I've only got quite a limited collection of patterns, but if you stir them around, one or another will usually fit. Circles, trees, mandalas, numbers, recursions, musical relations and, of course, these cards. And when the slip of paper pops out of the slot in your mind, you slap your haunch and say 'What an original lion I am!' Then you write a paper describing how you *deduced* the relationship. I have to stick my horn in my ear to stop laughing."

"Now look here . . ."

"I wouldn't start anything if I were you, Lion. The Master is watching us. With amusement. Has been, for some time."

"My God! Get your collar on! Give me that crown. Master, I'm sorry. We *are* off duty."

"So am I. You may both stand easy. I was listening with amusement. I have to congratulate the Unicorn. For many years I dined at that High Table without realizing that I was in the presence of an instructive parable."

"I did whisper it, Master. As loud as I could."

"In which case, I very probably heard you unawares. Which seems to prove your point."

"With respect, Dr. Whewell,* that mobile marlinspike has been insulting Science. Don't let him make a monkey. . . . sorry, Sir, that slipped out."

"I see no danger that he will impose on me, if that is what you mean. I heard your argument, and I tend to agree with him, though I must say that as a Christian I dislike his use of heathen auspices. Let me remind you, Lion, that I invented the word *scientist*. The view you put forward of scientific activity is that popularly held. It represents the way in which scientific inference is presented, but not how it is actually done. No general statement, not even the simplest iterative generalization, can arise merely from the conjunction of raw data. You have been reading the nonsense written by Mr. Mill, who criticized my ideas without com-

---

*William Whewell, D.D., 1794–1866, Master of Trinity College Cambridge, was a formidable polymath, a friend of Faraday (to whom he suggested that physical units of measurement should be named for eminent researchers) and the first writer to use the words 'scientist' and 'physicist'. His *Philosophy of the Inductive Sciences* (1840) is the first serious account of how modern research is actually done. He had a red face and a loud voice, and seriously upset the Fellows by including a laudatory inscription to himself on a new building he erected for the College, Whewell's Court, which still stands.

prehending them. Facts cannot be observed as facts except in virtue of the conceptions which the observer himself unconsciously supplies. Our friend here governs the unconscious supply. Which appears to me to be what he was telling you."

"That's precisely what I was telling you, Lion."

"With great respect, Master, if that is so, what stands between us and the idiot who thinks cards tell fortunes?"

"You do, my friend. The office of a lion is to tear to pieces every hypothesis which fails to accord with observation, and which fails to predict future, and as yet unknown, observations."

"Right on."

"But it is only recently that I became aware of the office of the Unicorn."

"Which is to fool around with silly pictures and drive every right thinking person crazy."

"Precisely. It is not so long since every right thinking person believed on the evidence of his senses that the Sun rotates about the Earth. Or that the Earth itself was flat and one could fall off its edges. They even interpreted Scripture in that sense. I have no doubt at all how science proceeds. It moves from interest in the observed to hypothesis, from hypothesis to verification, and that which escapes your jaws becomes for a while the knowledge of the time, until it is consumed by some grander generalization which extends its boundaries to new facts and new predictions."

"You preach a fine sermon, Master."

"So I am told. You are probably aware that a fellow clergyman said of me that my forte was science and my foible omniscience. I think that in my writings I stood on firm ground. What has amazed me is the fertility and boldness of those minds to which we owe new models of the world, in originality and complexity far exceeding the models which I knew as Master of this College. Some of these original minds sit at this table every night."

"I know, and if you ask me, some of them are as mad as hatters."

"There is an originality which looks like madness, Lion. If it is indeed madness, it is you who cut them short. But if it happens to accord with observation, and to lead to new observation, you have to let them pass."

"They're not crazy, Lion. They're just people with unusually good hearing, who listen to the stories I tell them, and instead of saying 'Bosh!', they say, 'I like that. I wonder . . .' and they're off."

"But never so thoroughly off that they forget that the stories which the Unicorn tells them by night, must get past the Lion next day. I wish you both a very good evening."

"Whew! That was sudden. Is he back in his frame?"

"Yes. Flat as a pancake once more."

"Always in a hurry—always was."

"He talks like a book. Pompous old josser, but bright—in spite of putting up that Gothic courtyard and having an advertisement for himself written over the front door. Fell off his horse in the end and broke his neck, poor old chap. After that, it says a lot that he puts up with unicorns. Makes a nice portrait."

"Well, perhaps now that you've heard him you'll believe him about the importance of creative imagination. After all, he should know. He practically invented science as a rational activity. Sandwiches? Alfalfa for me, raw steak for you. And the bread's too thick as usual. It's reassuring to have it confirmed that we're both needed."

"Hold it, Unicorn. We're not alone. Do you see what I see?"

"Where?"

"Up there. It looks uncommonly like a grin. An unattached grin. I dislike it. It's unnatural. I am about to roar at it. Grrrrrr!"

"Don't waste your breath, Lion. Give it time. It's only the Cat, a small relative of yours, I understand. Always hanging around, but he never comes out while the Master's around. Look, he's materializing nicely."

"Evening, all. Has he gone back into his frame?"

"He's gone. Probably for the night. Good evening, Cat."

"What is this Cat doing here anyway? Must belong to somebody. Cats do."

"Lion, I think you two should meet. Cat, meet this literal-minded Lion. Lion, meet Schroedinger's cat."

"*Whose* cat?"

"Schroedinger's Cat. The most celebrated scientific member of your family. I'm surprised you aren't acquainted."

"What does he do?"

"He bifurcates."

"Don't be filthy!"

"Explain to him, will you, Cat?"

"I'll try, if the Unicorn will comb my whiskers. It's a rather distressing story, and I need something to calm me if I recite it. Mind if I sit down? Thank you. You're quite sure Dr. Whewell isn't listening? Are you sitting comfortably? Very well, I'll begin. You have to imagine, Lion, that I am shut in a box."

"Why?"

"Because that was where Dr. Schroedinger put me. So that he couldn't see me."

"Not a very nice way to treat one of my relatives."
"I agree. But just listen to the next bit. In the box with me there is a large jar of poison."
"What sort of poison?"

"Does it matter? Well, if you must know, it's nerve gas on Mondays, Wednesdays and Fridays, and cyanide the rest of the time. Satisfied?"
"No. But go on."

"Over the jar of poison there is a hammer, and that hammer is connected to a counting device. The counting device is made so that it is controlled by a single quantum phenomenon. Between the time I go in the box, and the time Dr. Schroedinger opens it, there is just one-half probability that the hammer will fall. Picture my position!"
"Well, you've got one chance in two of getting out alive. Look on the bright side."

"It's worse than you think. Suppose the experiment lasts one hour. Just before Dr. Schroedinger comes to open the box, am I alive or dead? Lion?"
"It's evens."

"Wrong. Unicorn?"
"Half alive, half dead."

"Right. Quantum events are indeterminate, not just probabilistic. Until Dr. Schroedinger opens the box I am a coherent superposition, alive and dead. I only settle down to one state when Dr. Schroedinger opens the box, and then only in his mind. He becomes correlated with one eigenpussy (let us say the live one—naturally I prefer that). And the other one is . . ."
"Where?"

"Who knows? Lying dead in a divergent time stream to which Dr. Schroedinger has no access. Or put it the less pleasing way around: Dr. S has a dead cat on his hands, if he doesn't poison himself opening the box; and a living eigenpussy flies off at right angles, as it were."
"Into another world where, if Dr. S had poisoned himself opening his damn box, he too would be alive doing more experiments. . . ."
"Sequitur, Unicorn."
"And generating further bifurcations if he repeats the experiment, and so on ad infinitum."
"Baloney. I can see why you couldn't face Dr. Whewell."
"Unfortunately, Lion, that is what quantum mechanics indicates. Now we both know that if you were to do the experiment, not just imagine it, and keep repeating it, you would find live and dead cats with approximately equal frequency. Correct, Cat?"

"Probably. Schroedinger never tried, I'm glad to say. But that is simply because the other eigenpussy, the Duplicat, I call him, is fundamentally inaccessible once you are correlated with the observation. The maths work."

"I don't believe it."

"Let me present you with this thesis by Hugh Everett. You can check it for yourself. Got a pencil? Good. Let me hold your sandwich."

(The Lion sharpens his pencil, writes a large $\psi$ at the top of the sheet, and starts to repeat Everett's calculations.)

"Tell me, Cat, why won't you face Dr. Whewell?"

"Because."

"Don't tell me you're scared. He's a just man. He agrees that if a hypothesis is found to predict previously unmade observations, and is not controverted by critical experiment, we have to stay with it however insane it looks at first sight. Does quantum mechanics not stand up experimentally against classical formalisms?"

"Alas, it does. Even when it predicts the same particle can be in two places at once like a yogi."

"Then Dr. Whewell will have to take his medicine . . ."

"I know. But think of the strain on a great Victorian, who believed in the efficacy of First Causes and all that."

"You underrate him. You do, really."

"Well, maybe, later, I'll broach it to him gently."

"Sonofabitch. I don't believe it!!"

"Have you finished, Lion?"

"Must be something wrong. But I'm damned if I can find it."

"There *are* other explanations, hidden parameters and so on. Why are you looking at me like that?"

"Goddamit, Cat, YOU HAVE EATEN MY SANDWICH!"

"Dear me. So it has. What will you have for dinner, in that case, Lion?"

"I think, Unicorn, I will have . . . CAT."

"And I think it is time to rejoin my other eigenstate. A very good evening to you both."

"He's fading. Sit down, Lion. You can't eat a grin."

"I'll try."

"Well, the grin has gone now too. Have some alfalfa—it's very calming. Count yourself lucky that he left when he did. If you'd swallowed him during his transformation you might have found yourself transformed into a Metalion, and I'd have had to explain your absence to the Master. There, there, never mind. There's enough for two."

"It's not the alfalfa I'm crying over. It's the respectable world of sanity. Where cats don't duplicate. I'm shaking all over."

"Consider. The world is no different now, presumably, because we describe it in a different algebra, now is it?"

"I suppose not."

"So all is as it was?"

"I suppose so. This is all your doing, Unicorn."

"Not mine. I suppose you should blame the Master. He told people to check their hypotheses against Reality. The Cat is only one intellectual test of the quantum hypothesis. The Einstein-Podolsky-Rosen paradox is even worse, because it's an actual not a Gedanken experiment. Einstein thought it up to prove that quantum mechanics must be wrong. Unfortunately it's testable, and quantum mechanics works. If you want to go on living in a world made up of little billiard-balls, blame Dr. Whewell."

"I suppose you're right. But it's a bitter pill. Seems unBritish somehow. Duplicats! Oh, bugger science. Let's finish our dinner, such as it is, and get some sleep. We're on duty at breakfast."

# Chapter 2

# *MATHEMATICAL MODELS AND THE DEMONIC COMPUTER*

# 2.1

# Demonics: Talking to Gezumpstein

"Young man, in mathematics you don't *understand* things, you just get used to them."

Von Neumann

In 1781 Immanuel Kant pointed out that time and space are not phenomena or things, but ways of organizing data, thus effectively opening the way for Einstein. Kant gave to what we now call 4-space (space consisting of three linear dimensions and time) the title "a priori"—an invincible way-of-seeing with which humans are born. So convinced was he that this frame of reference *was* invincible that he cited the impossibility of imagining a non-Euclidean geometry to prove it.

Unluckily for this argument, non-Euclidean geometries not only can be, but soon were, imagined. The question must accordingly arise how many of the other a priori modes of looking at reality can be circumvented if once we recognize what assumptions our brains make for us in the process of constructing the world (middle-order-reality) in which we live.

This study—thinking of other ways in which thinking might take place—is called "demonics," a demon being shorthand for an imaginary intelligence which does *not* process inputs in human terms. One of the earliest and most celebrated demons of this kind was E.A. Abbott's character, A. Square, Esq. who inhabited Flatland. He was a being whose a prioris differed from ours in being able to handle intuitively only 3 dimensions (*x, y, t*) not four (*x, y, z, t*). A. Square's encounter with a discursive sphere, who tries to explain 4-space to him, was originally intended as a scientific joke, but it caught the imagination of mathematicians and physicists, and has been continuously reprinted. It has also generated sequels in which A. Square lives not in a flat surface but in the surface of a sphere, a cone, a cylinder or a torus, while still able to appreciate only 3-space (Rucker 1977).

Note that there is no point in asking "Are there any Flatlands?" or "Might we find a Flatland in outer space?" A Flatland is not a place—*it is the way-of-seeing of Flatlanders*, precisely as (3d + t)–land is the way-of-seeing of humans (and probably most organisms). A Flatland exists if and only if Flatlanders (those who happen to make these abstractions and have these limitations) exist. One could perfectly well devise a computer which, if put down in Hilbert space with an unlimited number of dimensions, would see, and consequently create, a Flatland.

The corollary is obvious, that (3d + t) or conventional 4-space has no pre-emptive claim on being in some way specially real compared with other possible algorithms, beyond the fact that it is a print-out of our Kantian a prioris. Just as a Flatland is the print-out of all-that-is-the-case produced by a Flatlander, so observed reality is the print-out of all-that-is-the-case produced by a human head. Flatland instruments might be expected to perpetuate flat vision, though from some of their readings a flat mathematician could arrive at something like a 4-space view. He could infer higher dimensional orders, but he could not empathize them. A third line orthogonal to both of two orthogonal lines would be as incapable of illustration, except in projection, as a fourth or fifth orthogonal is to us. What would a Flatlander do about any phenomena which persisted in intruding from a nonflat mode? He would ignore, reformulate, or flatten them.

Another demonic model is the planiverse, developed by Dewdney (1979). Whereas Flatlanders lived in a surface like a sheet of paper, and were aware of North-South, East-West, but not up-down, planiversals live on the edge of a very thin phonograph record and see forward-backward and up-down, but their world has no lateral dimension: in order to pass one another they have to climb over each other. Their world has a dimension of curvature of which they are aware (whereas if a Flatlander lived on a sphere, his world would be curved in Flatland hyperspace). Dewdney has designed a planiversal cosmology, including a 3-space periodic table of elements, and planiversal engineering including doors, cranes and faucets. Moreover, planiverses are inherently stackable, and if considered as parallel worlds separated in a space dimension, they will plot into each other. Events in planiversal space-time will be relativistic if adjacent planiverses are compared, because they can be rotated individually about the record player spindle; their displacements will affect simultaneity and the displace-

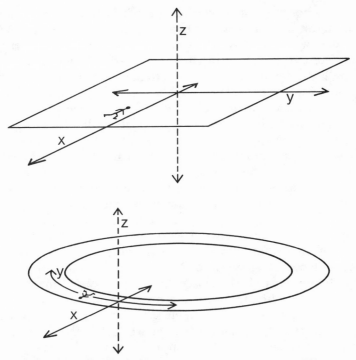

**Fig. 1** A Flatland and a Planiverse. The inhabitant can perceive two real dimensions (*solid arrows*), but not a third (*dashed arrow*). In a Flatland both the sensible dimensions are open; in a Planiverse, one of them is closed.

ments themselves are a Lie group, etc., etc. There is room for endless mathematical games, but Planiversals could not play them—they are inherently and invincibly denied access to the adjacent planiverses.

The aim of these exercises has been, among other things including sheer fun, to make hyperspace models of curvature more intelligible to general readers. They illustrate very clearly the difference between demonics and mathematics. If A. Square had been a mathematician, he could have imagined 4-space and done calculations involving it, but he still could not have *see* a sphere as a sphere. In mathematics we have a resource which Kant underrated—we can hypothesize and manipulate Euclidean and non-Euclidean surfaces as well as 4-, 5-, or *n*-dimensional spaces. Mathematical students learn to deal with the flat *n*-dimensional space called "Hilbert space" over which subatomic particles can be depicted as vectors. But we cannot see or empathize these constructions on a par with conventional reality. In this sense Kant was quite right, and the difficulty explains why, compared with the Copernican and Newtonian revolutions, quantum mechanics has had so little impact on general human thinking.

The point at which demonic models become most interesting,

however, is not in the appreciation of static geometry. With an effort, we can digest hyperspaces and hyper-hyperspaces. Far more difficult is the idea of a demon who did not share our a priori perception of *time*. In spite of the inseparability of space-time, time is still an outsider, owing more of its peculiarities to ourselves as observers than to any properties of reality. Flatland is relatively easy. In the first place, Flatlanders lack a dimensional perception which we have, so we can create their world by handicapping ourselves. In the second place, their referents are $x$, $y$, $t$, and $t$ is perceived exactly as we perceive it. But how about a demon, Mr. Semper, who also lives in a 3-space, but who sees not $x$, $y$, $t$, but $x$, $y$, $z$?

The other difficult human prejudice, not mentioned by Kant, but even more a priori than our vision of the time arrow, is positional identity (Comfort 1979B). This is the belief that there is an I inside (or, as some sensory experiments suggest, just behind) our heads, which is separate from what we are observing, and which is situated at this particular locus in space-time. Mathematics is not much troubled by this homuncular I, though much of the exposition of relativity involved getting around anthropocentrism. On the other hand, one of the consequences of understanding how this I functions, with its tendency to attribute identity (which we feel ourselves to have) to things, and particularly to things at a subatomic level, as well as the assumption that what we observe at that level are indeed things, has had an influence on physics. Particles differ strikingly from macroscopic things, nor can one speak, except for brevity, of a particular proton, as if it were one particular billiard ball. A billiard ball is assumed to have "transcendental identity" (this is the quality which Nāgasena denies)—it stays macroscopically the same object from the moment it is made until the moment it is destroyed; it can be identified by marking it, and once marked it can be distinguished from any similar billiard ball. Particles only have identity to the extent that, for example, a standing wave has an identity. How do we relate to a demon Mr. Ubique, who not only sees 360 degrees in all directions, like a rabbit, but who has *no* sense that he is in a particular position in space-time?

Computers have made it easy to generate simple demonic models, so that anyone with a small computer can recreate what A. Square could see and what he could not. Bigger computers can generate topological models which make difficult mathematical ideas visible as diagrams, though these can be misleading—quite a few students who have seen models of toroidal hyperspace may have come away with the idea that the universe *is* donut-shaped, rather than some of its properties are those of a toroidal surface. At the same time, since computer displays are meant to be intelligible to people, they fail to bypass all of the a priori transformations. Like Mr A. Square, they retain our conventional real-time perception (or have to transform it into some other kind of display). In order to program us to see events like Mr. Semper or Mr. Ubique, we have first to analyze exactly what difference our a prioris make, and then instruct the computer to display the difference as visible algebra.

The object of the demonic exercise is not to program computers, or to facilitate communication with any extraterrestrials we might meet who have other a prioris, but to make us look closely at the characteristics of our minds, which are the universal instrument in science and mathematics, so as to see how they determine the structures we treat as real.

As a matter of fact, it appears that human brains are quite capable of visualizing both Mr. Semper's world and Mr. Ubique's world at one and the same time during altered states of consciousness (oceanic states), which can occur spontaneously or can be facilitated by psychoactive drugs, religious and meditative exercises, or other traditional expedients. These experiences have been assiduously cultivated by large sections of the human race and provided the basis for Hindu and Buddhist philosophy. Although Hindus and Buddhists were not traditionally very interested in what we now call physics, the striking conformity between some of the intuitions drawn from oceanic experiences by people like Nāgasena and the mathematical models derived from quantum physics has led not a few physicists to recognize that while publishable results require mathematical analysis of regular experiments, there might be something to be gained if, indeed, the world model which follows from such experiments could not only be inferred but actually seen, as Newtonian mechanical models can be seen. There is no better answer to the flat-earth intuition (which was a priori for most Europeans until the sixteenth century) than actually to sail around the Earth, inverted kangaroos and all, or to see it from orbit.

Altered states of consciousness apart, however, there is no substitute for looking carefully at our a priori postures as a source of observer bias. This, of course, is where the imaginary demons are helpful. If we program them correctly, like good students, they will ask very awkward Socratic questions.

If we start this exercise at the simple end, with Flatland, we immediately notice something peculiar: although A. Square could see only a world of two linear dimensions and time, his *perception* is not strictly of 3-space. A demon whose mind was totally limited in all operations to 3-space could not manipulate it to discover all three coordinates—he would experience movement along the $y$ axis as a time-based change in $x$. Although A. Square lives in two space dimensions only, he is clearly able to construct mentally a *map* of Flatland, and a map is a schematic representation of a plane seen from a point in a dimension orthogonal to it. A. Square cannot draw a map, and has no experience of up or down, but his brain can add one. In fact, while a mathematical space is completely described by its dimensions, it can only be completely perceived if the perceiving system has a virtual dimension in hand. All Dewdney's planiversal machines have to be drawn for our examination in a dimension their makers would be unable to use. It was pointed out by Prof. H.A.C. Dobbs (1971) that this is true of 4-space also. Hinton (1904) had actually drawn attention to the same thing over 60 years previously.

The Necker cube illusion consists of a drawing of an open cubical frame which can be interpreted either as the front of a box seen from slightly below, or the back of a box seen from slightly above. Most people plump for one or another of these readings, but after a while the interpretation suddenly changes to the alternative, and then back and forth at a rate which varies for different individuals. This rate has been used by psychologists as an introversion-extraversion test.

Now the human retina is effectively flat, and the image produced by the diagram is identical with that which would be produced if this cube were a solid object. A solid object, however, produces no comparable alternation of states. What the brain appears to do is to map the reversal of a 3-D object: it behaves mathematically as if it had one hyperspace dimension in hand, orthogonal to the dimensions of the virtual cube.

Moreover we see that in a space which has $t$ as one of its dimensions, operations in this virtual or imaginary dimension $I$ (which exists only in the circuitry of the perceiving system) tend to be translated into the perceiver's reality as time effects. In the case of the cube, these are oscillations between the two ambiguous states, but what actually exists in the brain—if we can use the word *exists* to describe virtual images in an imaging system—is a coherent superposition of both states. Here we encounter another and more important a priori: a superposition is something which the human nervous system cannot accept in optical objects. For such objects, we write the logic equation: $a \cap a' = \emptyset$ which reads as "the intersection of $a$ and not-$a$ is null." This means that if we keep a box for storing all objects which are both $a$ and not-$a$, the box will be empty. For most purposes, this is true by definition. Unfortunately, in quantum systems the number of virtual objects which are both $a$ and not-$a$ (both waves and not waves, for example) is increasing steadily. What happens with the Necker cube is that to our a priori perception, the observing system splits into two time lines which are presented alternately. $I$, the virtual dimension in which these two time lines diverge, is in

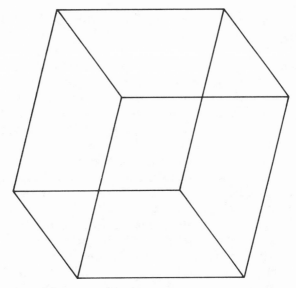

**Fig. 2**  A Necker Cube

fact an imaginary number in Boolean algebra, represented in this case by the usual behavior of a system fed a rule-paradox—namely, oscillation between two states (Pattee 1979).

A dimension in ordinary parlance indicates something in which measurement can be made, as when we say that the dimensions of $a$ are $b$, $c$ and $d$. A dimension in logic means basically a degree of freedom for nonidentities or opposites to coexist. Ordinary or Boolean logic starts by saying "$A$ and not-$A$ cannot both exist" meaning that yes and no, $A$ and not-$A$, cannot *ex hypothesi* apply to the same thing *at the same time or in the same place*. It is accordingly one-dimensional logic, represented in computer design by on-off. A practical example is Pauli's exclusion principle, stating that two particles (electrons, neutrons, and so on) cannot occupy the same state at one and the same time. In this regard they behave like billiard balls. Spencer Brown's logic exists in a planiverse and is two dimensional. To deal with imaginary numbers or with superpositions, one must burrow under or jump over boundaries in a third dimension, or introduce curvature into a 3-D transparent sphere, or as in a model developed by Kauffmann and Videla (1980), one must allow the boundaries to have oscillatory properties, i.e., to vary in time. When Kauffmann and Videla draw oscillating or degenerate circles to represent the role of the imaginary number $i$ ( $= \sqrt{-1}$), in the Cartesian plot of $a + bi$, the diagram looks remarkably like the planar projection of a hypersphere. Instead of $t$ they are introducing a hyperspace dimension. How many dimensions a space has in description depends on the dimensions of the logic we apply to it. Put down in a Hilbert space with $n$ dimensions, a two-dimensional logic sees a 2-space, a three-dimensional logic a 3-space, and so on. Minkowski diagrams and most modern physics and astronomy see a 4-space $(x,y,z : t)$ with the potential of hyperspace curvature in an unnamed fifth dimension. The logic of a Hilbert space itself is indeterminacy, and hence it is an appropriate algorithm for describing particle reactions. Whatever shape the cosmos is, Flatland is flat, because Flatlanders see only $x$, $y : t$.

The difference between an imaginary number such as $i = \sqrt{-1}$ and what I have called for brevity's sake an "imaginary dimension" would take us too far afield, and I am consciously trying to avoid the numbing effect of algebra on nonmathematicians. On the other hand, imaginary and complex numbers were devised specifically to deal with situations in which $a$ and not-$a$, or $a$ and $b$, both coexist or appear to alternate. The imaginary number $i$ is an alternation between $-1$ and $+1$—one can think of it as being in orbit around zero. There is no algorithm in ordinary either-or logic for the state called "iterative alternation with period two," i.e., $abababababab$. . . . If a process like this is viewed from what mathematicians call the "complex plane" (an imaginary surface divided by the straight line corresponding to the real numbers, . . . $-3$, $-2$, $-1$, 0, 1, 2, 3, and so on), it becomes manageable. We make the complex plane by drawing another axis, $z$, at right angles to the line of real numbers, and calling its divisions $ai$, $2ai$, $3ai$ and so on. From this, and the complex space (which has one real dimension, the number line, and any number of imaginary dimensions), we derive the equipment to deal with alternations and superpositions. In the Minkowski diagram of space-time (see page 104), $x$ $y$ and $z$ are real dimensions of space, while $t$ is a complex dimension with different mathematical rules. It is the dimension in which we perceive succession, alternation, and sequence. Nonmathematicians to whom these ideas are unfamiliar or opaque, should read Penrose (1978) or Kauffman and Videla (1980) for an explanation.

Nonmathematicians having taken time-out until the next page which has no equations on it, I can point out that Kauffman and Videla (1980) appear to have invented a new type of number, which is neither real, complex, nor hypercomplex, and which is useful in modelling some of the ways in which the brain generates reality—the alternate iterant. This is introduced for the logical superposition:

$$a \cap b : a = {\sim}b, \; b = {\sim}a$$

as an alternation in any real or imaginary dimension of $a$ and $b$ with period 2, which causes the Brownian boundaries $\overline{a}|\;b$, $\overline{b}|\;a$ to take the shape of a continuous waveform:

$$a \underline{\phantom{l}} b \overline{\phantom{l}} a \underline{\phantom{l}} b \overline{\phantom{l}} a \underline{\phantom{l}} b \overline{\phantom{l}} a \underline{\phantom{l}} b.$$

We shall write this operation on a pair of states $a$, $b$ as:

$$I_2 \, (a, \, b)$$

the subscript being the period. The conjugate alternation is obviously:

$$I_2 \, (b, \, a)$$

which is opposite in phase. This method of resolving a superposition is very much like the way that the brain treats the Necker cube (Dobbs 1971).

The relation between iterants and complex numbers opens up a large field of creative algebra which relates Brownian iteration to quantum theory, and which is being pursued by Kauffman (personal communication), so I will not trespass on it. The problem which interests me arises from the following considerations.

(1) Where $a = \sim b$, $b = \sim a$, the boundary waveform, as Kauffman and Videla depict it, is a square wave; there is no intermediation, no real point at which $a = b = 0$, and neither $a$ nor $b$ is differentiable. The transition between them is a Dirac function, which has zero value at all points but one—where it is infinity. The waveform generated by the unit circle of $i$ in the Argand field is by contrast sinusoidal, and $\frac{\delta i}{\delta \theta}$ is meaningful. One might get a square wave out of the "infinity of synchronized circular orbits" derivable from the expansion of the real-number line (Kauffman and Videla 1980), but there is a problem in bridging the gap to the required Fourier series for a square wave with vanishing transition time:

$$4E_{max} \sum_{}^{\infty} \frac{1}{n} \cdot sin \, (2\pi n \, \frac{t}{T})$$

(2) One naturally treats iterants as temporal, i.e., $t$ is the line along which $abababababa$ is arranged. Nearly all iterants, and nearly all physical waveforms, are of this kind, and in consequence, one can transfer formalisms using frequency

$$\omega = F(t)$$

directly. Now in the case of $i$, one can continue the analogy by using the idea of succession: there is no time frame to the orbit, but every $-1$ operation must be succeeded by a $+1$ operation. Succeeded in what? Obviously, in $t$, if we are performing the sums. But this obscures the fact that time is a human injection; abstract iterants are freestanding numbers or operations, with no more obligatory temporal component than the statement that for $a$, $b$, $\in S$, $b$ is the successor of $a$. The line of march of

$$I_2 (a, b)$$

lies in a wholly abstract dimension.

(3) Not only is the "buzzing alternation" between $a$ and $b$ a Ding-an-Sich, not a time sequence, it is also effectively quantized, for there is no intermediate state. One could very well write:

$$|a - b| = k\hbar$$

and the expression would make sense. In this case $a$ and $b$ are accordingly eigenstates of the wave-function:

$$\Psi I_2(a, b)$$

so that

$$\exists v: Tv = \lambda v; \lambda = a, b.$$

There is no particular point in pursuing the vector formalism here, but the link between iterants and a large body of quantum algebra may be important. Quantum alternations can be separated in time, but they do not have to be; more commonly, they are irregularly iterant superpositions which coexist. In that case, what happens when we collapse the wave-function could be that we stop the apparent motion of

$$I_2 (a, b)$$

by grabbing hold of one state for the record—an interesting reinterpretation of Everett, since the iteration itself is beyond reach. Actually, what we grab is one of the two states, $a$ or $b$, plus a phase relation.

## THE CONCEPT OF VIEWPOINT

Viewpoint is a naive, not an algebraic, factor. We view the Argand plane from a point in a dimension orthogonal to it. A Flatlander, who lived in it, might infer but could not draw it. This, of course, makes no difference to the mathematics of such a plane, but in the case of iterants it may.

For a start, the insertion of $t$ represents a viewpoint. In spite of the insertion, we actually represent *ababab* along the *real-number axis* (not along $t$ in a Minkowski manifold, which would land us in among tiresome hyperbolic functions), and the sequence is flanked by $z$ and $\bar{z}$ in the complex plane.

Kauffman (personal communication, and in press) has pointed out that

$$\begin{bmatrix} a & z \\ \bar{z} & b \end{bmatrix} = \begin{pmatrix} a \\ b \end{pmatrix} + \overset{\bullet}{\iota}\begin{pmatrix} z \\ \bar{z} \end{pmatrix} \equiv \begin{matrix} & & z \\ & a & \\ \bar{z} & & z \\ & b & \\ \bar{z} & & z \\ & a & \\ \bar{z} & & z \\ & b & \\ & \bar{z} & \end{matrix}$$

From this beautifully simple and original approach, which consists in essence of viewing the iteration *ababab* from the complex plane, flanked, as it were, by $z$ and its complex conjugate, there springs a whole sequence of relationships between the algebra of iterants and that of modern physics.* I had the privilege of being introduced to this concept in a note written by Kauffman on the back of a reprint. It not only gets over the intuitive placing of

$$I_2(a, b)$$

in time, but by transferring it to the complex plane, one can, for example, proceed to write:

$$H \begin{bmatrix} a & z \\ \bar{z} & b \end{bmatrix}$$

and so on, with a 90° rotation over *abababa*. This approach represents the analysis of a superposition. What we actually see, and what constitutes the existential character of any natural nontemporal iterant, is the alternate appearance of $a$ and $b$—in other words, in a superposition we view *abababa* not from the flank but end-on.

One way of effecting this would be to take *abababa* into a second complex plane, orthogonal to the Argand plane and vertical and edge-on to the Argand diagram, by another 90° rotation $(a, bk)$, so that the direction of *abababa* is along this $w$ axis. Evidently, a solution to the problem of getting time out of the frequency formulae is to cause the half-phase time of an alternation to tend towards zero and the frequency to tend towards infinity. This is precisely the effect of perspective as the rotation of *ababa* into the $w$ plane tends toward 90°. The line of march of *ababa* is an infinite vector:

$$(\infty, 0, 0)$$

along the real-number line (where it does not really belong) which we shift to:

---

*To be developed shortly by Kauffman in a paper entitled "Sign and Space"—in press. See also Kauffman, "Complex Numbers and Algebraic Logic," Proc. 10th Intl. Symposium on Multivalued Logic, 1980.

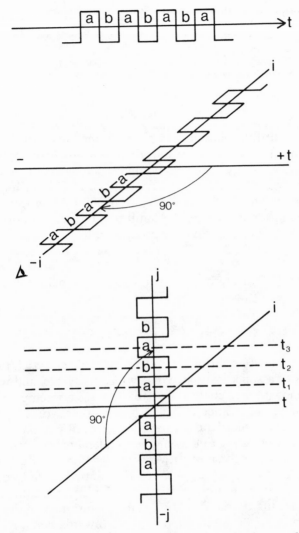

**Fig. 3** Rotation of an iterant in a complex space to display parallel "time lines."

$$(0, 0, \infty)$$

along the second complex axis. Its first complex (Hermitian) component $H[Im]$ develops along a vector:

$$(0, \infty, 0)$$

Since it happens that the $w$ axis corresponds to our viewpoint as we look at the page, we see *ababa* end-on as an infinite regress of superposed *a*'s and *b*'s. Moreover, what we have from this change of axis is an unconventional spinor $(x \ Re; z, w, Im)$. Looking at the Hermitian rank 2 matrices giving $(a, b, z, \bar{z})$, we find a rather close structural analogy between a Brownian iterant period 2 and a particle with spin ½. Having waded in so far, one might ask whether there is a Brownian iterant formalism which would translate the Einstein-Rosen-Podolsky nonlocality into a phase shift between

$$\overline{a|} \ b \ \text{ and } \overline{b|} \ a$$

The remainder of this argument must be submitted to the Journal of Unsupported Speculation. Its point, however, has been to indicate the conceptual importance of Brownian iterants as a relatively novel addition to the formalisms in which observables can be expressed. Spencer Brown clearly appreciated this when he proposed not these, it is true, but the related imaginary numbers in Boolean logic: "What is fascinating about the imaginary Boolean values is the light they apparently shed on our concepts of matter and time. Why, for example, does . . . [the Universe] not appear more symmetrical?" (Spencer Brown 1972). One must congratulate Kauffman on being the first to subject them to rigorous treatment.

The particular logic of the Necker-cube, in which $I$ is an imaginary number, was actually worked out, not to apply to physics or physiology, but for the peculiar inclusive-allusive mode called "primary-process" thinking, which represents the logic of the unconscious (Blanco 1975, the only logician I know of who is also a psychoanalyst). It is not identical with the imaginary number logic developed by Spencer Brown (1972), but it is cognate with it. The trouble is that propositional calculus logic is static. If we write:

$p$ and $\sim p$ cannot be simultaneously with regard to the same thing

the unanalyzed portion is and. At different times or in different places, $p$ and $\sim p$ can be compatible. Moreover, in any situation where $p$ and $\sim p$ appear to coexist, generating a paradox, in order to apply any logic, one must separate them in time (the brain's solution to the Necker paradox) or in space, or in a virtual dimension created for the purpose. If $p$ and $\sim p$ exist as a superposition—say, as square and not-square— we cannot envisage them optically as showing tendencies to be square and to be not-square, but only as alternately square and not-square, or as one behind the other in a dimension $J$ in the axis of which we imagine ourselves to be viewing them—which is exactly what superposition means. In other words, "the notion of the law of contradiction cannot be formulated without making reference to the spatiotemporal notion" (Blanco 1975). If we use Spencer Brown's notation, depending on the crossing of boundaries, $p \cap \sim p = \emptyset$ if we draw the boundaries on a plane surface (boundaries are anyhow a spatial meta-phor), but not if we draw them on the surface of a glass sphere. There, to the equatorial viewer, $p$ can partially or wholly include or overlap $\sim p$, for the plane enclosures are only nonporous if we happen to be in a Flatland. Moreover, in writing that

$$\overline{p\|} \ = \ \text{identity operation}$$

(moving from $p$ across the border into $\sim p$ and back effects no net change), we are preserving precisely the metaphor of spatial motion to which Blanco refers. "Die Welt ist alles, was der Fall ist," and we subdivide it dimensionally by mentally moving parts of it about. Wherever this shuffle leads to a planar-logic paradox, we must either displace one of the parts in time—usually, if the superposition obsti-nately stands its ground, by alternation—or displace them in a virtual dimension, like the tunnels or wormholes burrowing under the walls of Spencer Brown's enclosures and letting the contents out. The in-trusion of this unwanted echo of optical Kantian experience into logic is one thing, but it is also basic to mathematics, as we shall see in a minute.

This is one of the practical reasons that the transcendence of local-reality models in physics gives us so much mathematical trouble. It is a major piece of procedural contraband in the quantum-observer paradox—the fact that in any quantum observation, the act of obser-vation converts a superposition or range of tendencies into a yes-no event. One interpretation of this paradox, from Hugh Everett (1973), is that when a wave function (indeterminate) appears to collapse into a definite reading, i.e, when a yes-no measurement is made, *both* alternative events occur. What happens in observation is that viewed by a human (largely optical) brain, the superposition splits into sepa-rate time lines. This split is repeated for every quantum choice: the result is the so-called many worlds interpretation of quantum logic. In this case, since observation is indirect (we cannot see particles, with the single exception of a photon striking the retina), there is no alter-nation, and the observer, who cannot disobserve, is irrevocably com-mitted to one particular time line. As Everett's extremely elegant mathematics indicate, however, he can *infer* separate Everett worlds for each option, and these are separated with dimension $I$, which is treated as orthogonal to the time-arrow. What exists in reality is an array of wave functions or "tendencies to exist." The manufacture of specific choices is, on this theory, a result of our a priori operations to render these into a model. (Quite apart from the argument from irreversible memory, any recursion from 0 to not-0 would effect such a split. The universal state function actually defines all the ways in which a plenum can split into 0 and not-0).

In fact, the manufacture of optical objects from wave functions is one of the most striking activities of human brains—the more so if human visual input is indeed represented in the brain not optically but holographically. Holograms can and do accept wave functions, but in order to survive in a middle-order world, organisms have had to learn to organize these probabilistically and transform them into manageable objects. A cannonball, as Everett points out, consists of a very large number $N$ of subatomic particles, with a state function of $3N$ dimensions. Luckily for us, the centroids of all these can be treated as if they were a thing, which makes real life cannonballs easier to avoid than if we treated their constituents in quantum terms.

If, as some physicists think, one can extend Everett's model from single particle-events to macroscopic systems (so that there exists a time-stream parallel to "this one," identical but for the fact that there is no Empire State Building) the consistency of what we call causality gets odder still. Consider a sequence: an employee smokes at work $(p_1)$ is seen and fired $(p_2)$ revenges himself by putting nuts and bolts into the bread dough $(p_3)$ and I break a tooth on a muffin $(P)$. If we take the bifurcation broken-tooth, no broken tooth $(P, P')$ our time-stream has to include $p_1 \ldots p_3$ and (since this argument generates a regression) all the past events which "caused" $p_1$. By Pangloss' Theorem (things are as they are because they cannot be different) we need $p_1$ to produce eventually $p_n$, and we see why empirically there is no jumping between time streams in common experience. But streams can converge in the particular $P,P'$: the bolt might have fallen out of the mixing machine—but then $P,P'$ would not coexist with the bifurcation in which Joe Blow was fired; it would be a different stream, even though $P,P'$ was represented as a bifurcation in it. The real singularity of $p_1 \ldots P$ is that we consider ourselves to be in it, which is where we came in.

One can do a magic trick with one demonic model to illustrate a "many worlds" state—not Everett's, but a Gedanken one. Returning for a moment to Dewdney's planiverses, which occupy a 3-space, imagine them to possess infinitesimal thickness $\delta z$, of which plani-versals are unaware, and to be seen by us in a 4-space, stacked like phonograph records. For $n$ such planiverses, the minimum height of the stack must be $n. \delta z$, and $n$ can be any number. Even if $z = 0$ and they are mathematical ribbons, one can still envisage any number of discrete planiverses stacked in a 4-space world. Suppose, however, that they exist in a true 3-space: then either they are unstackable, so that no more than one such planiverse can exist (though it may con-sist of discrete parts in the same plane) or, if we consider the original stack in 4-space, as $\delta z$ tends to zero, the stack of nonidentical, non-communicating planiverses must be reduced to a coherent superposi-tion, while remaining mutually discrete in the virtual dimension $I$.

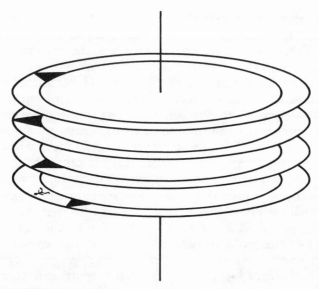

**Fig. 4** Stacked Planiverses

The Gedanken problem is as follows. Consider a stack of plani-verses of equal radius, $P_1 \ldots P_n$. One can think of them as records on the spindle of the Divine record-player. Each $P_x \in S_p$ has a single feature (say a pyramid), and one of them, say $P_1$, contains a planiversal observer, observing the feature which is separated from him by the radial angle θ. Now if each planiverse has infinitesimal thickness $\delta z$, the minimal height of the stack is $n.\delta z$ and the sheets are separated in $z$. But if they have no thickness, and are genuine mathematical ribbons, $n.\delta z = 0$, and the elements of the stack are collocal, i.e., the corresponding points in each of them have the same spatial coordinates $(x, y)$:

$$(x,y)P_1 = (x,y)P_2 = \ldots = (x,y)P_n$$

Now if the pyramid feature in each $P \in S_p$ plots exactly into the pyramid feature in all the others, the observer in $P_1$ has no problems, and presumably no need for any awareness of the stack, since features coincide. But suppose that the feature in successive planiverses does *not* coincide and let it be rotated in each planiverse by the angle θ. *What does the observer in $P_1$ see?*

The sane answer is that he sees (or could see, if he could climb over each of them) $n$ pyramids at intervals corresponding to θ, an identical finding to that of a 4-space observer looking down in dimension $z$ on the covering space of the stack. But the correctness of this depends on the neural and software basis of a planiversal observer's inability to see $z$. The insane answer might be that for a superposition in $z$, O still correlates with one $P \in S_{(p)}$ and is unaware of any change.

$P_1$ still contains one pyramid only, and the others, although they are all describable in the same space, remain totally invisible to him! How do they manage it? In the same way that Everett worlds invincibly remain invisible to an O who is once correlated with one of them. They too are collocal, though their separation is immediately obvious if we plot the corresponding eigenvectors. A covering space which displayed all of them would be a mathematical confection, not a topology of real 4-space. The dimension in which we treat them as separate is a logical or Spencer Brown dimension—a confection of the human way-of-observing, which collapses wave functions—not a feature of real space.

The analogy, of course, is mathematically false, in that separate planiverses in a stack are not eigenstates of a wave-function, having no absolute existence apart from it. But they do resemble the achronal slices of space-time commonly used by topologists, and if for some reason O were to travel up the stack from $P_1$ to $P_n$ with time, $t = z$, the analogy would be complete (in which case, the feature would appear to O to be displaced at a steady rate $= \theta.dt$: one sees that $z$ is now plotting $t$). There is a rather striking resemblance between this behaviour and the successive explications of an implicate proposed by Bohm, with the pyramid feature doing duty for an electron.

The interest of collocality in planiverses is that it introduces the counterintuitive idea that a number of universes, plotting into one another, can coexist, and that the mental inhabitants of one of them may be irrevocably committed to that universe simply by being irreversibly correlated with it (See Misner, Thorne & Wheeler 1973). The idea of a stack of steriverses, or 4-space universes, potential and actual, has been taken to follow logically from the mathematics of hyperspace distortion in high-gravity fields, as well as in the algorithm for observer-correlation which led Everett to infer the existence of a many worlds system. The two stacks are entirely different, however. In the case of Penrose's "anti-universe" and "other universes," it would in theory be possible to gain access to them by travelling great distances in space-time in order (if that were possible) to dive through the hole in the doughnut-shaped singularity, inferred to exist in a black hole with spin (a Kerr black hole). In Wheeler's model (Misner 1973) the structure of the stack is different. But if these additional universes exist in different hyperspaces which plot into one another (are collocal in some virtual dimension), movement in normal 4-space might not be inherently necessary to gain access to them. In order to travel directly from one to another one would need to reach superluminal velocity, which is why it cannot be done without the help of a deformation of hyperspace. But it is difficult to exclude the science-fiction possibility that correlation may not be absolute for all aspects of mental processes, and the alternative members of the stack might be mathematically if not empathically present to experience, but filtered out, rather as all television channels are present in the antenna circuits of a receiver but only one is selected. 4-space is, after all, *our* Flatland. Heady stuff of this kind is the motive for a close look at observer correlation, and hence for the study of demonics.

Collocality in planiverses, like the planiverse itself, is a Gedanken situation. Its interest comes from the one hypothetical instance where steriverses can be said to become collocal by compression, namely in the focus of a black hole.

Black holes are structures which appear when stars run out of expansile energy and collapse under gravity. If the star is sufficiently massive, exceeding the Chandrasekhar limit (1.4 times the mass of the Sun), its electrons are pushed bodily into the nucleus by gravitational attraction, and convert its protons into neutrons. At about 2.8 solar masses, even neutrons are telescoped, and matter as we normally describe it disappears, leaving an enormously dense object whose gravitational field is so great that the escape velocity from it exceeds the velocity of light. Such a black hole produces an extreme distortion of space-time into a funnel-like form (an Einstein-Rosen bridge) which emerges into a different order of space-time: either elsewhere in the universe, if the universe is closed (like a spherical Flatland) or hyperbolic; into a totally different universe if not. The theoretical properties of static, charged, and spinning black holes differ, but all are characterized by extreme deformation of space-time and a range of paradoxical consequences on the perceptions of an imaginary observer passing through one. (Since in a spinning or Kerr black hole the mass singularity is toroidal, it might even be possible to pass through the hole in the donut without bodily dissolution.)

Since Clifford, some speculative physicists have played with the idea that heavy particles may be the event horizons around micro-black-holes. This model raises cosmological problems we will not go into here. In a static macroscopic (Schwartzschild) black hole all bets are off—matter, atoms, and particles cease to exist as they are pressed into a singularity. How (and, in fact, whether) this occurs is at least as speculative as the mathematics of planiverses. At the point where exclusion fails, however, particles presumably cease to be manifest as such or are displaced into superpositions. More interesting from the collocal model of planiverses is the speculation as to exactly where the lower sheet of an Einstein-Rosen bridge is situated with relation to ordinary space-time. In a closed or hyperbolic universe, the two sheets might be continuous (the wormhole model). The stacked planiverse model suggests another possibility: the two hypersurfaces are in fact collocal, but separated in *I*. The notion of collocality implies that stacking does not involve displacement in any but a virtual dimension. It is being described by observers irrevocably committed to correlation with one element of the superposition and in that case all manner of possible stacks can be imagined, ranging from Everett worlds to the alternating universes and antiuniverses in Penrose diagrams of spinning black holes.

We are obviously in an area where any language save math is very close to burn-out. It rapidly becomes obvious that the system breaks and anomalies we experience or infer with very large or very small systems—galaxies or particles—originate through the way we handle middle-order reality, particularly time, and that this, then, is the place to start. In order to see the kind of issues which are involved, we set out to explain to a demon named Gezumpstein how a chess game works.

## TALKING TO GEZUMPSTEIN

Gezumpstein is a universal or fundamental demon; that is to say, he has no a prioris and his vision is inclusive and nonpositional. This means that anything which mathematics can describe, Gezumpstein can see. He is also a mathematician, able to describe what he sees algebraically, and interested in our viewpoint. If we can represent it precisely, he will comprehend it.

Gezumpstein has serious problems with chess. He sees that it consists of meaningful quanta (moves) represented graphically in a 3-space. But unlike us: (1) he does not read $t$ unidirectionally and accordingly his concept of correlation, which takes the place of our concept of cause-effect, is symmetrical; and further (2) he does not attribute transcendental identity, which means that although he can tell a pawn from a bishop, he cannot discriminate individual pawns or individual bishops of the same color except as tracks (vectors) in a 3-space.

As a result Gezumpstein sees, first of all, not a chess game but the coherent superposition of all imaginable chess games with each component of the superposition having limiting states. In one state, the pieces are arranged in facing rows $(x_1, x_2, \ldots x_8, y = 1 : x_1, x_2 \ldots x_8, y = 2)$ for White, and so on; thus, Black and White are 2 matrices of 8 columns and two rows which map into one another with one singularity, K & Q. The other state involves a constellation of coordinate positions surrounding a King. Gezumpstein identifies these in a matrix table of all possible situations giving mate. But he sees a game as the set of transformations by which one of these becomes the other, not as a sequence with a start and a finish.*

Gezumpstein also attempts to understand our extraordinary no-

---

*He would indeed need to be outside time to do this, since any practical algorithm for the number of choices involved can be shown to be transcomputable.

tions about the dimension $t$. For him, whether the ordered transformations are plotted in $t$ on a plane board or in another spatial dimension $z$, using a pile of boards to give a 3-D matrix, makes no difference at all. His natural bent is to analyze processes in terms of becoming, not of things. If we explain that we have access to $t$ only through a moving slit which "scans successive slices of space-time" (de Broglie), he has great difficulty in depicting this mathematically, and probably tries to do it via set theory, using successive moments $a<b<c \in T$. But then we have to explain also that time is probably not composed of quanta, so for every $a<b \in T$ there exists an $a + \delta a$ which follows $a$ but precedes $b$:

$$\forall a,b, \in T : a<b \; \exists \delta a : a<a+\delta a<b$$

This still does not explain what exactly is contained in the time-slit, though its width is of the order $\delta a$, nor why we invariably associate our world line with $t$.

The real crunch comes, however, when we try to explain to Gezumpstein the difference between this (real) chess game now being played and the superposition of imaginable chess games. Gezumpstein asks, "By what mathematical singularity can I distinguish the class of games or universes you call real from the general universe of chess games or universes?" And that is quite a poser. Like it or not, even with a system such as chess, we are back with the question put, but not answered, by Neill Graham in his critique of Everett's many worlds model: Why we should assume our own real world to be typical, and if not, in what way is it singular?

There is really only one way of expounding human experience to Gezumpstein. We tell him that in a 4-space with dimensions $x$, $y$, $z$, $t$, we can see the whole of what goes on in $x$, $y$, or $z$, but we see $t$ only through a narrow moving slit which appears to travel along $t$ in one direction only. For every successive point $p$ lying on the axis $t$ which goes past this time-slit, we have a second record called "memory." Any configuration of $x$, $y$, $z$, which we record at $p$ we call "real," and once we have recorded it, the record is frozen, though our storage isn't perfect. In fact, at $p + n$ if $n$ is large, soft errors get into the memory tape, chiefly in the form of loss of detail, so we often rely on accessory records such as notebooks and photographs. Incidentally, our cameras are optical and have the same time-slit as we do: they only show what was 'there' at time $p$, so it can't all be in our heads—our measuring instruments function likewise. Now quite often we know from other evidence that what was there at $p$ wasn't an either-or event but a coherent superposition; however, we can never see this. For macroscopic objects, the state functions average out, both for us and for our cameras, and for most purposes our reality consists of optical constructions, which is why we talk about seeing the point of an argument or the solution to an equation. If we assume that two random chess playing machines are playing each other, so that every game is equally likely, nonetheless, for a game to be real, we have to mean that the probability of that game is 1 and the probability of all other possible games is 0. At which point Gezumpstein says either "Why?" or "These carbon-based units can accept only Boolean, yes-no, logic. Strange!"

It must already be obvious that it is futile to send Gezumpstein to talk to Popper, and get the explanation that the real represents a compromise based on the absence of refutation. One can arrive in physics at a model in which $a \wedge \sim a \neq 0$, and show this to be upheld by experiment, but the observation plays Popperian hell with any system which assumes that $a$ and $\sim a$ cannot both be true. If we define reality as that state in which $A \supset a$, $\sim A \supset \sim a$, Gezumpstein will point out that there are systems in which both possibilities observably coexist, so that we can apply experimental refutation to the hypothesis that they do not exist; thus, there is a limit, which we cannot decide a priori, on the kind of hypothesis to which a Boolean-type logic can be applied. This logic, accordingly, cannot be set up as a refutatory means of identifying the real—and we have ourselves applied it to show that the real includes coherent superpositions. By the a prioris we have inserted into it, Gezumpstein's world is indeterminate and consists of coherent superpositions—even in areas such as chess to which we do not ourselves normally apply them. The statement "this move mates in three" is a testable hypothesis, but only if we treat chess by our logic and not his.

Gezumpstein also does a demoralizing magic trick to illustrate in simple terms von Weiszäcker's (1979) reasoning that $t$ itself is a virtual dimension—in other words, not an object of knowledge but a cerebral and perceptual ordering operation, just as much as $I$. The fact that it looks extraordinarily concrete to us does not negate such a hypothesis: if it were an obligate cerebral operation, it would look concrete. The idea is a difficult one, but Gezumpstein proceeds to illustrate it as follows.

He would point out that mathematics, as a cerebral operation, makes its living by explication of implicates: the binomial theorem is a simple instance. Given an implicate $x$, if we can extract:

$$\sqrt[n]{x} = A, \ A = a + b : x = (a + b)^n$$

this is one unfolding and we can go on and spin a thread:

$$x = a^n + na^{n-1}b + \frac{n(n-1)}{2!}a^{n-2}b^2$$
$$+ \frac{n(n-1)(n-2)}{3!}a^{n-3}b^3 + \dots + nab^{n-1} + b^n$$

with further unfoldings equal to the number of terms. We can then proceed to conduct operations on these to which the implicate was opaque. We only need to take hold and pull, and $x$ unwinds like the core of a golfball. The essence of explication is that an implicate is unfolded in this way and the unfolded components (terms), while remaining, as it were, inside the envelope $(a + b)^n$, are rendered discrete and ordered. Now the terms of a binomial expansion are not things or events: one canot pick up one term and take it home. The demon, and some intuitive mathematical minds, can see these terms simply as a grain or Tao existing in $(a + b)^n$. Knowing this, a human, discursive mathematician, in order to open these terms up to discursive manipulation, is obliged either to write the terms on a blackboard (separate them in space), read them out, or print them successively into a computing system (separate them in time). Whether one goes on to express this kind of explication as an ordered set $(a,b,c,\in S)$, a matrix $(A_{ij} = (a+b)^n)$, a vector space, or any other sort of mathematical confection, one is using the separation of terms in imaginary dimensions as a means of interfacing them with our processing mechanism. In fact, if one wanted to operate *simultaneously* on the second term and the last term but one of a set or a binomial expansion, one would have to transform them mathematically into a single expression. Moreover, this injection of dimensional graphics into mathematics is not a topic of mathematical consideration, at least up to the level where the term *space* is used algebraically, any more than and has been in logic, because it has no more to do with the implicate concept $(a + b)^n$ than has the process of pressing keys on the calculator: it is a purely mechanical interjection necessary to enable our brain to handle the relevant logic linguistically. There is no physical sense in which the first term in such an expansion exists before the $n$th term, or "in a different place from" the $n$th term, or even at all; but the terms are ordered and the first term ordinally precedes and is discrete from the $n$th term in the process of explication, even though the order is arbitrary (we could rewrite it backwards if we wanted). The prize question, Gezumpstein points out, is how far this sort of ordering applies to all conceptualized experience, and how far experience and reality are explicates demanded by evolution in response to the inability of organisms to react appropriately to large lumps of the implicate Brahman. Given such a computing system, $t$ may be no more phenomenologically concrete than a column or row vector, and its arrow may reflect only ordering vis-à-vis a mnemonic system (Pattee 1979).

Yet an organism could very well be a pocket calculator programmed on such a row or vector, or occupationally tied to one term of a mathematical expansion. One can do far more horrible things to an indefinite $x$ than expand it binomially. For all we know, brains may be trapped in such corridors (even if they are not the brains of mathematicians) for one can construct machines which are structurally bound to them. Organisms might prove to be just such machines, just such systems, and the worlds they construct might be similar to Hofstadter's patterned and recursive printouts, or the drawings of M. C. Escher. Reality may indeed be there, solid-looking, amorphous, and black-box-like, without windows, hatches, or handles, but if we take hold and pull. . . . For example, suppose the function given above were a description of $x$, and organisms were occupationally obliged to be aware of one term?

Von Weiszäcker (1979) has pointed out that a tense logic is inherent in any system which bases mentation on experience. A wholly instinctual animal uses a demonic logic devoid of tenses because its experience is irrelevant, and its operating instructions are provided, like those of the imaginary computing system called a "Turing machine." This might suggest that a serial ordering of time, like the generation of optical objects, is an adaptation: it gives the option of self-programming and feed-forward (learning) instead of instinct and feedback, just as optical construction gives the option of sensory coherence. Constant demonic thinking is a substantial handicap, and not only in a society which thinks conventionally. Much of the balance of appropriateness in human brains appears to reflect a balance in restricting superpositions (relevance); this is disturbed in schizophrenic thinking and we know that affective disorders often involve a disturbance of tenses (loss of futurity). Time metrics in nonlearning organisms tend to be cyclic (circadian or lunar, for instance), although some, like the successive roles of worker bees, are sequential.

Moreover, once the Adamic unicellular organism, or whatever, develops a measuring system for some explicate term in the cosmic implicate—say, the third term of a binomial expansion—it has already committed Original Sin and its increasingly complex descendants will be stuck with explicates: Time, Space, and saṁsara generally. They are all committed to losing sight of the wood for a virtual ordering of imaginary trees (at least until their computing powers become complex enough to be self-critical or to develop incidental states of mind in which the original implicate is perceived as such); the more discursive they get, the more ingrained their acceptance of the explicate expansion as normal or intuitive or real. Brains do not operate by mathematics: mathematics is a critique of the mode of operation of our brains. In this case the a priori time arrow may be linguistic in the sense that it defines the ordering of operations in a non-Abelian group—this is a possible start in explaining $t$ to Gezumpstein, who is still trying to handle it as an uncountable set of moments.

Anyone who wants to argue further with Gezumpstein will do

well to read the massive symposium on the study of Time which appeared from Springer Verlag in 1972. Gezumpstein, however, has a few considerations of his own to add. We are actually saying, he points out, that we define the present as a moving point in $t$ to which we have access at any moment. But in point of fact, we have no direct access to $t$ at all, because in order to perform any operations on it we have to encode it, and that, in a neural system, takes a non-negligible time in itself. In fact, the only thing to which we have access is the tape recording, which is frozen (it cannot be disobserved; what has happened has happened). So how do we know that the kind of correlation we call "causality" works one way only? We shall get eventually to the future, but so far as the past is concerned, we only have our tape recording. How do we know that the past is not different now from the state which we recorded? We say the present, whatever that is, is real, the past is no longer real, and the future is not yet real, but since the present is a perceptual construction of our own, Gezumpstein finds this kind of metaphysical shenanigan hard to take seriously. Does Gezumpstein mean that he is a determinist, who can see exactly what must happen next? "Nonsense," says Gezumpstein, "your past, present and future all consist en bloc of tendencies-to-exist which are probabilistic or strictly indeterminate or both, and which cannot be explicated together in your frame. You still haven't proved to me that this present of yours has any singularity to give it an ontological premium, beyond the fact that your system for some reason records it preferentially. I shall have to know more about your nervous system. Nature isn't the problem, you are." And his parting shot is that if we are looking at $t$ through a slit, we must be looking at it in a dimension orthogonal to $t$, or our brain is constructing one, and that this is our old friend $I$ again, the dimension in which Everett's time streams are distinct.

By this time most straight scientists will have come to agree with the Church that talking to demons is a bad idea and likely to generate confusion if not damnation. Much simpler, then, to stick to intuitive 4-space and deal with any overlaps by straightforward, metaphysic-free algebra. If a Hilbert space or a Grassmann algebra gives a serviceable description of particle behavior for heuristic purposes, one can learn its mathematical properties and use them. The question of whether reality is a Hilbert space, or is an explicate derived from a subjacent implicate, and the attempt to see these models with unsuitable equipment are all useless if not mischievous and generate nothing but mystification. Causation may not be respectable in quantum logic, but it is a useful convention. Particles may be treated mathematically as doing contrary things in other time streams, but what matters to us is what they appear to be doing here and now in useful devices. If the damn thing works, who cares?

This view—which is really the so-called Copenhagen solution in quantum physics—is at least robust, and a recognition of how science actually proceeds. The trouble is that a science which makes no attempt to come to terms with the awkwardnesses arising from its ad hoc models, is inclined either to get stuck or to receive a practical and heuristic shock. It is fortunate that no nineteenth century physicist tried to make a large uranium sphere for a purpose other than causing a spectacular release of neutrons. He might have surprised himself. At the other extreme, this kind of no-nonsense empiricism is apt to dismiss soft observations or hypotheses as impossible *ex hypothesi*, because it has not fully explored its preconceptions. Precognition is a nice case in point: the evidence is appallingly soft, many of the investigators remarkably credulous, and some may be overmotivated or frankly fraudulent. Intense skepticism is therefore mandatory. At the same time, if we told Gezumpstein that humans have often had the conviction that they could forsee the future other than by inference, would he find it more surprising than the prosaic experience of reality we just tried to explain to him, or point out that the universe could not possibly admit an observation of this sort? Quite possibly not—though that does not, of course, mean that the belief is true.

Demonics is an instructive philosophical exercise, and the closer we get to the limits of the instrumentation contained in our nervous system, the more instructive it gets. Since anyone can design his own demon, it will not be of real scientific use unless it produces some testable prediction which would not otherwise have occurred to us. It is also important if we cherish the hope that manmade systems might ever make such predictions better than we ourselves can. To bring this about, we would have to analyze our own built-in program in order to free the machine to transcend the program if it could. J.B.S. Haldane once said that nature may not only be odder than we think, but odder than we can think. In brief, the aim of demonics is to see exactly what are the constraints on what we can think, so as to extend them and move towards experimentally testable predictions.

Hinton (1904) had the ingenious idea that our 4-space experience actually has infinitesimal 5-hyper-space thickness, with dimensions $x$, $y$, $z$, $t$, $\delta I$, and that neurones are in some way susceptible to, or able to operate in, $I$. If so, particles might be hyperspheres, and might miss each other when on a collision course. This is probably unnecessary, so far as our brains are concerned, since a computational system can process in any number of hyperspace dimensions we care to write in. Goedel's (1959) view of en bloc space-time with "closed" time could be rewritten to accommodate $I$ as a dimension orthogonal to $t$, so that we can view time in the equivalent of optical perspective. Far more interesting is the fact that in Blanco's dream logic, superpositions in both space and time are permitted as such. One way of experiencing *I* canvassed by occultist aficionados of a fourth dimension is the trick of awakening oneself while dreaming into a second-order dream—the equivalent of a second, square, bracket (push) in computer programming. There is an amusing account by Rucker (1977), a mathematics professor, of how he tried this, and scared himself so badly by the assault on prosaic I-ness which resulted that he gave it up in short order. He suspected that the amateur yogi from whose book he got the technique eventually frightened himself into a heart attack. Other intronauts are apparently less easily scared. The interesting thing, Gezumpstein would say, might be to ascertain exactly what range of inputs from external reality gets into our brains before the filtering and sorting process takes over. With this in mind, such experiments make a kind of sense, even if the theosophical interpretations placed on the results by soft-nosed enthusiasts trying to experience an astral body or the like do not. Those results closely resemble the "push-pop" sequence described in near-death experiences. It would be extraordinarily odd, and extraordinarily instructive, if the filter could be circumvented in this way, even allowing for a great deal of misconception about the objective significance of unusual states of mind, which are apt to carry as disabling a sense of enlightenment as does prosaic reality itself. "Try it," Gezumpstein might say. "It's how *I* see things, and it might save you a great deal of hard work. At the very least, it would loosen up your rigid attachment to optical and linear experience." He would add that nobody takes dream states overseriously— not even psychoanalysts—except as occasional sources of scientific or artistic inspiration. Such insights still have to be written out in plain for heuristic testing before they become respectable.

# Interlude: Gezumpstein's Teaching Tape

"So why exactly did you conjure me, Master? It wasn't, I'm sure, for the pleasure of my company."

"I assure you, Gezumpstein, the reasons are practical, and quite important in the world I live in. You don't mind? After all, you've still got all the time in the world."

"Of course, though I don't perceive it in the way you do. But I'm getting used to your peculiarities. You do realise that it's risky, talking to demons?"

"It's been traditionally thought so."

"But not for the reasons given. Why take the risk? Pure devotion to knowledge?"

"No. As a matter of fact . . ."

"That's a relief. One thing we demons do *not* provide under any circumstances is knowledge."

"As a matter of fact . . . I'm embarrassed to tell you."

"No need for shame! Treat me as your psychiatrist. Demons are utterly shameless and utterly disreputable. They will provide a framework for anything."

"It's NASA. They want to 'send a message' to potential extraterrestrials who might get hold of their latest piece of peripatetic machinery."

"So they write them a letter. Or send them a tape. Or draw them a picture. Or a theorem."

"They did, they did."

"You brought it down on yourself?"

"Alas, yes."

"You pointed out that the little green men might just possibly not share your Kantian a prioris? That they might live in a planiverse? That they might read your insufferable confection $t$ from back to front?"

"Fool that I am, I did."

"And fool that you are, they said Wow! we never thought of that. And obviously the right consultant for this project is somebody who is *used* to conversation with unconventional intelligences—I mean unconventional by your standards, of course. Fool that you are, you took it on."

"Indeed, indeed. I was flattered."

"Oh well, so am I. We're none of us flatterproof. Not even demons. So now you're lumbered with it. We'll work on it indirectly, however, simply by continuing our conversation."

"You've become strikingly fluent."

"I may later on become less so. This is pre-taped—I knew what you'd say. Normally the idiomatic program uses too much of my circuitry, and I turn it off. But before I do, listen to my consumer advisory. The dangers and uses of talking to demons."

"I'm listening."

"CAUTION ONE, then. DEMONS DON'T PRODUCE KNOWLEDGE. DEMONS PRODUCE MODELS. AND NOTHING ELSE. If you trip on that you'll do yourself a serious injury. Mammals have four legs, yes?"

"If they don't have flippers."

"Are there any five-legged mammals, freaks excepted?"

"None."

"But if you asked me for a model which accounts for the five-leggedness of mammals, I will *give* you one. And if you don't watch it you'll think you have proved that mammals have five legs. Take a piece of soap and write this on your shaving mirror:

$$A \supset a, a, a_2, a_3 \ldots a_n. \text{ If } \sim(a_x) \text{ for all } a \text{ then } \sim A.$$

Rider: if $a_1\ a_2\ a_3 \cdot a_{(n-1)}$, then $A$ will still be in good shape. BUT SOME DAY IT WILL RUN INTO

$$\sim a_n.$$

"Obviously!"

"Obviously! But if $A$ is ornate, or antique, or holy, or highly original, and I write it

$$\mathcal{A}$$

your're going to forget, and every time you forget I'm going to print out

# A

or similar. I proceed. CAUTION TWO (it follows from #1). DEMONS CONSTRUCT PROOFS ONLY IN MATHEMATICS. NO MODEL CAN BE PROVED—IT CAN ONLY BE DISPROVED. View the display. I intend to blow up this balloon."

"I'm viewing. What a beauty! It's enormous! It has this incredible structure of interrelations on its surface! Don't blow it bigger, Gezumpstein, I want to take in its detail . . . Gezumpstein, it burst. What happened?"

"It unfortunately brushed against an empirical observation, $\sim a_n$. In other words, a fact. We demons refer to those sharp little objects as poppers."

"It was a thing of beauty."

"Yah! Of course, they don't all burst. When that $\sim a_n$ comes along, as it will, sometimes

$$A \rightarrow B \subset A$$

and a bigger balloon swallows it up completely, though you can still see $A$ floating around inside. But most of them that demons inflate, burst. Be warned."

"Still listening."

"CAUTION THREE: DEMONS DON'T ONLY SELL BALLOONS. THEY SELL INTUITIONS, WHICH ARE UNINFLATED BALLOONS. THESE ARE PARTICULARLY VALUABLE AND PARTICULARLY HAZARDOUS."

"I see hazardous. Why valuable?"

"It's the way they're stored. We keep them in a large wooden case. It stops them blowing themselves up. But as they continually try, the case is always full, and there's a lot of pressure. So, most of them are nothing, and burst at once if you don't keep them well away from facts. But the ones at the top, the bottom and the sides, take the grain of the wood, and those are something else. We call them 'clicks'. Often sell them to mathematicians; *they* don't keep sharp objects around. Only get burst when they play with them outdoors."

"Do they last any better?"

"Oddly enough, they do. But no balloon is popper-proof. Sooner or later $\sim a_n$ will come. I sometimes hope to find one with the grain of the wood all over it, and then perhaps it will inflate and inflate until it contains both of us. But it's unlikely. Still, every balloon which is reasonably well-formed with the grain is serviceable. You could play with some of them on and off for several of your centuries. Even let one down and blow it up again years later."

"What's the chest made from?"

"Alles, was der Fall ist. Everything which is the case. What else would *you* make a case out of? Want to go on?"

"Yes."

"In spite of the consumer advisory?"

"Yes. I might get one of those balloons with a pattern on."

"Very well. Let us begin."

# Demonics and the Phenomenal Time-Arrow: The Nine Lives of Schroedinger's Cat

If that's what history says, history is bunk.

Attributed to Henry Ford I.

Quantum logic models of reality—both those which depend on universal wave mechanics (Everett 1972) and those which postulate, with David Bohm (1980), that "the fundamental processes of nature lie outside space-time but generate events which can be located in space-time" (Stapp 1977)—can be addressed by imagining a computer which would operate in demonic (Comfort 1979B), i.e., non-homuncular, non-spatiotemporal terms.

Such a computational system might be physically feasible, at least in part, but even if treated as a hypothetical device with inferrable properties like the Turing machine, the exercise of designing it is useful as a point of access to the homuncular bias, as well as calling for full elucidation of what exactly Stapp's model means.

The basic issue is the ontological status of middle-order reality—of this particular chess game, now being played, as against the matrix of possible chess games—and how this chess game differs from other chess games which do not appear to us phenomenally as being played on this occasion. It seems clear that if reality has even a tenuous and experiential meaning this real game must differ other than arbitrarily from hypothetical, possible, or imagined games. The demon Gezumpstein's initial position will be that he sees the superposition of all possible games. Leaving aside that he also sees play nondirectionally (he has no preconceived time arrow, entropic or empathic, to indicate that the game starts with all pieces present and ends in mate), and that he does not attribute transcendental identity to individual pieces, how do we explain to Gezumpstein what we mean by "this 'real' game"; how is this singularity to be demarcated in his analysis, and by what signals?

In past materialist-idealist disputation the traditional, hard-hat model of reality is that the real is the domain of matter and its interactions. An object consists of matter, or is associated intimately with it, and possesses some measure of transcendental identity for the optical observer. This optical-materialistic stance would probably have been Newton's formulation. The most striking and neglected philosophical spin-off of particle physics is not so much that matter is a virtual object (so, after all, is a cloud, and on a longer timescale, a dog), but that wholly virtual particles are ontologically indistinguishable from 'real' particles. In both cases, unlike a Democritean cloud or a Democritean dog, there is literally *no thing* there. In contrast to Nāgasena and thinglessness, there is an implication, though not a demonstration, that since 'real' objects are image-formations from a ground, software virtual objects of other categories (such as the program underlying morphogenesis or regeneration) are likewise ontologically equivalent to hardware objects and hardware virtual objects. This possibility is immensely important in biology, because it gets rid of entelechic vitalism by a radical surgery. Which of these intervalent categories includes 'mind' is unclear. This implication certainly represents a strikingly neo-Buddhist revision of epiphenomenalism. Plato missed the same conclusion by a few centimeters, and may actually have grazed if not hit it squarely , but he muffed the exposition. Even the Nonconformist Conscience is an ontological object like a dog if it can be shown to be a consistent program influencing events and behaviors; most primitives would have reified it as a goddess, and reification (thing making) is the underlying process of optical transformation. For the enthusiast it also leaves open Brahman-perceiving-Brahman models for human brain function and ideation, which at the moment are more intoxicant than heuristic, but need filing for future reference in dealing with several problems in physics and linguistics which at present tend to circularity between the observed and the language and mathematics of the observer.

Popper's answer to the problem of "What is real?" is that there are three orders of discourse: physical objects, subjective experiences, and statements. The point of this is to differentiate thought processes from statements, the computer program from the print-out. In such a system, the top layer (statements) only interacts or interfaces directly with the bottom layer (objects) through the layer which lies between, namely, mental software (Popper 1974). As to statements, there is no contest, because they are a human artefact; the problem, not only in physics, but throughout this discussion, is to unscramble the other two layers. If a determined sophist refused to admit any difference in this respect between the status of an electron, a dog, a goddess, and the Nonconformist Conscience, he could probably be managed, but only with some difficulty. The key phrase in so dealing with him would probably be "optically transducible," which pertains to a category of virtual objects representing either naive experience (dogs) or an inference one order down from naive experience (electrons, which one cannot see, but the effects of which one can see en masse). But this is a poor and equivocal shadow of the material-immaterial contrast which has so long been the distinguishing point between real-real and virtual- or figurative-real.

In order to avoid giving a metaphysical hunting license whereby *any* coherent system which can be imagined or abstracted may be said to be real (i.e., any possible chess game is ontologically equivalent to the game now being played), we add the requirement that the real must be observed, or strictly inferred from observation, and that the inference be then predictive in heuristic terms. The whole question of observation, however, now raises difficulties at the practical level in the interpretation of physics, and once considered, these spill over into the nature of human observation in general. Apart from being the end of the road for classical realist-idealist disputation, this type of consideration chimes well with growing neuropsychiatric recognition of the extreme arbitrariness of the Cartesian I, and growing self-satisfaction for adherents of mystical traditions which regard the homunculus and the phenomenal world as equally virtual, as manifestations of *māya* or *saṁsara*.

A biologist has to be impressed by the fact that, thoroughgoing mystics apart, most of the classical post-Einsteinian space-time models are mathematical and topological (i.e., the universe is like that) rather than psychoneurological (the conceptualizing system which we obligatorily use has the following built-in program). This arises largely through the agility of mathematics (an evolutionarily uncovenanted capacity of our brains, considering that they are by all arguments adapted to handling middle-order events) in getting around the adaptive, object-generating, optical preconceptions on which practical behaviors depend. Now our computer may in fact be able, via topological models, to form an analog of various models for the Universe as-it-is, but in any model interfaceable with human brain there is an inherent confusion with the universe-as-mental-construct—not as a

94 REALITY AND EMPATHY

Goedelian system break, but simply for reasons as crude as those which cause my pocket calculator to reject expressions involving negative square roots, or to treat numbers greater than 99,999,999 as unmanageable: the necessary hardware may not be there. Pauli and Jung originally made a start on the connection between archetypes and mathematical-cosmological visualization, but archetypes like myths are an empathic metalanguage, not an exhaustive one. Dobbs (1971) addressed the experience of time as against its geometry, but that was before we got evidence of imaging systems in the brain which, being holographic, are theoretically capable of handling quantum-type models (or generating them) if the interface with the rest of mentation happens to be able to accept such models. In order to look at this kind of question we need a brain of a simple order in which the character of the programming is known.

The problems of homuncularity in relation to physics come from discomfort over empathy, not from physics—in this regard they resemble the flat-earth intuition (which was fortunately rather easy to overcome since the alternative model could be experienced directly). For the homuncular, conventional observer, observations appear to be concrete: when we observe chess, we observe one chess game which appears to be extended in time. For quantum physics using rules of indeterminacy, observations are not definite and extension in time (irreversibility) is a statistical property of macrosystems. For heuristic and predictive purposes, these algorithms consistently work, which is the meaning of the proposition that they are true within the universe of discourse. In another mode, our conventional 'real' (nonmythological) perception is one which inherently accepts true-false, yes-no, on-off Boolean logic. To interface wave-mechanical models with this, the wave function has in some way to collapse, and it is this interface which presents the empathy problem.

Strict physics offers several models to get around the difficulty. The name of the game, initially, is "avoiding metaphysics." The biological psychologist would have to agree with this, but unfortunately 'metaphysics' is here another name for the idiosyncrasy of the perceiving system, namely, the human brain. A device which measures and records, the usual surrogate in quantum models for O (the observer), is not a true transduction of psychophysical parallelism, since O, so far from being a see-and-record system, has several highly configured chips intervening in the recording process. These program the conceptual and the mathematical models involved in the observation, the apparatus, and in the theory evolved afterwards. In fact, even in a true-false, nonquantum situation, Schilder's maxim that "perception is construction" applies a fortiori since in an indeterminate situation we still get true-false or event-nonevent answers.

The models available to get over the interface problem are various. The Copenhagen solution (chiefly an intellectual holding operation) was to say that state functions are not a comment on 'reality', which is probably unknowable, but are algorithms (useful mathematical shenanigans) which empirically predict particle behavior under existing experimental conditions with human observers. Some physicists, notably Wigner, are ready to admit the cerebral program on a level with the inputs to it, but tend to treat the interface between wave function and Boolean logic as a kind of psychokinesis. Respectable evidence for observable psychokinesis might improve the odds on this approach, but straightforward archetypal image-formation would probably do as well. Classical quantum theory generates paradoxes (notably the Einstein-Rosen-Podolsky paradox) which could be resolved by adding a further (extradimensional, transluminal) layer to the reality model, and this is Stapp's solution. By far the most elegant reduction, however, is the Everett-Wheeler-Graham universal wave model which shows that using classical mathematics, it is possible to incorporate all these paradoxes on the assumption (or more correctly, with the consequence) that all possible concrete derivates of a wave function in fact occur, but in distinct time streams. That in which we as observers currently find ourselves has no singularity, but inheres because all other streams are inherently inaccessible (the many worlds theory). As an exercise in the descriptive power of mathematical formalism Everett's papers are masterly. They do not rely on speculative metaphysics to bridge system breaks, but neither do they properly exclude metaphysics, as Everett asserts, because the conceptual process which generates particles, mathematics, physics, physicists, and the concept 'reality', is in fact taken as given: even mathematical consistency involves linguistic coaptation to a human logic system. By contrast, Bohm's implicate-explicate model does take in the observer, and Grassman, indeed, devised his algebra as a means of examining the sequence of ideas, not the behavior of objects.

This limitation may in effect be as absolute as the implied impossibility, in the many worlds model, of transfer other than by magic from one such Everett world to another. The aim of demonic computation would be to see what are in fact the constraints on conceptualization imposed by the brain. Mathematics can already get round some of these, but not the constraint that brains would imagine or construct Gezumpstein. The metaphysical datum would therefore be exactly the same as in mathematical analysis. Moreover, a demon programmed on any mathematical construction would work and provide answers which agreed with its own parenthood. This limitation could only be overcome, or commented on, to the extent that Gezumpstein was given the capacity to program himself for maximum reduction with minimum naive homuncular preconceptions. One can see in retrospect that such an autonomous demon could have produced most of prequantum relativity by being nonpositional in space-time. Going beyond crude space artefacts is going to be harder, and there is the possibility that an autonomous Gezumpstein would produce matter tautologous, vacuous, or comprehensible only to a hypothetical inhabitant of Hilbert space. One could only ascertain this by trying. The demon Gezumpstein might well sound like the purported ghost of F. H. Myers trying to get through to a 4-space brain.

Models from oceanic philosophies, which go back to Schroedinger (1964) and are now increasingly in favor with popularizing physicists, are not particularly helpful with the demonic computer problem. Yogis do not, and philosophers until recently did not, program or design computers. Given the intuition of a field-type reality manifesting in space-time, the standard approach of Oriental oceanism has been that extradimensional reality is invariant and diamond-like while phenomenal reality is simply illusional as dreams are illusional. Questions as to whether phenomenal events affect the field, whether the manifestations of an adamantine or nonchangeable field can be other than deterministic if seen in real-time, and, incidentally, how a wholly virtual or illusory brain contrives to think itself, are rarely addressed by Buddhist philosophers. In our context they are seen as belonging to physics. Some Buddhist philosophers (notably Nāgārjuna) address the origins of "forms," but in Platonic-idealistic terms. The traditional conclusion would no doubt be that extradimensional reality (Brahman or Sunya), because inclusive, cannot be interfaced with any discursive phenomenology, i.e., the computer which empathized it, like the yogi who empathizes it oceanically, could not talk intelligibly or exhaustively about it in any space-time model other than "neti, neti" (not this, not that). This idea is no different from the inaccessibility of other time streams in the Everett-Wheeler-Graham model, for example, which might be fundamental—though nobody likes postulating entities or states which are fundamentally inobservable. It will not do for physics, however, where the inference that there may be a subjacent non-space-time reality comes from experimental observation and mathematical analysis. Aspect's experiment on photon polarization, for example, is designed specifically to demonstrate insufficiency of conventional space-time as a basis for particle behavior. This experiment confirms the Einstein-Podolsky-Rosen paradox using photon polarization instead of particle spin.

Any theory which addresses epistemology from the mental or constructional end has to pay regard to problems in strict quantum logic, but is obliged at the same time to use hybrid language, since it is addressing the modes of experience and the perceptive system by which quantum models are seen to be mathematically logical. There is really no sensible way to break out of this circularity beyond pointing it out, since any strictly mathematical construction is a means of abstracting interrelations in a manner logically palatable to the human system: it avoids asserting incompatibles or formulating equations which are illogical, such as $2 = \sqrt{2}$, and those constraints are linguistic. These considerations apply to the demonic computer—which has the assignment of seeing how much linguistic-cerebral pre-bias it can omit while retaining intelligibility. Its initial use is not in the field where strict quantum logic was developed, but precisely in hybrid and interface fields, particularly biology, where strict indeterminacy may not (and probably does not) apply, but where state functions can be calculated nevertheless. All state functions in these macrosystems are, from the microphysicist's point of view, contaminated by mass effects and by thermodynamics, as well as by biological 'information' which represents a different order of effect. Its only likely bonus for the particle physicist is as a source of possible information on the machine with which he is working—the cerebral computer—leaving aside the serendipitous possibility of finding that a universal wave equation was descriptive in areas for which it was never intended. That conclusion would raise the strong probability, not that we have uncovered Brahman, but that we are taking away the number we first thought of, i.e., the conformation is in the observer.

At the same time, several mathematicians, notably Wheeler, see no way of limiting a general model, such as the many worlds hypothesis, to submicrophysical events—only that the streams generated by macro-birfucations like the death of Schroedinger's cat are likely to be so widely separated as to be practically unimportant. We have to take this view into consideration in determining how the demonic system will proceed.

Since the object of the exercise is psychological, with subsequent possible application to complex or middle-order systems, I have in this chapter deliberately chosen to start with naive or intuitive, rather than quantum-mechanical or other rigorously mathematical models. The strict amplifications will be limited to satisfying physicists who mistake the starting point for their own and think that the conclusions of quantum theory have been misunderstood. Their turn, as it were, will come when the naive constraints on a demonic model have been determined, and the time actually comes to construct one. At the same time a demonic model closely resembles a universal wave theory in which state functions are arbitarily reconstructed to know themselves, so to speak, as if, in spite of indeterminacy, they had been transduced without a human observer or mechanical apparatus. Naturally this is a fiction—the observed values have been homuncularly determined using apparatus. Lacking ESP, the demon we create can only know the observer-containing universe and then endeavour to take the observer, naive or quantum-mechanical, out of it. In the naive model, then, we begin by addressing not the relativistic but the naive model of time, since it is a major component of homuncularity-as-experience which relativistic and mathematical models themselves aim to circumvent in abstracting reality from intuition.

A strictly apophatic computer (one which could only say what Stapp's, Bohm's or Everett's field is *not*) would be of limited use. What one would ideally aim at is a cataphatic system, which could make positive heuristic inferences, for example, about the meaning of Stapp's statement that extradimensional reality generates events which appear in space-time. This system would preferably be of a sort that clarified the nature of phenomenal reality, particle interactions, and unified field theory, giving rise to experiment as well. The reason for using a mechanical system is to avoid the inherent limitations of an identity- and position-based brain, the homuncularity which all pictures, mathematical or logical-reductionist, of matter, energy and the like are at root attempting to circumvent. Our brains have devised quantum logic, but to see its implications we require a different sort of brain, which is not biased to geometry and optical transformation. The only way to obtain such a brain other than by mystical exercises is to construct one.

We now have to address in detail some of the logic problems which come to mind in considering how this might be imagined and, perhaps, eventually done.

## LOGIC AND MATHEMATICS OF DEMONIC SYSTEMS

There is no difficulty in imagining a mechanical system which processes events as wave functions. The difficulty is in determining how it deals with the collapse, in phenomenal reality, of a particular wave function. Here our experience seems to resemble a sharp object moving through a field of balloon-like envelopes and collapsing them into points.

At the naive-perceptual level this presents no problems—it is simply the chopping of a probability distribution. In order to comprehend why it presents such epistemological difficulties at the strict quantum level, it is necessary to remember that the quantum uncertainty is not statistical but fundamental, so that if an observer $B$ observes an observer $A$ who is in turn observing a process $P$, either $B$ is precluded from applying a quantum mechanical description to $A + P$, or if $B$ assigns to the situation a state function $\psi A + P$, $A$ will be incorrect in the state function which *he* has assigned. They cannot both be correct in assigning the same result to the experiment, and the discrepancy can be amplified at will to give a catastrophic regression by adding more observers. The alternative, proposed by Everett (1973), is to adopt the general validity of pure wave mechanics—without any statistical assertions—in all physical systems including observers and observed. Aside from generating a state function for the entire universe, the model also generates the existence of bifurcations in the time line. A full consideration of the mathematical consequences of "conservation of eigenstate" is given by Everett (1973): observation does not change the universe, it simply correlates the observer to the universe. It also resolves the Einstein-Rosen-Podolsky paradox without recourse to transluminal hypotheses. The demonic computer is a nonpositional, noncorrelated observer (i.e., it excludes psychophysical parallelism) and programmed, if we follow Everett, to the universal wave function. Its metaphysic is not psychomechanical but more like the Hindu-Buddhist formulation of observerhood: the observer is Brahman observing Brahman. It is possible to treat primary state functions as stochastic and observerhood as a form of chopping, but this works badly in terms of wave as against particle mechanics and is a less reductionist treatment of the observer-observed complex.

One might ask why our instruments share our rather restricted view and collude in collapsing wave functions. The short answer is that "instruments" are by definition systems which give distinguishable macroscopic readings, not fuzzy ones: our design criteria are drawn from hands-on, anthropic reality. A rather longer answer would be that because most of the phenomena involved in studying quantum processes are submicroscopic, we detect them by using thermodynamically metastable systems (photographic plates, cloud chambers) as amplifiers. But these systems, which come rapidly into equilibrium with one initial state of the wave-function, also have a Schmitt trigger effect—their thermodynamic component squares-up waveforms into yes-no answers. Given the size of the "instrument" system compared with what it is recording, the time necessary to establish coherent overlap of the wave-functions $\Phi_n$ would be greater than the age of the universe (Davies, 1974: Gottfried 1966). Short of reading-off wave functions by telepathy, "instruments" are accordingly in the same bind as are brains.

Suppose that one designed an instrument which could register both states of a coherent superposition, but constrained it to display them on a single meter. We would have no use for a reading which averaged them, or for a system which "hunted." What we would settle for, in all likelihood, is a Necker-cube type solution, in which the two eigenvalues were presented alternately by way of a readably slow alternation—in other words, an *iterant* (see p. 68 & appendix).

As with so many philosophical models, the "many worlds" interpretation is an old one. It appears in the *Brahmavaivarta Purāṇa* (Zimmer, 1946)—although Hindu thought probably regarded separate time streams as cyclically rather than simultaneously related—and in the Cabbala as the "kingdoms of Edom" (parallel realities with which God was unable to make contact because they contained no experiential human time line.) The interest of mythological models is that they are pointers, like the demonic computer, to finding an appropriate metalanguage to amplify experience, but our problem is that a persuasive metalanguage has to be heuristically useful and interface with mathematics as well as empathy. If the demon Gezumpstein, in dealing with wave functions in nature which we collapse experientially into points (specific observations) encodes the collapsed point readings, his viewpoint is homuncular and spatiotemporal. If he deals only in probabilistic envelopes, he tells us nothing about the uniqueness of *this* chess game, which becomes merged in an inclusive Brahman, jelly-like, and therefore unmanageable. Starting from state functions, the Everett-Wheeler-Graham model requires the reality of each exclusive choice in different time streams; for a wave function, this implies an infinity of time streams if the function is continuous. How and why does our sensorium choose among them?

Presumably in Bohm's (1980) or Stapp's (1977) model, the subjacent field which "displays invariance outside space-time" is itself in some sense formed or modified by the middle-order manifestations, which spring from it, when these are manipulated (otherwise it is hard to see how space-time events appear to modify one another other than deterministically.) Unless we accept thoroughgoing determinism for time-sited events, one definite consequence is that causality will almost certainly appear to the demonic system less as a homuncular illusion than as a symmetrical process: rather than one-way correlation, an intervention affects not only the future but also the past. This is possible because the demonic computer is bound to distinguish between the description of the time arrow in phenomenal events (historicity) and the way in which it perceives the same events extratemporally. To Gezumpstein, mnemonic history may be bunk. Very possibly, one consequence of his counterintuitive mode of processing events will be to show that historicity is an artefact based on the human use of memory.

## DO PAST EVENTS EXIST?

This question becomes, first of all, much less perverse in a relativistic context. To forestall a general assault by physicists on what follows, let me make it clear that this discussion is not concerned with the pure topology of space-time and time asymmetry, but with the much more hazardous interface between these pure models and empathy (psychological time). If "relativity physics has shifted the moving present out from the superstructure of the universe, into the minds of human beings, where it belongs" (Davies, 1974), we still have to address the resulting interface questions. If physicists, who should know better, still muddle "this dubious psychological concept of 'becoming'" (Davies) with structural space-time, the whole of non-physical science, including evolutionary biology and morphogenesis, continues *in statu quo ante* relativistic cosmology, while explicitly treating cosmology, biogenesis and evolution as one coherent process. It is difficult to be happy about this two-track approach, particularly when there are practical aspects: not only would it be a good idea to forecast the *empathic* effects of thinkable exploits in space travel before they become practicable, we may in fact be missing important regularities in middle-order nature by persisting in taking the motion-of-time experience as a solid viewpoint when no theoretical physicist regards it as other than a subjective preconception. The difference between middle-order and relativistic systems is not one of discontinuity or scale: in the first our viewpoint has not been updated to accomodate knowledge, while in the second it has. One way of attacking the implications of an update is for the unregenerate to ask naive questions of the enlightened.

In Bohm's model the phenomenal world is an explicate representing the sensible mapping into (Kantian) space-time of an implicate which has no such dimensions, which exists en bloc, and is either of high dimensional order or not dimensionally describable. The empathizing reader is going (and who could blame him or her?) to ask how the implicate can be visualized. The stock answers are: "By mathematics" or, more accurately, "It can't be," or "Not by you— possibly by Gezumpstein." The point is that 'visualize' implies translation into dimensional terms. If we are invincibly unable to visualize a hypercube, even if we work regularly with spaces of 5, 6, 7 or $n$ dimensions, we are not going to visualize an implicate. We can model it (we shall be discussing a number of models), present it in parables, most of which indicate what it is not, or mathematize it by creating a descriptive algebra. The temptation (which Bohm avoids) is to go in for portentous statements, such as "the surface of reality is configured," or (better) to use myth instead of math and present what amounts to a partial artistic impression. No man hath seen God at any time, and no man has seen an implicate at any time, for the rather different reason that seeing it would be one of the modes of explication, or making it amenable to our a priori, fixed circuitry. There is nothing unusual in a 'real' model which we cannot handle optically—the same would go for a hologram (though we can see that, we cannot see what it represents), or for a mathematical possible such as toroidal hyperspace. That a real system cannot be visualized is not evidence that it is either supernatural or fanciful, but simply that visualization is a 4-space process, and like the Flatlander we do not have the necessary circuitry. Moreover, what we 'see'—namely 4-space—may in fact not be there, at least as primary structure.

I strongly suspect that when the Hindus make Mahākālī (Great Time) the goddess who generates the entire real world display out of an underlying implicate order, they have got it right. Time is the critically unmanageable part of experience: it is mathematically an imaginary or complex quantity, but it determines our notions of causality, historicity, determinacy—in fact our entire analytic posture, where processes have a built-in arrow, a start and a finish. One can imagine a Flatland with $(x, y : t)$ but not a Flatland with $(x, y : a)$, $a$ being some other slicing of the salami. Fanciers of the implicate order have very commonly made the point that for an order of regularity to be truly implicate, it cannot be expounded, for all exposition is explication: trying to *expound* one's way through *māya* to the underlying Brahman is self-defeating because all one gets is more *māya*. One ends with the model of the apophatic mystics in which the underlying reality can be experienced in toto but not described. As a matter of fact, what appears to happen in this kind of global apperception is that all our customary frames for structural description are collapsed by the removal of $t$, or by the equivalent of a 90 degree shift (seeing $t$ end-on): in the result, "the end precedes the beginning, and all is always Now" (T.S. Eliot). So the problem of getting mathematically closer to the descriptive algebra of an underlying implicate resolves itself into finding a way of performing a rotation on $t$—something like $t \rightarrow a + jt : a\ Re;\ j\ Im$ (easy enough algebraically) and then absorbing, empathizing or visualizing the result (difficult and possibly misleading unless we can find some experimental pegs on which to hang the visualization). The whole of phenomenal reality as a display is generated by the fact that $t$ is a built-in *way of ordering experience*, whereas we treat it as an object of knowledge. We have to work with a cerebral pocket calculator which displays its results in this form, and the problem getting around apophatic or blob-type models is to devise the appropriate low cunning to enable the calculator circuitry to get around its own design limitations. If this cannot be done, Krishnamurti and the older mystics are right, and there is no way we can plug in to unprocessed reality except by "being there" at a nondiscursive (and therefore, to science, an unsatisfactory) level. It is worth a try. Since they describe but do not explain, mathematics seem the most promising start, provided that we realized that what they produce are algorithms (statements of regularity, function relations and so on). Māya (common experience) produces a different set of algorithms, and what may be instructive is the comparison of two viewpoints.

It is already clear that an observer-astronaut who travelled at a sizeable faction of the speed of light would experience very odd subjective effects. It was, in fact, the attempt to work out how it would feel to ride a light-wave as a surfer rides a breaker which set Einstein's speculations in train. With advancing exotic technology, there is always a fair chance that linear, experiential $t$ will start generating sorethumb-type anomalies, not in the remote world of microphysics or cosmology, but in actual experience. Remote singularities such as black holes do not raise this possibility so long as we cannot get at them; if we could get at them, they would stop being algorithmic and directly affect our perception, probably in a very anomalous way. If this were to occur, we would no doubt realize that similar anomalies due to our assumptions about $t$ were present in far less exotic contexts, only we had not noticed them. What we need is some kind of jolt to break into the circular process of a priori perception. If we got it, what is now relevant only to models in physics would become existentially relevant as well.

The relativistic picture of space and time can be shown rather simply in a Minkowski diagram (fig. 5). What is plotted here is the movement of a photon (light) from $A'$ to $A$, or $B'$ to $B$. At time $t'$ in the past it was at a point $a'$ in space. At O, in the middle of the diagram, which corresponds to our experience of "now," it reaches us and we see it. At time $t$ in the future, the velocity of light being constant, it will have reached point $a$ in space.

Several things follow from this figure. First of all, there are two areas of space-time, the triangles A'OB and AOB', about which we can know nothing at time O because no physical signal from them can reach us. In order to do so, it would have to travel faster than light. Minkowski labelled these neither "past" nor "future" but "elsewhere." Obviously, because of our experience of the time arrow, O will appear to us to 'crawl up' the $t$ axis, revealing successive slices of these triangles as light has time to arrive from them. We also, by definition, know nothing about BOA. Why? The commonsense answer is "because it has not yet happened," but this may well be a tautology for "we cannot receive signals from it." If there were such a thing as anti-light one could, from this model, see forward into BOA—a nova occurring at place $a$ and time $t$ might be visible at O, exactly as if it occurred at place $a$ and time $t'$ in the past. The photon, however, is its own anti-particle: it does not exist in symmetrical varieties with regard to time. In fact, going from the Minkowski diagram alone, one

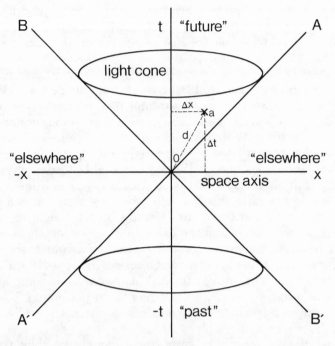

**Fig. 5** The Minkowski Space-Time Diagram.

The axes represent $t$ and one spatial dimension. We are viewing it in a second spatial dimension, perpendicular to the page, but it is not possible to draw *four* orthogonals. Note that $t$ is an "imaginary" or complex dimension, so $d$, the length of the line Oa, is given by $\sqrt{\Delta t^2 - \Delta x^2}$ not $\sqrt{\Delta t^2 + \Delta x^2}$

as it would be for two real or spatial dimensions. Instead of all points equidistant from O being defined by a circle with center O, as they would be if $x$ and $t$ were both real spatial dimensions, points equidistant from O in $t$ lie on a hyperbola. In other words, $t$ is quite a different creature from ordinary, spatial dimensions.*

might say not that "the velocity of light is constant, and it travels forward in time" but "time as we observe it is a statement of the properties of $c$, the velocity of light."

The Minkowski diagram is not a time-and-motion graphic: what it shows is the "space of simultaneity" of an observer. The "past light cone" contains all the events from which a signal travelling at or below the velocity of light could reach O "now," and the "future light

---

*To make matters more complicated, topologists now suggest that a 4-space can exist in two distinct forms. The relationship between these is too involved to elaborate here, and it is by no means clear what significance this finding might have for physics (See *Science* 1982 217: 432–433).

cone" contains all the points which a signal emitted "now" at O could reach. All events which are really *simultaneous* with point O, lie in the "elsewhere."

A real interval (in a real dimension) is described as "time-like," an imaginary interval as "space-like." Where the separation between two events is space-like, their apparent sequence will depend on the relative position of the observer. This is the structure behind the Einstein effect, the famous paradox of the difference in time experience between the crew of a moving space shot and observers on earth.

Stable causality is usually taken to be a desideratum for topological models of space-time, i.e., they should avoid any closed time-like curves. Singularities apart, some coherent topological models do admit these, but most mathematicians would clearly rather that they did not.* A closed time-like curve through a point $p$ implies that an individual at $p$ would in theory be able to influence his own past, for instance, by shooting his grandfather in the cradle and preventing his own birth. "One might argue that endowing individuals with this ability violates our most basic conceptions of how the world operates, and so it is entirely proper to impose, as an additional condition for physically acceptable space-times, that they possess no such causality violations" (Geroch and Horowitz 1979). On the other hand, as the same authors point out, counterintuitive ideas commonly lead to new discoveries in physics, and the possibility of causality violations has to be taken seriously. The test is heuristic, not intuitive.

Note that if Buck Rogers can abolish his own grandfather, return to the present, and still find himself in *statu quo ante*, then events in middle-order human experience, viewed as a sequence, must be

---

*To visualize a spacetime which does admit closed time-like lines, imagine the Minkowski diagram drawn on the side of an enormous donut with a very small central hole: the $t$ axis is parallel to the axis of the hole. The circumference of the donut represents any of the three space dimensions, assumed to be closed—the journey round the side of the donut, passing through the hole, represents closed time. In this model, all of the past of $p$ lies also in its future—but in order to get there, and return to $p$, one has to go through a singularity (the hole), at which point all the spatial dimensions have collapsed. The universe so modelled would go through a series of cycles in the form of big bang-expansion-collapse-big bang and so on indefinitely. Note that if this model were correct, either the past as well as the future is quantum indeterminate, or the universe is locked into a series of endless repetitions down to the last detail.

Closure of any dimension would accordingly not have to be obvious—that would depend on the radius of curvature. If spatial dimensions are closed, one might have to travel for billions of light-years to return to base: if time were closed, one might have to pass through an entire universe cycle to reach the second screening of the movie. A toroidal model $(S^1 \times S^1)$ and a cylindrical model in which time but not space is closed $(S^1 \times R)$, are both examples of space-time topologies which admit closed time-like lines. See Geroch and Horowitz (1979) for a technical discussion of this whole problem.

like regulative morphogenesis: if, within limits, we tinker with it, it gets back on course by a different route. Reflection on the implications of a many-worlds or many-tracks model will suggest that this is another artefact of our memory-perception system, and exactly the artefact we might expect: indeterminacy would always look *to us* like determinism.

The double take is between the fact that for all cosmological purposes, past and future are treated as existent en bloc, and the obligatory emphasis of humans on a nonsingular and illusory reference point called "now." Unfortunately, the fact that humans, including physicists, do have this experience—which has to be addressed in making sense of the link between middle-order and cosmological realities—means that what can be rendered into mathematics cannot be readily rendered into empathy. It also means, as Geroch and Horowitz say, that we draw mathematical models with an eye over the shoulder to commonsense, which is probably a bad idea, since, as we noted earlier, "Nature may not only be odder than we think, but odder than we can think" (Haldane). From this source comes the constraint that although the past-future antithesis is illusory, the future can be modified (which is experientially true) and the past cannot (which, because we have no direct access to our past world line, is totally speculative).

There would be no trouble with an en bloc model in which neither past nor future could be altered, except that this kind of determinism defeats causality altogether. Past and future could also be both homogeneous, seen *ab extra, and* modifiable. In effect, this is the many worlds model (De Witt and Graham 1973) in which the texture of the manifold is more like a sponge than a surface. Our past track appears linear because we can accept into consciousness only one eigenchoice at each potential bifurcation, the other representing different time streams with which the observer at $p$ can never correlate: in the forward light-cone, the sponge is still a sponge or a labyrinth without Ariadne's thread. Since we are talking about the neuropsychology underlying physics, it has to be pointed out that the implications of such a view for the hard-hat, Helmholtzian, epiphenomenal mind would be catastrophic. In fact, it has been taken out root and branch, since unless we reckon that Helmholtzian mind is a one-track mind, and somehow contrives to throw away all the alternative eigenstates, both body and 'mind' must also subdivide, as Schroedinger's cat bifurcates into one live and one dead eigenpussy. There exists a time stream, albeit remote, in which Julius Caesar or Moses is still alive. One could take this kind of model if it were confined to exotic particle events, which in any case are virtual, and a transduction, in all probability, of a "something else" to a positional observer. But, as Wheeler has pointed out, there seems to be no way of limiting a many worlds model once it is adopted, except that the time stream containing a still-preaching Moses is so remote in the imaginary dimension $I$ (hypertime, orthogonal to the $t$ axis) that it resembles probabilistically the likelihood that a television set or Charles Darwin will emerge fully formed from a black hole (Hawking and Israel 1979).

What is anomalous, clearly, is not the en-bloc substratum of reality, but the human construct derived from it. This construct has the same artificial relation to "reality" as a film or a videotape has to middle-order reality: one can create anomalies (jump-cuts, reversals and so on) in a film which do not exist in middle order reality. Middle-order reality, being itself an artefact, can generate anomalies not present in unprocessed reality, and so on. In the light of this, the possible consequences of closed time-like lines which allow the modification of the past, and hence by feedforward through conventional causality, the present—beside bedevilling time travel as a plausible topic for science fantasy—raise a question which is not strictly dependent upon whether such lines exist or not, namely, "Is the past real?" All topologies which proceed by the slicing of space-time accord a certain degree of privilege to the slice containing the junction of the past and future light-cones (now,) which coincides with empathic human observation. Most of them, however, in spite of using models in which the slice presupposes the existence en bloc of the entire salami, incorporate the intuitive perception of the time-slit. 'The present', to an observer at a given locus in 4-space, is 'real' and may be said to exist (even though it is mathematically illusory); 'the past' no longer exists, and 'the future' does not exist yet. But in any consistent model of space-time what appears to O to exist, to have existed, or not yet to exist, can be altered, and the categories transposed, by moving O to a different stance within the light-cones, and topologies have been proposed (e.g., Goedel 1959) in which by reason of nonsimultaneity, relativistic space-time cannot be sliced into a stack of 'nows' in any unique way. The Kruskal-Szekeres model for black holes contains two singularities, "past" and "future", with equal reality. Topologies are slightly more ready to face forwards, and treat the future, though indeterminate, as an extant part of the surface model, than to look backward and enquire what the past of an observer at $p$, the focus of light-cones, is doing now. Rather than a slice situated elsewhere on the $t$ axis, the past is more commonly seen as the causal origin of the situation at $p$ involving very disparate events in overall space-time, especially for the cosmologist whose information arrives from varying distances at the velocity of light.

As Geroch and Horowitz point out, the acceptability of models at the point when they are translated from the language of mathematics into quasi-experiential terms still turns on their capacity not to violate middle-order a prioris. We may be forced to swallow such violations, given sufficient evidence, exactly as we have learned to handle curved space, but we are uneasy with them and leave them until last. Accordingly, the influence on theory of the perceived time-slit does not seem to have been wholly thought through. It is obscured considerably by nonsimultaneity when one is dealing—as cosmological topologists do—with macroevents: The slices which make up middle-order experience lie on a scale where relativistic effects are unimportant. Unless one argues, however, that this microstructure is in some way locally singular, the same considerations have to apply at the local and at the cosmological level; otherwise, one would have to treat the local structure of event-sequences as 'grainy', with different topologies within the grains from the overall characters of the macrosurface. One would, in fact, be intuitively happier with a symmetrical model in which past and future were both indeterminate, because fluid and modifiable, rather than the past fixed because it is past and the causal source of a present, while the future is undetermined because it is a substrate for causal interference. There is here a possible rough analogy with the finite velocity of light: a cause might resemble a photon packet emitted by a distant object which is free thereafter to disappear, or change its activity, while the emitted signal is on its way to the now sited at the apex of the past light-cone.

There are two blocks to a modifiable, existent past: one is the absence of plausible examples of retrocausality (in which the present is seen to be receiving causal inputs from the future); the other is quite simply the intensity of the human perception of reality as being located within the time-slit. The point as to the reality of the past is, of course, implicit both in Goedel and in Park's protest (1972) against the tendency of nonphysicists to 'animate' the Minkowski diagram, so that its focus 'moves' in time. Physicists accordingly do see past and future as existent and present as merely a reference point. The trouble starts when we address modifiability. Incidentally, biologists, when first confronted with Minkowski space or a model such as toroidal hyperspace, almost invariably treat it as a *chart of movement*, not a topology—so ingrained is the movement of time. The error can run the other way. Reichenbach, a mighty stalwart, gets into terrible trouble with biological time by confusing middle-order reality with a special space-time topology (Reichenbach and Mathers 1959).

Everett worlds are one model in which "the past is fixed and the future is yet indeterminate" (Penrose 1979), and other causes of time asymmetry can be modeled. Penrose's interest is in the space-time adjacent to singularities, where space-like and time-like lines may be transposed. Our present capacity to examine the interface between space-time and experiential time is a brilliant testimonial to the ability of mathematics to get around Kant. It is likely to be some time before any one can actually test what deformations of space-time around a singularity actually do to empathy. It is possible in principle, however, and might eventually be practicable, to do some experimental philosophy and examine the empathic effects of approaching such a singularity (picking a rotating example to minimize the risk of catastrophic effects on the investigator). Even in the vicinity of a Kerr (rotating) black hole, one can draw time-like closed lines from which one could emerge earlier than one entered them. In conducting such an eventual experiment, one would have to hope that the demon is correct. Commonsense (if indeed it is applicable to such contexts) here strongly suggests that a space-like time reversal could not be deterministic; otherwise, a probe following such a trajectory would revert via nuts and bolts to its original raw materials, but as a preliminary, it would have to retrace its course out of the critical region in which space-like journeys are possible. One way out of this would be Tipler's (1974) suggestion that a time singularity acts as a duplicator of matter, with horrendous energetic implications arising from $e = mc^2$ (we should meet ourselves coming back, in other words, with enormous energies needed to construct the replica). Neither of these difficulties would arise, however, if the non-mnemonic past is itself modifiable, or if we concede that matter can exist in two places at once as a combination of superpositions, of which the two states of the probe, before and after space-like displacement, are two differently computed centroids. In that case, space-like travel would involve displacement not into the mnemonic past, which is artefactual, but into "elsewhere"—viewed, if we please, as another component of a stack of space-times if we try to transduce what has happened to an observer by using middle-order formalisms. This would render the journey less disagreeable to the passenger, who would be spared the necessity of unlearning physics and reverting via a zygote into the component cells of his parents, and so on. He might, however, find himself irreversibly disjoined from his original world line, including his place and time of departure.

The object of our exercise is not really to discuss time travel, nor to solve the paradox that "a time machine would never require to be invented, only copied." It does aim to suggest by introducing the Gedanken demon that after a period of creative mathematics and a great influx of information, cosmology is going to have to get over its tendency to equate neuropsychology with metaphysics (bad) and start to address the idiosyncracies of the apparatus which is doing the observing and conceptualizing (good, but neglected). Neuropsychologists have a vested interest in bringing this about, even though once it occurs they are in for a rough ride, having been far more uncritically committed to the nineteenth century's epiphenomenal mind\* than most of them would care to admit. This area is still jealously guarded against demolitionists for fear of letting in a horde of waiting theosophists and Californians ready to pounce at the very idea that all bets are off. It is the opinion of this author that science is now old enough to deal with these enthusiasts, and has no ground for anxiety. At the very least, it seems impossible to go on with the heuristic modeling of space-time without observing and dissecting the hyperloop, in which material objects and their relational topology are studied by 'mind', while 'mind' is held to be mediated by a subsystem of material objects—brains and neurons—which demonstrably distort the model of which they are a part.

Going back to our question "Is the past real?" the answer "yes" inheres in a consequence of relativity—the virtual character of simultaneity. Kurt Goedel (1959) drew attention to this but oddly enough, his admirers rarely refer to this paper, possibly for lack of a clear perception of what he is talking about; but if correct, it is fundamental to demonics and to world-modelling alike. Goedel's argument is that given the relativity of simultaneity, de Broglie's (1959) "slice of space-time" is not a correct description of 'now', since relativistic space-time cannot be sliced into a stack of nows in any unique way. Past, now, and future must exist en bloc. He illustrates this by imagining a rotating universe, in which "the local times of certain observers cannot be fitted together into one world time," i.e., some of their world lines would appear to us to be composed of simultaneous events. Clearly their experience of change would be a subjective, not an objective, phenomenon—with the implication that this is what we mean by change, both in relativistic 4-space, and in general: change is not a thing but a way-of-seeing. Einstein himself clearly agreed, but put it a good deal less bluntly, in the form that 4-space is not a thing but a structural quality of a field. For some extraordinary reason, the penny never seems to drop, in any of the subsequent discourses on the character of mind, intelligence, cerebration, and the like, that this realization has a neuropsychological dimension—not even in Hofstadter (1980), who is the most devoted of all Goedel's interpreters. We assent happily to relativistic 4-space in cosmology and go on treating linear experience as in some way given. This hyperloop is one of the singularities of human perception which we shall have to discuss presently. The difference between past, present, and future not only patterns all of sci-

---

\*"Epiphenomenal mind": this phrase is unfortunately used by different writers in different senses—"mind and brain are separate but parallel manifestations," or "mind is an irreducible expression of the processes occurring in brain." I am using it here in the second (Helmholtzian) sense.

ence, which subsists on causality, but also our domestic perception of living and our anxiety driven zeal in confabulating world models. But rather as passers-by fail to notice even an enormous statue in a square unless it is newly erected, this piece of patterning gets by unnoticed.

There is no problem, of course, in seeing the simple relativistic point. A nova occurred one year ago at a point two light-years distant from an observer. In that case, assuming that observer and event keep relative station (their relative mutual velocity is zero) does the event exist? And if so, does it exist in the past, the future or the present as viewed by the observer's time arrow?

The relativistic and historical answers here coincide. The event is in the observer's 'past', though he does not know it; its consequences exist, and their existence will become evident in the observer's 'future' i.e., one year from now. In this respect they do not differ from a letter posted by his mother last week which will be delivered tomorrow. Moreover, since space-time is inseparable, one observer's past is another's future, but the sequence is nonetheless historical in form to a third or omniscient observer. The trouble with this is in defining the existential status of an 'event'. An event without consequences, a non-event in the media sense, is a contradiction. There is no meaningful way of separating the event—a nova—from its consequences. The nova itself is a conspicuous member of a chain of physical events occurring in a star. Its consequences include the emission of energy in the direction of the observer. These photons are still on their way, and accordingly to this extent the future vis-à-vis the observer is deterministic: there will be a nova to be seen even though no observer at that point survives to see it. Only in more complex models can the event be separated from its manifestations—posting a letter, not the letter itself, is an event.

So far so good. If one asks philosophical questions one gets silly answers. But once we start designing the demonic computer and programming out homuncularity, it gets harder to exclude the 'reality' of past events in nonrelativistic models. The Dow Jones was 805 on Jan 1 and 813 on Jan 10. What was the Dow Jones on Jan 1 on Jan 10? An observer ten light-days away will hear 805 on his radio, but he is after all only in the same case as the investor on a remote lighthouse whose Wall Street Journal takes ten days to reach him. But if the speculative lighthouse keeper phones his broker, he will find the figure 805 is no longer 'real'. The cosmic investor cannot call his broker, because by any spatiotemporal means, it will take him another ten days to place an order.

In terms of quantum logic, however, reality transduced into the homuncular time-slit is something else again—the moment of decease of Schroedinger's cat. According to this view, the whole resultant series of skullsplitting paradoxes comes from the homuncular model, including its time arrow, and the manner in which we synthesize it, not from the oddity of the universe. A computer programmed to be strictly nonhomuncular might generate counterintuitive data but would avoid system breaks, and this would be the test of its nonhomuncularity.

## CAUSALITY AND THE HOMUNCULAR TIME ARROW

It is not, in fact, self-evident that cause exclusively precedes effect in middle-order, experiential reality, even if it seems to do so by definition. What is self-evident is that cause precedes effect and is not also retroactive *in our experience*. There exists no way in which we could detect a retroactive action of a middle-order cause which was also prospective, because *we have no direct access to past events*.

Causation in its phenomenal form is a major determinant of the intuitive time arrow. Experience—evident from the first occasion on which we bite out of a nursery rusk—is that 'the future' is modifiable by intervention in real-time while 'the past' is not. This is, however, a constructional inference, since we have no real-time access to either past or future, only to 'the present', defined as that condition to which we have sensory access—a slice (de Broglie 1959) of coherent spacetime.

Consider a quantity $a = (f)T$. If from consecutive observations $a_{t1}, a_{t2} \ldots a_{tn}$ we determine $\frac{da}{dt}$, the phenomenal readings represent successive now's in real-time: there is no way of observing $a_{t1}$ at $t = 2$, though we can infer or extrapolate $a_{t(n+y)}$ and eventually observe it in real-time for fit when $t = n + y$.

A simple model of the neuropsychological experience of the time arrow, which generates causality and historicity, is in fact not very easy to make. A Turing machine model in which a moving paper roll is scanned by a slit corresponding to now will not do, since interventions in the slit, like a pencil mark, travel successively into the past but are incapable of affecting the future. It would work only in a deterministic setting where the roll was preprinted (in this case causality would work only in reverse). One needs a film of a developing zygote such that if from a given frame we delete a gene or an organ, subsequent embryogenesis is affected in the remainder of the film, while the deletion moves into 'the past'—a very odd and awkward model. Nevertheless, it implies the prosaic experience that if we alter the value of $a_{t1}$, then at $t = 2$ the new value of $a_{t1}$ exists in the record, and $a_{tn}$ will be modified accordingly.

Consider first the viewpoint of the demonic computer in trans-

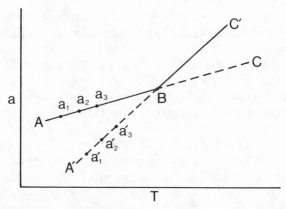

**Fig. 6** Heating of a Wire with An Intervention

ducing not observer participation in a quantum-type event, but prosaic participation in a middle-order process by *intervention*, for example, in a mechanical or thermodynamic middle-order system.

As Meredith (1972) pointed out, Einstein's universe includes only
incidental observer intervention. Nothing in it is motile or propelled,
and nobody fires any retrorockets. The result on Gezumpstein may be
instructive or farcical, experientially and mathematically, according
to taste.

Let us turn to a simple nonrelativistic class exercise in a classical
thermodynamic system (for a discussion of "mind-reversibility" in a
true wave-mechanical system, see Cooper and van Vechten 1973). We
can observe successive values of a real-time, or middle order function
against time by heating a wire with an electric current and reading
off $a°$ each minute, and find that it follows the straight line $ABC$
over the period of study. At $B$ we perform some intervention (increasing the current) which, given the equilibrium with loss from the
wire, now alters the slope of the line to $BC'$. What is encoded by
the demon?

The historical record will show $ABC'$, which is what we have
experienced as 'real'. But Gezumpstein does not treat time as a prefer-
ential or special dimension: he encodes *and* extrapolates. If he encoded
$ABC'$ he must be deterministic—it will appear to us that since he is
atemporal, he had foreknowledge of $C'$ with which we merely com-
plied. If he encodes $A'BC'$, he is exhibiting retrocausation and adjust-
ing $a_1$, $a_2$ to unhistorical values. What he does has to be intermediate
between the two. In the Everett model, he encodes both $ABC$ and
$A'BC'$ with a changeover at $B$ due to what was done there: $AB$ and
$BC'$ are in real-time, $A'B$ and $BC$ somewhere else. More probably,
Gezumpstein must encode the "tendency to exist" of $a_1 \ldots a'_1$ and
$a_2 \ldots a'_2$ probabilistically (we see their probabilities absolutely as 1

and 0 respectively). In this case he would treat macro-observations as effectively wave-function-like, and their arbitrary collapse into discrete readings as a cerebral expedient to achieve cognitive coherence (there are no real readings $a_1$, $a_2$ or $a'_1$, $a'_2$), but how does Gezumpstein treat the singularity at $B$? He observes a rule for $ABC$ and a rule for $A'BC'$. How does he designate the changeover?

At this point the mathematician will infer either that Gezumpstein is innumerate or that the demonkeeper has grossly misunderstood the range of validity of quantum theory. Statistically, macrosystems do not behave indeterminately; the molecular movements composing temperature are stochastic, but in spite of theoretical reversibility, the demon has no excuse for blind retrodiction. In any case there is no need to drag any of this into a situation which can be dealt with by classical mechanics, and Gezumpstein's speculations about the tendency to exist of something which did not happen are vacuous.

To which Gezumpstein replies, "Either I don't see your problem, or you don't see mine. What I see are equations yielding straight-line plots, based on values you got by averaging molecular states observed in your reality continuum. You relate these to a dimensional ordinate $t$ which seems to have special religious significance for you. I can see they intersect at $t_b$ with an angle $\theta$. What I don't comprehend is the singularity of $t_b$ such that you treat $AB$ and $BC'$ as ontologically distinguishable from $A'B$ and $BC$. And I don't understand what you mean by retrodiction. Is this another singularity of $t$? I am simply extrapolating." When we explain what we meant by blind retrodiction, Gezumpstein points out that what we call statistical treatment involves an observer entry located in the dimension $t$ (quite apart from our physical intervention in turning up the heat at $B$) which interchanges information and correlation. Our simplest way of making him see the singularity of $t_b$ is to explain that for all values of $a$ located on $AB$ we have a subjective 'second record' called "memory" which gives the values as existential premium over mere extrapolates. "But," says Gezumpstein, "in that case is $B$ real in your terms or not?"

If we reply "Yes, because at $t_B + dt$ it will be in the record, and at $t_B + 1$ there will be an observation point lying on $BC'$," we will have him foxed—and thinking in the observer correlation terms of an observation set which looks to us like everyday, classical physics. The demon has no idea of the nature of intervention either as a specific human act, or in its relation to a homuncular observer. Furthermore, if we say that in *our* logic $a_1 \cap a_1' = \emptyset$, it says "Why?"

Causality and sequence both appear to be the artefacts of a homuncular viewpoint. The problem in demonics is to anticipate how the nonhomuncular demon will represent them. The demon's trans-duction (whatever our choice of universe models in physics) is almost certain to be a "manifestation in space-time of a field situated outside space-time" by virtue of his terms of reference. (Since we have to make the demon, we have to choose this model by a process of trial and error—it could be Hilbert space, a matrix based on Hamiltonian quaternions, a holographic power spectrum, or some topological confection based on Menger's "topology without points"—the choice is open for grabs.) Now if the slit representing $a_t$ scans some derivate of this factitious model, a modification in the slit will affect all parts of the pattern (changes are translationally invariant). The slit itself has no singularity, so these changes will affect the encoded values of $a_t$ whether we see them as past, present, or future. If there exist interventions (causes) operative in middle-order reality which are reflected in the field, Gezumpstein must see these as operating both backwards and forwards in relation to the motion of the slit, or be restrained from doing so because we wrote into the print-out conditions intuitive rules which prohibit it.

Nor is all this simply a product of the Department of Tiresome Ingenuity, because what are effectively demonic models of subjacent reality are being seriously bandied around (e.g., Stapp 1977). Leaving aside naive problems as to how a "reality outside space-time" is to be considered as changing at all, and in what dimension, and how it contrives to be translationally invariant except in a graphical 4-space model (which are no heavier paradoxes than the existence of angular momenta without actual rotation) causes will appear to operate symmetrically to Gezumpstein, but will be seen by us as operating forwards only, because and only because $a_{t1}$, $a_{t2}$ are 'frozen' as observations by the motion of the slit. This would apply to a straight class experiment, but has no heuristic value: when we get to particle situations, using for example S-matrix formalisms, Gezumpstein might turn out to be right, and the intuitive bar to rewriting history might be experimentally inappropriate.

The demonic exercise, even if it looks at first flush a little like one of *Scientific American*'s mathematical games, is worthwhile chiefly because it focuses attention on the time-slit. Transducing the experience of time is the fundamentally unmanageable part of the homuncular experience, for there is no conceptual problem over simultaneities in 3-space. A positive result in nonlocality experiments is odd, but the idea that apparently separated events could be coherent is manageable because we experience analogous situations in middle-order reality, even though the explanation is different. Dipoles are a conventional experience, monopoles are not.

Gezumpstein also fails, one might add, to derive comfort from thermodynamic explanations of why middle-order processes cannot be run backwards in time, self-evident as they seem to us.

The usual argument is that experiential time is a measure of entropy, so that in middle-order experience it cannot be run backwards, because of the second law of thermodynamics. If we look hard at this, however, it is tautologous: time cannot be run backward in middle order systems, only in single-particle interactions, because this is our experience, of which the second law of thermodynamics is a concise statement. Subatomic phenomena escape, because they are not part of middle order experience, not only because they are thermodynamically distinct from mass effects. Gezumpstein understands thermodynamics, but reads the situation without our bias.

We could, if called on, explain middle-order experience to a non-positional demon. This is a necessary exercise for cosmologists, for as long as commonsense continues to intrude into their models, they need to identify exactly what the middle-order experience contains. The explanation would have to run something like this: These carbon-based units, in spite of their vivid illusion of a moving 'present' in one-way time, have in fact no direct access to their 'past', 'future' or 'present'. All their inputs from the world manifold take a finite time to encode and process; 'present' accordingly monitors the instantaneous state of that processing. The processing system we have seen prints out two categories—'now' and 'real'. In the course of doing so, it also deals summarily with wave-functions, collapsing them into $p = (0 , 1 ,)$. What happens to the rejected eigenstates is a matter of argument. The processing system converts interference patterns into objects, and makes objects out of centroids: in fact, simplification into optical objects is one of its leading principles, which is why 'objects' of a Democritean kind have hagridden physics against its better nature.

This highly processed information is transferred to a tape called "memory," which cannot be disobserved, though it loses definition with time. All impressions which have been coded 'now' and 'real' are transferred to memory with the same coding. In referring to 'the past' we are talking about the content of the memory tape, which is fixed. Accordingly, $t$ is scanned through a 'moving' time-slit. Let $t_{-5} \ldots t_{+5}$ be imaginary divisions of experienced time $(\in S_{(t)})$ then at $t_0$, which is the point of record, the memory contains $t'_{-5} \ldots t'_{-1}$ which represent successive records of $t_0$ and nothing else. If in the tape $t'_{-5}$ contains $(\alpha, \beta, \gamma, \delta)$, that was what $t_{-5}$ contained at $t_0$. "However," says Gezumpstein, "adopting the convention of moments, compartment $t_{-5}$ now appears to contain $(\alpha, \beta, \varepsilon, \tau)$." "That," we reply, "we wouldn't know."

Note that for Gezumpstein, there is no convention that because the content of $t_{-5}$ at $t_0$ had causal effects which appeared in due course, human-style, at $t_{+5}$, that content is immutable: in his view it has, as it were, "done its stuff" in fixing our record of $t'_{+5}$ when that appears in our time-slit, and is at liberty to vary without our being aware of the fact. In fact there is no motion of $t$ and there are no successive slices. They are as much human position artefacts as the undisobservable memory tape, but all human algorithms are modelled by our odd habit of breaking up the time-space manifold and recording the instantaneous products—which is very like the decomposition of a field into lines and frames for television transmission, but without resynthesis into a picture (our set appears to have no tube in it). We view physics, therefore, in terms of linear causation, and evolution in terms of historical sequence. To Gezumpstein, who sees both as field-determined, this linearization is distinctly odd. He applauds our praiseworthy ingenuity in mathematics, which enables us to get around our brains by low cunning, but condoles on our inability to empathize the results and alter our mode of processing experience. He is greatly disturbed by our confusion between the memory tape of our experiential world line and the actual state of space-time within the past light-cone. We are making trouble for ourselves by failing to let knowledge override empathy. The content of $t_{+5}$ may correlate with what was in $t_{-5}$ when its rank in our processing system was $t_0$, but by the time it has reached $t_{-5}$ position, that correlation is over and done with.

What Gezumpstein finally concludes is that in the experiential model, causes have a fixed "velocity" closely analogous to $c$, the velocity of light. So much for Buck Rogers' grandfather.

Moreover, to make things worse, time as we perceive it could quite possibly turn out to be quantized—to consist of discrete very short sections, as a film consists of frames or a video picture of rasters, between which there are gaps of time-out. Very brief gaps, certainly, but quite big enough to make utter nonsense of transcendental models of identity or of becoming. Śiva destroys each moment to create the next. This presents no problem to Gezumpstein, who is looking at the covering space made by cutting the film into frames, putting them en bloc, and looking through the assemblage as if it were a single frame, but it plays hell with most conventional models of what constitutes objective reality. Perceived time does not have to be a thing for this to be possible; after all, local phenomena such as electrons are not things, nor are they present continuously, but in our brains they have a certain algorithmic continuity. Whether the statement "time appears to be quantized" is true heuristically seems doubtful at present, but there are models which involve its being so, and the fit is plausibly good.

Quite obviously, Gezumpstein is not saying that for every $|t|$

there are ghostly particles, physicists, aunts and uncles pursuing separate existences. Unless time is indeed quantized, Buddhist-style, they would have a job remaining separate, since

$$\Delta t \rightarrow \delta t$$

and their behavior would have to be integrable. The "set of moments" is a clumsy construction, but it will have a use, in Gezumpstein's thinking, as we will see in a moment. Recall that he does not attribute "transcendental identity" to any structure and is consequently not bothered to assert the continuity of the particles, etc., which our Procrustean experience of 'reality' imposes. There is actually a respectable formalism for what he *is* saying concerning the 'reality' of the past. This is Bohm's (1980) model of continuous explication: this *does* contain "moments," but they are defined not in $t$ as such, but by the successive explicates making up one virtual object. The 'past' of each of these certainly exists, as does its 'future'. The test of whether the experiential past of a system is fixed or not fixed is, quite simply, to rotate the cylinder in Bohm's droplet model backwards. If we get a reversed replay of the virtual droplet, there has been no perturbation of its 'past' in the meantime. If its 'past' has now altered, there will be no replay, but a different explication. In this model, incidentally, it is open to Gezumpstein to treat $t$ itself as a topological slice (presumably of a hypertime, one of the spaces defining Bohm's implicate if it were reduced to vector-space form). In at least one thinkable model, therefore, there seems to be no logical contradiction between observed causality and a mutable past, since causality itself becomes correlation within a field structure, not the result of atomized events.

The sum of Gezumpstein's argument is that (1) both our past and our future are indeterminate and in constant motion, if we insist on subdividing the manifold which contains them; (2) both these imaginary parts are subspaces of a unified vector field, the structure of which determines the apparent events displayed at $t_0$; and (3) "there is no cause and effect in Nature—Nature simply *is*. Recurrence of like cases exists but in the abstraction we perform for the purpose of mentally reproducing facts." (Mach.) Of course, if I put a match to my house it will burn down, and if I take poison in sufficient quantity I will die (or that of my eigenstates which takes it will). And the demon may be fundamentally mistaken, because the universe may in fact have a topology which is asymmetric to time. But conversation with him—allowing for the established risks of converse with demons—is a useful preliminary to permitting commonsense to censor cosmologies.

One could, of course, go on and quiz the demon about matters such as nonlocality, which are intellectually difficult; they are however, far less seriously affected by our a prioris than the time-causality-asymmetry problems (probably because time itself is a more existentially anxious topic). Cosmology does not address the dangerous $64,000 question of epiphenomenal mind. If it wipes out Helmholtz, it is likely to do so incidentally, and, since cosmologists are not usually neuropsychologists, without noticing that it has done so. Our naive experience of flowing time has always been around to haunt cosmologies. Probably the reason that we now have to come to terms with it (and neuropsychologists have to come to terms with physics) is the increasing evidence that the universe is noticeably singular and that singularities may actually exist, and in considerable numbers, which, if approached, would overturn the forward light-cone.

Our understanding of the phenomenal time-slit is crucial to demonics. It is a structure situated both in physics and in neuropsychology—with three out of four legs in the second, because we use brains to do physics. Experientially the time-slit prints out three superposed modes—'I', 'now' and 'real'. The circuitry depends heavily on a series of internal operations which are equally coherent but which are coded 'not-real'. These include wholly internal transactions and the memory with which they interact, but items in the memory which have passed through 'now' and 'real' (i.e., objective experiences) carry a coding of 'real' and make up experience of the past. This code is particularly important in learning behaviors. Of the three primary signals, 'I' is the general homuncular viewpoint (Comfort 1979B); 'now' is the most closely linked to the coding of 'real' as a specific, discrete state of experience. Time is one-way because there is no provision for dis-observing (Park 1972).

Taken from the other (physics) end of the system, where most of the hard-data work has been done, the characteristics of the experiential time-slit can be summarized into three.

(1) It apparently cannot handle $\psi$ or $P$ as such, but reduces both wave functions and probability functions to (1,) or (0,). This generates serviceable objects of knowledge in the case of most structures larger than the subatomic, i.e., over middle order reality and a little beyond, but fails at the particle level. There is an analogy here, and maybe a homology, to the optical reduction of waveforms to generate objects in vision.

(2) Something critical happens during this processing into 'now' and 'real' which concretizes process into a mental replica discrete from whatever it is that generates the inputs. This is the process of 'participation' (in fact, the entire work of the perceiving brain is the process of participation) which creates objects out of waveforms. The most interesting twist in this model is that the brain gets its visual

input in the form of light waves, but we have no specific awareness of any input of probability, which, as a model, we have had to construct by intellection. Quantum reality being what it is, probability may be simply delivered with the groceries, or if not, we have to hypothesize some other form in which it arrives or is constructed, since in doing physics we only 'perceive' particle phenomena by complex inference, not by photons hitting the retina. The simple answer is that since we normally see objects, we look for objects in our models, using the same visual-optical, image-constructing circuitry for intellection as for sensory coherence.

(3) What is meant by 'participation' is clearly crucial to any clear statement of an explicate-implicate model. The notion that our involvement somehow intervenes to kill Schroedinger's cat (and hence modify the Implicate) is more theosophical than simple. Correlating now the quantum and experiential levels, all that is modified by participation is the tape or record which is 'peeled off' from any implicate order in the time-slit. Rather than Everett-Wheeler-Graham's multiplicity of time streams, it seems more economical to visualize in this case one solid block of permissive implicate relations from which our own time stream is peeled off by the substitution of (0, 1,) for a continuous statistic, with all the alternative choices remaining en bloc. Such a time model does not ramify—it looks more like the process of a lathe turning a fine shaving from a rotating stock, by throwing away the off-diagonal terms.

We cannot, however, infer at what level such a system elects to call a probability distribution (0,) and at what level it elects to call it (1,). A demonic computer could be adjusted to select this arbitrarily, accepting rare events as having occurred, since it could score either the leading or the trailing edge of a probability distribution as (1,) and the peak as (0,) and generate a different tape devoted to highly unlikely events. The result would probably be mere confusion, but a finer adjustment might produce a different time stream, rather as in some driving simulators, one can choose to turn right or left at an intersection with a different subsequent display. (If not physically instructive, this might be marketable as a form of entertainment.)

Coherent physical theories need to be mathematical in order to take advantage of the power of mathematics and to conform to the social requirements of science as against science fiction. But since the aim of a demonic computer is not only computation but, if possible, transduction to a point of empathy, no harm is done by loosening-up the subject in this style.

Probably the main use of the imaginary demon is in making visible the distinction between mnemonic and non-mnemonic systems

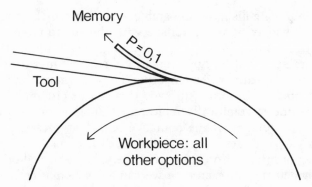

**Fig. 7** Memory as a Detachable Layer


(Pattee 1979). Although, as Dobbs (1971) suggests, perception appears inherently to require one more dimension than description, it is the mnemonic property of brain which determines most of the paradoxes surrounding time. There are physical and mathematical ways of describing phenomenal irreversibility—the Wheeler-Feynman model, for example, which indicates how the advanced wave may be cancelled out. The chief alternative to this is the statistical model: it is scattered according to Bayes' principle and accordingly not coherently displayed in the time-slot. This alternative is worth considering for the macroprocesses in which time dysymmetry is most strongly intuitive, in view of attempts to draw cosmological conclusions from Wheeler-Feynman. Very fortunately, we do not have to involve ourselves, or make Gezumpstein involve himself, in another set of arguments over the meaning of the momentary and the continuous or particulate character of time experiences. It suffices to take Gezumpstein by the hand like a child and instruct him *ex cathedra* that when he tries to understand seriality, two 'instants' $a$ and $b$ are sequential and do not overlap and that no arbitrary subdivision of time is exhaustive since $T$ is an uncountable set. We leave it at that.


## CONSEQUENCES OF DEMONIC COMPUTATION

One has to reiterate that demonics is not "about physics" but rather about brains and their consequences. Fortunately, too, we do not have to wrestle in advance with the *kind* of subjective analysis of time which has occupied Whitehead, Husserl, or Merleau-Ponty, or even to analyze its experiential relation (e.g., to memory) except by comparison. For the demonic computer problem, it is enough to assume that there is a transformation or operation performed by the slit and its associated circuitry which is impartial—so that if Gezumpstein produces an implicate display comparable with that which generates the 'real-world' display, it will interface with the slit to produce our acceptance of it as quasi-real, i.e., resembling conventional experience. One constraint is that for normal states of perception, the display has to be extended-in-time to be empathic, i.e., it cannot simply be algebraic or geometric in form. But even this can be circumvented if extension-in-time is graphically represented in some other way which indicates a singularity at the point we regard as 'present'. 'Present', moreover, can be treated as a convention, as a refinable set with varying degrees of information, and 'past' treated as a peeled-off memory trace, provided that in each case we can see schematically what the Gezumpstein is doing and recognize what we have put into its program. The check on circularity is then to see whether counterintuitive predictions by Gezumpstein are (a) verifiable or (b) refutable by analysis of some derivative in which the slit process is not involved. But it may also offer access to the character of the slit transaction and the nature of the artefacts, if any, which it generates. We could use the demonic system to supply the slit, namely the observer, with displays which test its discrimination, since unlike O and conventional reality, Gezumpstein's output can be controllably programmed—though we may need to construct rather than design it to see what actually happens.

With regard to causality, not all correlations are causal, of course, nor all causal correlations simple: crime may correlate with poverty through a complex network of interactions with other factors. Normally we use the word *causal* to mean the type of correlation which can be put in a figure looking like (though not quite analogous to) a Feynman diagram:

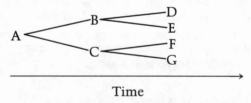

Time

We do *not* apply it to figures which run:

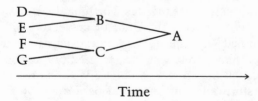

Time

or if we do, we treat $D-G$ as multiple causes of $A$. Gezumpstein has no such ideas: he would be equally at home reading $t$ from left to right in a context of matter or reading $t$ from right to left in a context of antimatter, or an intermediate state which took it as static or read it boustrophedon (alternately left to right and right to left) like some ancient scripts (the Greek name means 'turning the oxen', and refers to plowing back and forth in parallel furrows). Given our preconceptions, we might be able to recognize $D-G$ as multiple causes of $A$, but more likely than not, we should never appreciate the correlation at all, or treat it as an acausal coincidence of the kind which exercised Jung and Arthur Koestler. Gezumpstein's formulation is simply $A \ \wp \ D \ E \ F \ G$, with no directional arrows at all except in cases where the correlation is noncommutative (thermodynamics might be one such case, though he might read that backwards too).

As a matter of fact, if we take an actual Feynman diagram, in which a proton emits a positive pion, which is captured by a neutron, causing the nucleons to exchange "identities," and the newly-formed neutron emits a negative pion, restoring the status quo, argument as to what if anything caused what is not part of the convention of the diagrams—leading on to an S-matrix formalism in which the events are depicted simply as a black box with particles in and particles out. From this it would not be self-evident that anything had occurred at all. Gezumpstein does not handle macro-events quite like this, but he handles them in very much the same spirit, i.e. by a demonic, not a causal, descriptive logic.

Our demonic computer might find that causality-correlation in middle-order reality anterior to the slit is retroactive as well as anteroactive; it might equally have to treat determinism as an illusion due to our mode of perceiving, in that an extradimensional substrate might be both invariant and nondetermined when viewed from a dimensional standpoint. Something of this is foreshadowed in de Broglie's (1959) or Goedel's (1959) pictures of the human time-slit as successively scanning slices of space-time which are both present en bloc ("all is always Now") and at the same time nondeterministic in that events viewed in the time-slit affect what will 'next' be manifested there. Testing this hypothesis against quantum logic would be achieved by devising a means of instructing the machine to think 'illogically' in the middle-order terms (a difficult exercise for the programmer used to excluding incompatibles) and transferring the system break into our conventional mode of reasoning (the machine's logic is correct, ours is contradictory). One would then see what consequences flowed from the paradox. This is a much harder exercise than, for example, starting a geometry from non-Euclidean postulates,

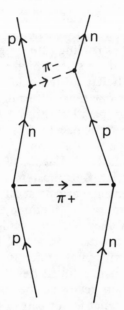

**Fig. 8** A Feynman Diagram

because real computer systems have been selected and designed to copy normal middle-order logic models, not quantum logical models. Computer systems are transduced to human real-time, and a machine incorporating unconventional logic modes could not be assembled by standard methods from standard Boolean logic-gate chips. Trials of illogical or nonlinear logics in mechanical systems may in fact prove an extremely fertile source of insight as expertise in computer manipulation grows, enabling us to try counterintuitive models for fit and select whichever are congruent with experimental results. A computer able to scan or select various logics for maximum reduction is not a fundamental impossibility—it would become a mechanical philosopher rather as a calculating machine is a mechanical arithmetician.

One might quite reasonably ask how Gezumpstein's universe (or for that matter any other universe in which it is possible to 'see forward' in time, or in which space-time exists en bloc) can be other than deterministic. As a matter of fact, it does not have to be. Imagine a maze divided into two halves with the join between them representing 'now'. At now, our track through the first half of the maze is determined in our experience: we are correlated with it in our memory and cannot disobserve it. There were numerous possible alternative tracks through it, however; to a demon adopting Everett's model, all of them will be on an equal footing, exactly as all the tracks in the second (future) half of the maze are on an equal footing in our, conventional, or freewill view. When we have in fact traversed part two of the maze, so that it constitutes our 'past', we will have reduced all the possible eigentracks to yes-no choices, which is our habitual way of treating wave functions. At the same time, both we and the demon will agree that the *whole* maze existed en bloc throughout the process. Without getting into the Byzantine notion that possibly there is a separate eigenself pursuing an insulated and wholly inaccessible course along each possible track, Gezumpstein's view is that past, present, and future are equally indeterminate, and historicity (which is determinism run backwards) is a human position artefact, not a feature of reality. As to the old chesnut about time travel ("What if I were to go back fifty years and alter the course of history so as to produce an inconsistency, say by assassinating Hitler?"), this kind of operation would clearly involve switching eigentracks: we could hardly expect to get back to the situation in which we think we started unless our own experiential timeline is regulative in the morphogenetic sense, and able to "heal" itself when tampered with. Gezumpstein's model would take this for granted, as a consequence of māya. Our more literalistic view finds it rather hard to swallow. The notion of dodging about in time, though contentious, is not now something which we can rule out ex hypothesi. Whenever a paradox like this arises from physics, it is usually safe to assume not that nature is irrational, but that the limitations of our a prioris are preventing us from reading its structure correctly. The point about Gezumpstein is that he does *not* share our a prioris. Not only does he see the future as en bloc but indeterminate, he sees the past as en bloc and indeterminate also. This makes conventional conversation with him both difficult and confusing. Messy as his model looks to us, it is not irrational.

A demonic computer would not negate Copenhagen-type or general quantum logic problems in *philosophy* regarding the participation of the observer, simultaneity, the interpretation of coherent superpositions, or any of the other headaches which arise from homuncularity. It might provide an alternative language to language, and in fact, an anthropologist shown a topological model which purported to schematize some aspect of participant reality would be quite justified in categorizing it as a *myth*. In this regard, the advantage of a demonic computer over anthropological myths is simply higher economy, and the fact that since the transduced display is visual—the preferred human analytic mode—the brain's analog system can get to work on it intuitively without having to break for language, conceptual or mathematical. If this seems an odd way of using a computer in doing science, it is no more unconventional than quantum logic itself. The kind of defeatism (adopted reluctantly by scientists and enthusiastically by theosophically inclined devotees) in accepting ineffables of various kinds, arises mostly in semantics. Given a topological display, what is 'ineffable' could very well be visible (with a back-up mathematical language into which it can at least be transduced for manipulation without getting into homuncular languages). Quintessential suchness is heuristically an extraordinarily unuseful concept. 'Ineffable' here only means so strongly counterintuitive that any intuition-based language addressed to a homuncular audience by a homuncular lecturer is downright misleading. A computer has only those ingrained superstitions which we incautiously build into it. The essential exercise in imagination is to construct the hypothetical demon.

What we really want is a prosthesis for our 'right hemisphere' not in strictly neurological, but in Californian, terms, as effective as the prosthetic use of computer logic by our 'left' hemisphere. It might well prove that this simply takes the form of a pattern-making machine, generating the topological equivalent of Lissajous figures from wave functions. Now, so far from negativing participant interpretations of ontology, this technique agrees with them, because the perception of coherent pattern is a cerebral function: the display not only projects the implications of an algebra derived from experiments on 'reality', it *also* provides a substrate for human pattern detection (and consequently a way into the analysis of that detection) which is the observer component of reality models. The interaction might possibly go beyond the esthetic, which is basically the right name for our satisfaction if, for example, we feed the machine the results of measurements and it presents a tidy topographical model of a hydrogen atom. Since the brain itself is a computing system, and probably in part holographic in form, we may detect actual resonance between the dynamic patterns on the screen and our intellection. (The really humbling thing would be if it were given the 'ontological' data and started displaying traditional *maṇḍalas*—which is not entirely a flippant comment.) These fundamentally unconventional uses of computers, not to compute but to render empathically manageable, are a direct answer to the impasse of finding a language for observed reality, and call for creative exploration.

There was formerly a schizophrenic patient in Portmarnock Hospital who devoted all his time to superposing perforated zinc and plastic sheets with different sizes and repetition-frequencies of holes, and deriving from them all the organic forms in nature. He possessed a demonic viewpoint of considerable profundity, and it is unfortunate that he was not a mathematician. He did, however, spend his substance in printing booklets which characterized the perforated sheets he used to make each organic form, and one could reduce them to equations. The whole exercise would have been very simple with a computer display and a pattern-generator. This man's brain, though dysfunctional in dealing with middle-order activities, was interfaceable with nonhomuncular models. If he had had the idea and the requisite knowledge, he could have applied the same field formalism to developmental forms. As it was, all he had to work on was a static series of shapes clipped from old zoology books. I introduce him here not to suggest that a demon could only address those whose consciousness is unusual, but to suggest that it may need to address inclusive logical perceptions, which we normally suppress or translate into equations, in order to transduce normal into unconventional perceptions—and that the brain has the capacity to accept these with suitable persuasion. Most perceptual-mathematical systems have reserve capacity: Stonehenge *could* have been used to compute eclipse calendars, and whether or not it was actually so used by its builders would have depended on their seeing how it could be done.

## EXPLICATE AND IMPLICATE IN THE COMPUTER MODEL

The computer faces the same difficulties as the discursive sphere which visited Flatland, though in a much harder form. It is *not* insuperably difficult to model mathematically Bohm's postulated implicate reality or Everett's universal wave function. The problem is to transcribe this model back without explication. If it is transcribed, it becomes conventional, for otherwise, the postulated implicate is discrepant from what we observe, rather than the basis of the explicate. If it is not transcribed, the model is inclusive, and as difficult to apprehend as the phenomenon it is modelling. Nobody will get much from an ineffable model unless they can already intuit one.

On the other hand, since all results are processed by homuncular brains, a demonic computer, if it were practical, could do the following:

(1) It could indicate or negate the validity of whatever implicate model it adopted by correct prediction of known results.

(2) It could be applied to unknown results, with special emphasis on any of its predictions which appear paradoxical or counterintuitive. If a computer programmed to quantum logic had been available to Einstein, it would have modified his formulations.

(3) It could be applied heuristically to areas where quantum logic is not usually adopted, for example, speciation and morphogenesis, to see what happens.

The most important part of developing a new paradigm is probing for areas where the old paradigm does not fit. Normally, the critique of a paradigm depends on accidental instances of this kind. A computer programmed to a novel paradigm which produced counter-intuitive or 'irrational' results, which could then be subjected to direct verification, would be a new and accelerated tool. Ideally a computing system could be fed with paradoxes in one paradigm and programmed to develop a different paradigm which unified them. Thus, thinkably, a system fed with data about particle interaction without preconceptive bias could develop quantum logic on the pure grounds of mathematical coherence. One would have to provide this system with a repertoire of transforms and geometries similar to that of the mathematicians who developed quantum theory—only it would work a great deal faster, using serial comparison at high speed in place of mathematical creativity. Such creative machines are thinkable and possibly designable. But the initial step in any clearly practical project of demonic computation would be to make a machine which modelled the mathematics which we believe may apply to implicate reality and use its treatment of explicate reality as a commentary both on experimental results and on the theory. In spite of the logical problems involved, that step looks feasible, and may indeed have been undertaken already. Spinelli (1970), for example, has developed his OCCAM memory-model which combines modular and waveform functions so that both spectral and group models are represented.

## DEMONICS AND THE BRAIN

The most striking fact about computer demonics, however, is that they may not be necessary, and the Gedanken experiment may be sufficient simply to make the point. The ideal demonic computer may actually be the human brain with the Kantian filter removed, and improbable customers like Ouspensky (see page 19) may actually have seen what they claim to see.

On respectable evidence, the brain appears to contain a column-matrix structure through which topological images are transportable en bloc (Edelman and Mountcastle 1979). It seems to combine this system with, or use it to process, Fourier-type inputs—Pribram's holographic or non-optical system. If one were to set about designing a demonic computer to handle quantum logic models based on wave functions, one might adopt precisely this circuitry. If so, the brain is probably infinitely better suited, mathematics apart, to perceiving the implicate than the conscious Kantian mind which is our normal scientific and observational referent. The perception of Bohm's implicate may well be constantly present, figuring as part of the psychoanalytic (especially the Jungian) unconscious, other time lines, wave functions, alternative eigenstates and all. The brain might simply strip off the off-diagonal terms, as we pull layers off an onion. Bergson (1913) made the penetrating remark that the brain may be a device for filtering out impressions irrelevant or confusing to middle-order, Boolean experience. The Kantian a prioris are imposed on all our mental operations at the conscious level by an extremely tight filter, which regulates the print-out so that even if all Everett worlds are represented in the input, only one, complete with a causal and tense logic, is expressed. This possibility throws a very unusual light on the nature of repression of primary-process thinking. Without Bergson's filter, we might experience "buzzing, booming confusion" which had mathematical pattern but was not conducive to the formation and handling of optical objects, or their cousins, language and concepts. With this consideration in mind, and the fact that throughout human natural history—possibly from very early times—models very like those of quantum logic have been intuited, it becomes highly important to address the question of where Ouspensky, or the long tradition of Buddhist philosophy based on meditation, got their models. We do not know the phylogeny of Kantian-Cartesian thinking. Jaynes (1977) has suggested, in a slightly confused hypothesis, that it may be relatively recent. On the other hand, dogs and dolphins appear to treat 'objects' exactly as we do, and to see experience sequentially; thus, more probably, our added circuitry has given us an uncovenanted bonus. Dogs do not have crazy intuitions or do mathematics. Mathematics seems to bypass Bergson's filter through the creation of a special form of linguistics. One might add, to repress certain enthusiasts, that while artificial psychedelics seem to upset the filter, schizophrenics are not spontaneous mystics. In their case the filter is simply malfunctioning, and generating noise in the process of middle-order perception. On the other hand, in view of the primacy of the logic system, we can use it to examine any other potential modes of our brain. This is a Buddhist technique, well exemplified by some guileless exercises on the nature and virtual character of I-ness and 4-space perception, devised for an American audience by a traditional Tibetan lama (Tarthang Tulku Rinpoche 1980). If we could in fact see as Gezumpstein sees, we would not need to imagine or to construct him. And when schizophrenics "hear voices" or are "influenced by waves," one cannot help wondering exactly what if anything is leaking through the filter—neurological noise *tout simple*, other hemispheric patterns, or signal?

If the brain does in fact have access to wave-function models, other than by computation, the implications are interesting. Massive thermodynamic systems such as brains inherently chop such distributions (which is why they create a "hands-on" world): if $\psi_n$ proves to be somehow represented intact, as it were, then one might have to infer that in the course of evolving circuitry for complex memory-storage and imaging, human brains had acquired as a bonus the capacity to reconstruct wave-functions, as they have acquired the capacity to compute them mathematically. The ability to do higher math was probably not selected as such: the type of brain which is capable of mathematics was. On a computer analogy one might also suspect that the two capacities (to reconstruct $\psi_n$ and to do matrix algebra) use the same circuitry.

# Commercial Break: Gezumpstein's Charmed Balloons

"Gezumpstein, this last balloon you gave me is holding up."

"I'm delighted to hear it, Master. But so long as you don't actually *inflate* it, it will."

"But I have inflated it."

"Strange. To me it appears to be in its original condition. Are you sure you haven't found a way of blowing it up with radius *I*—blowing it up cerebrally, I mean?"

"All I did was blow air into it in the conventional manner."

"Let me look at it. Yes, as I thought, I've given you the wrong balloon. This is a charmed balloon. Take this one instead."

"I want the *original* balloon, Gezumpstein. I inflated it perfectly normally with radius *r*."

"They're not meant to be treated like that. They're dangerous. We only give those to mathematicians, and only after we've inflated them ourselves. I'll blow this one up. Watch the viewer. There!"

"It appears unchanged to me. Anyhow, it was blown up already."

"That's the trap. I propose to inflate it a *third* time. No change to you—still blown up. No change to me—still uninflated. One more time. No change? No change. That's a property we call charm in balloons. Actually, you know, you blew yours up twice. Before you brought it back."

"Once."

"Twice. Once in *I*, once in *t*. I feel it in my bones. I'm putting this one back in the balloon case."

"Don't."

"Well, at least let me check its *mantra*. . . . Good, you can have it. This one's harmless. Only an imbecile could make a world model out of it."

"What *mantra* does it have?"

"Well, of course, it can't be spoken. Except by the balloon. But *you* can see it, written all over it—it looks inflated to you."

"A very beautiful and elegant expansion . . ."

"Now let the air out."

". . . of a continuous fraction. Well worth a Ph.D. One might get a degree, Gezumpstein, by inflating balloons."

"Most people do. And you did blow it up with *I*. I smelled it coming out. You can have this one—it's charmed, but harmless. Might do you good to familiarize yourself in case you get another one. With tense charm."

"Tense charm?"

"To remind you that *you* can only inflate it with your infernal *t*. Won't blow up in any other way. Some are quite large. You can easily find yourself inside one. Has serious consequences, I mean, like entropy, mortality, acute depression and addiction to balloons."

"Gezumpstein, I think I *am* inside one."

"Did you intend to emphasize 'am'? I mean, was it conversational, or philosophical 'am'?"

"Say again?"

"Do you mean that you happen to find yourself inside a tensely charmed balloon, or that you owe your existential viewpoint to being in a t.c.b.?"

"I meant the first. I now begin to perceive the second."

"Good. There are moments when being a demon is quite rewarding. Want to try popping it and joining me?"

"I daren't."

# Chapter 3

## TIME AND BIOLOGY

# Interlude. How the Bird and the Snake Played Evolutionary Scrabble

Darwinism is not a testable scientific theory, but a metaphysical
research program—a possible framework for testable scientific
theories.

Karl Popper

"Ouch! Stop that! Give over!"

"Then get out of my nest. I do not tolerate snakes here. I am
programmed to clobber snakes which put their ugly heads into my
home."

"I'm only trying to get my dinner. Snakes have to eat. I'm surprised at you. Don't you know snakes are venomous? You might well
be bitten. And it wouldn't be my fault. I am programmed to eat eggs.
I have a special vertebra for cracking eggs. It protrudes into my gullet
like a natural can opener. Nature is wonderful. Allah is great. Now I
warned you. . . ."

"No dice. You can't scare me. I'm programmed to defend my
nest."

"Even if you get bitten?"

"Even if I get bitten. And you're a superstitious reptile. Why is
it always thieves, snakes, and politicians who talk about Divine purpose?"

"But you said it yourself. You are programmed to lay eggs, for me to eat. And you are also programmed to defend eggs, even at great personal risk. Why, do you imagine?"

"So that birds will survive. And birds with courageous parents will survive in greater numbers. That, you overgrown earthworm, is called Natural Selection."

"Your answer is incomplete. Birds must survive in great numbers, or there wouldn't be any eggs for snakes to eat. The whole biosphere was clearly designed . . ."

"Bah!"

"By an omniscient Snake. This is an Ophiomorphic Universe."

"Balderdash. Let me tell you something. We are as we are . . ."

"How about my built-in can opener?"

". . . by reason of the straightforward operation of population dynamics. I don't clobber you out of personal courage. Clobbering snakes is written in my genetic code. My fledglings will inherit the same behaviors. And there are going to be more of them than that pusillanimous finch will rear. You cleaned out *his* nest, and all he did was chirp."

"There are a hell of a lot of finches, however."

"They have other selective advantages."

"More finches than mockingbirds."

"Well, that's natural—we need bigger territories. Don't interrupt my argument. At some time among the generality of birds, there was one unusually aggressive individual who happened to get the right hand of genetic cards. Nobody ate eggs out of *his* nest. So more altruistic, plucky birds were born, and more of them survived."

"So now the world should be feet deep in avian kamikazes, and I should by rights be dead of starvation. Allah tempers the wind to the hungry snake. Your bluster is his device to ensure that there are enough mockingbirds—they lay superior eggs, and snakes might eat themselves out of a living. Surely Allah is merciful."

"Just the sort of remark I'd expect from a snake. No, keep your distance. One more slither and you'll lose an eye."

"I was talking to that Gila monster the other day—the fat chap with the stripes, who looks as if he might start off in either direction—and *he* says we are distant relatives."

"You and he, perhaps."

"No, you, he, and I. Your feathers are homologous with my scales."

"Very probably. You see what can be done by spirit and initiative."

"I thought your spirit and initiative were genetic."

"They are. They run in our family, the Mimidae."

"And the feathers, and the hollow bones, and the fixed all-up weight?"

"Very necessary. Try flying with solid bones and indeterminate growth."

"I was wondering about the feathers."

"It has been argued that at some point scales must have enlarged as a means of temperature control."

"Here we have a very educated bird. We do find temperature a problem. Cold weather turns me off. So suddenly a lizard with an overcoat found it could fly?"

"Well, not suddenly. Probably over a relatively short period, if you look at geological time."

"So it took off, solid bones and all, and crashed. And that was so adaptive that it went from strength to strength."

"Don't show your ignorance. Hollow bones came first."

"I didn't know that. But I'm still bothered about those feathers. I mean, it must have been awkward while they were evolving. Do you moult?"

"One pair of feathers at a time. It all fits."

"I agree, it has to. Allah is merciful. Suppose you moulted half your feathers at once?"

"Don't. I can't bear to think of it. I would be grounded!"

"Quite. You'd be in precisely the situation of that lizard with the overcoat. Knowing it had a great future, and surviving on the strength of it. And all those little lizards, buoyed up by the knowledge that their progeny would fly."

"They ran on their hind legs! They went in longer and longer hops!"

"Now I know why you're called a mockingbird. You've got to be kidding."

"And snakes are the symbol of insidious sophistry. Teleology is the coward's way out. The actual Darwinian process is far more marvellous."

"My can opener, I can understand. I do better with it. It makes me a more adapted animal. But in a pinch I could do without it. Many snakes do. It just gives me an edge. But not feathers. You can't half-fly."

"What you theists always ignore is that we are seeing a process in retrospect. If you roll an egg down a slope, it follows a geodesic. But to the naive mind it will appear to have been guided by God. All it did was to follow the only course open to it."

"When I was at snake school, which was a considerable time ago, that was called Pangloss' Theorem. It states that everything is as it is because it couldn't be otherwise. Always struck me as vacuous. How about you?"

"It's only vacuous as perverted by snakes. Natural selection alone certainly didn't explain everything. You have to consider linkage and recombination."

"The card shuffle?"

"Precisely. Those you now see are the descendants of ancestors with stochastically good hands. Nor can we exclude the possibility that selection operates to control linkage."

"Doesn't that beakful simply mean that Allah is all-wise?"

"No, it doesn't. What's your name, if snakes have names?"

"They do. It's Wilberforce."

"I might have guessed it."

"Let me guess. Is yours by any chance Jacques Monod?"

"No. It's Mimus Polyglottos."

"No sense of humor."

"Good morning all. Somebody discussing Monod? Always nice to meet well-read people."

"Good morning, Monster. Excuse me shouting. You can't come up here, and I'm not leaving this twig while the Snake is around. I was trying to explain to him. . . ."

"I heard. The bird's right, Wilberforce."

"What do you mean by right? About lizards going in longer and longer hops?"

"Not precisely. But the model he's giving you is in outline correct. Have you actually read Monod's *Chance and Necessity*?"

"Snakes can't read."

"Neither can Gila Monsters, but I obtained a tape recording. I'll play it for you, when you have time. It'll bear rehearing. Quite the best account of what is wrong with teleology."

"There is no God but God!"

"*And* vitalism."

"Dixit insipiens . . ."

"Hold it, hold it. I think you misconceive the nature of science. Nobody's trying to talk you out of religious conviction. But that's a different order of discourse. If you want to argue that God is so smart that he hides, and only lets us see *how* he operates, I won't quarrel. But science it isn't. We're concerned simply with whether stochastic and genetic explanations are sufficient. And I think you'll agree, if you study the evidence, that in general they are. And looking for exceptions. That's the critical part of it—looking for exceptions."

"How about First Causes? I was at Jesuit snake-school . . ."

"Thomist argument is fallacious. It doesn't recognize that causality is a human construct. It is a special case of correlation."

"How about the chicken and the egg?"

"Not my egg! You keep your distance."

"You show me a chicken without an egg. Or an egg without a chicken."

"All you're saying is that chickens and eggs are correlated. Anyhow, if you recognized that religion is a matter of personal experience, or lack of it, not positivist science, you'd stop being so aggressive. I'll even let you postulate the undemonstrable, so long as you don't assert the demonstrably false. Agreed? I thought this nineteenth century argument was over, even among Jesuits. Anyway, the reservations on pure genetic-stochastic selectionism are of a rather different order."

"Aha! So there are reservations?"

"Well, you pointed to one yourself—passage through a stage of relative disadvantage on the way to better adaptation. Try evolving into a bird."

"??"

"Like this:

```
s   n   a   k   e
*   *   *   *   *
*   *   *   *   *
*   *   *   *   *
b   i   r   d   s
```

You know the ordinary acrostic rules? One letter at a time and no nonsense combinations."

"Proves my point, precisely."

"Well, you are probably allowed *some* nonsense combinations because of redundancy. In fact, if the whole coding actually runs:

t w o b r i g h t a n d a g e d *s n a k e* s w h o o n c e w e r e c a d m u s a n d h a r m o n i a

it's more than likely that you could scramble the "snake" sequence provided the rest stays unchanged, and provided 'snake' isn't critical."

"Of course it's critical."

"He could actually do it, Monster."

"Go ahead, bird."

"Well, he could evolve into a starling."

"Expound."

"Like this:

```
s   n   a   k   e
s   t   a   k   e
s   t   a   r   e
```

In short order. Stare is an archaism for starling."

"So I evolve into an obsolete starling. Der Gott scrabbelt nicht!"

"Well, very probably some mutative sequences are of that simple kind. The question which I don't think is really sewn up is a matter arising from your egg-rolling experiment."

"My eggs don't roll."

"You used the model yourself, to illustrate Pangloss' Theorem. The egg rolled down a topographical surface. Now some of its topology represents selection pressures. Some of it represents genetic endowment. The question is, whether it is coherently patterned in any way *as well*."

"Draw it. On that flat patch of sand."

"It'll take me a minute or two. You carry on doing acrostics. I'll be as quick as I can. There you are!"

"Monster, how well you draw!"

"Thank you, Bird."

"May I ask what it is?"

"You're looking at a sloping awning, down which you are going to roll the egg. The contours are presumably determined by genes and by the process of growth, in which adjacent cells interact positionally."

"Lucid. The genes determine the surface. When they change, it changes."

"Actually, this is the *epi*genetic surface. It models how egg grows into bird. You realize, don't you, that the same gene-strings are present in every cell, and the same lexical information has to produce a beak in one place and feathers in another. It's very like evolution, only this is morphogenesis. If you wanted to make the awning model an evolutionary surface, you'd stand some weights on it to represent selection pressures, and you'd give a rule that where the surface goes down, a gene is pulling it, like an elastic."

"One thing strikes me as odd. I may be an ignorant snake, but am I right in saying that while we argue that evolution doesn't have a pre-program, we strongly assert that morphogenesis does?"

"That is precisely my point. It is an inconsistency. It could be got over in one way by asserting that egg-into-bird is also strictly stochastic, but with fewer degrees of freedom. Or of course, one could treat both imaginary surfaces as being pre-configured by some other set of correlations."

"If the first, more of my wife's eggs should be addled."

"Good point. And the fact that they aren't suggests that morphogenesis is highly channeled, and includes adjustments for drift. All that."

"You've spoiled my day, Monster. I thought we'd laid Bergson to rest, and here you are back with another version of vitalism. It's *adaptive* to have accurate development. It's an evolved, covert adaptation."

"True. And it would also be adaptive to have a patterned evolution. It would work out if the pattern could itself be evolved.—That would be called orthogenesis. It may be due to immunological sub-selection. As to vitalism, I agree entirely with Monod. It's bunk."

"I'm trying. About orthogenesis. I think that model is recursive."

"It's getting too hot. I'm going shortly to have to move into the shade. But just let me hint that we haven't exhausted the subject. Another time, we could get into the origin of social insects. However, for now, evolution seems to us to be extended in time and to be conducted in a 4-space. That may be a viewpoint artefact, you know."

"It may be another way of saying something about the order in which transformations occur. Those acrostics—if you include meaningfulness as well as letter order—they're effectively non-Abelian under permutation."

"Admirable bird. Go to the top of the tree!"

"Not while *he's* hanging around."

"All I'm suggesting—too hot to fill in the details—is that some of the field theory formalisms from physics might have relevance to evolution and morphogenesis. We're all three of us obliged to read evolution with a time arrow. It's probably a superposition. It's an idea worth digesting. It may be totally erroneous. After all, this is a different order of hierarchy from particle physics. I just throw it out as an idea."

"May I ask, Monster, what your world model is? Mine is perfectly simple—Allah is great. Any field around is *his* thumbprint."

"I thought you'd say something like that. Do you want to visualize my world model?"

"I'd very much like to see it. I may be a mere snake, but what you say sounds to me uncommonly like sophistry. You're more superstitious than I am. My God and your Field are both immune to refutation."

"Well, see it you shall. Oblige me by coming down here. You can't perform the experiment there."

"If this is a practical joke, Monster, we shall quarrel."

"Not at all. Oblige me now by carefully putting your tail in your mouth. You are immune to your own venom, aren't you?"

"You bloody well put yours in your mouth!"

"I'm not flexible enough. It has
to be a snake. Good. Perfect. You now represent my world model,
as a rough graphic. I'll explain when it's less hot. Don't stay too long
like that if you aren't accustomed to yoga. Good-day, gentlemen."

"Snake, you look a Charlie like that. That stuff of his sounds
like Bergson and splash to me. But he's got you out of my bush, and
I'm grateful for small mercies. See you, and stay out of my nest!"

# The Death of Vitalism: Implicate and Explicate in Biology

Genera and species . . . depend on collections of ideas man has made, and not on the real nature of things. . . . Our distinct species are nothing but distinct complex ideas, with distinct names annexed to them.

Locke

The idea of a good species . . . is generally without foundation— an artifact of the procedures of taxonomy. These procedures require that distinct clusters be found and assigned to some level in a hierarchy.

P.R. Ehrlich and R.H. Raven, Science 137: 652 (1962)

Plant species lack reality, cohesion, independence and simple evolutionary or ecological roles. The concept of species . . . can only serve as a tool for characterizing diversity in a mentally satisfying way. Diversity is idiosyncratic. It is impossible to reconcile idiosyncrasy with preconceived ideas of diversity. . . . The concept that is most operational and utilitarian . . . is a mental abstraction which orders clusters of diversity in multidimensional character space.

D.A. Levin Science 204: 381 (1979)

Modern evolutionary genetics is now an extraordinarily well-oiled machine which yields both intellectual consistency and good practical results. It also has the immense advantage of being an intuitively acceptable model: it has a few difficult passages and a few areas where, in the interest of the consistency of the model, we have to invoke Pangloss's theorem. Symons (1979) gives a nice example of this kind in an ironic form, when he assumes the *opposite* of what has actually happened in the matter of human estrus, and then adduces evolutionary arguments to show why it "must be so." Another such area is Maynard Smith's [1970] acrostic paradox. But for a well-performing and intelligible model that sort of thing is tolerable—especially where it deals with processes we can no longer observe, like anthropogenesis, so that they must be inferred *a posteriori*. It looks perverse when an intuitive model is available to propose examining a grossly counter-intuitive one. This happened in regard to the Newtonian universe only when we were obliged by experimental *force majeure* to stop relying on middle-order conceptualization. On the other hand, there are reasons derived from the striking success of the quantum universe as a heuristic model to try the counterintuitive model for fit and see what happens. The overriding argument, for me, is the power of the demonstration in physics that positivist reality models are metaphors designed to be operated by, and intelligible to, a time-and-place oriented homuncular observer.

Evolutionary (and even creationist) models of phylogeny are *historical*. That in itself makes them members of the family—they result from the application of inference and experiment to the way in which humans experience phylogeny. We mate and produce offspring, we have or become ancestors, we see our domestic plants and animals doing the same. Mythological accounts of origins deal with ancestors; historical accounts catalog them. In the creationist model all species came into existence simultaneously in a big bang, but even a big bang is a historical model. Darwin took the descriptive Linnean account of species and gave them a family history; Mendelian genetics proposed mechanisms to expound the process of inheritance and modification over time. Now if time is metaphorical in particle physics and part of the attempt to transduce phenomena to a temporal observer, what would be the formalism which, in the same way, treated time as a viewpoint artefact in discussing evolution? Moreover, since evolution is a middle-order process, is there any useful purpose other than mystification to be served by trying non-middle-order formalisms on it to see what happens?

The second question can only be answered by trying. The problem is to consider how 'evolution' would look to Gezumpstein, who has no sense of temporal position, which is the short answer to the first question.

Underlying both these questions, of course, is a far more interesting one: whether quantum models of reality have any general validity, or only a special validity at the fine structure level. If they do indeed

represent a point of general access to observer-bias due to our homuncularity, then biology, precisely because it is, or looks like, a manageable middle-order process, is an excellent test case to look for them.
Does our intuitive view of such a process pattern the 'reality' we see
in the same way as it patterns our attempt to systematize particle
events? Can we use quantum theory to get around the bias?

## EVOLUTIONARY METAPHORS

Conventional phylogenetic and morphogenetic theory uses one of
two diagrammatic models. One is the pedigree or tree:

the other is the flow or injection of material into a virtual tree-shaped
mould:

The second includes elements corresponding to the active moulding
and segregation of species and evolutionary lines by environmental
pressure, so that it is treatable as a representation of the movement of
matter under gravity on a shaped topological surface, the Waddingtonian model of creodes and canalization. This second model, accordingly, involves a factor corresponding to the slope of the topological
surface which causes the evolutionary 'stream' to move, i.e., a vis im-
pellatrix which has no counterpart in post-Bergsonian biology. Most of
us are content to square off the model by simply assuming potential
energy at the point A and not pushing the construction too hard. The
first, or simply historical, model is far less obviously a graphic metaphor. We are familiar with family trees in other contexts, and the
initial response of biologists and nonbiologists alike to the diagram
is that it is a straightforward chart of an objective process—errors
and omissions excepted, this is what actually happened. Both models
illustrate constraints on inheritance. They exclude action-at-a-dis-
tance (genetic transfer across mating barriers). There is no crossing
between separate limbs of the tree, no counterpart of 'tunneling', and
the lines of flow in the topological model follow gravity wells and
neither cross, nor perch on the top of, ridges. This does indeed happen in exceptions to the model, such as transfers of genetic material
between bacteria, by way of virions or plasmagenes, or of humoral
information in the embryo: they represent systems breaks which may
or may not prove to have been of great evolutionary importance,
but can be taken into the model if necessary. There are analogies to
quantum phenomena—highly canalized states resemble preferred orbits, ridges represent prohibited states, changes proceed theoretically
by genetic quanta—but these are very superficial analogies involving
nothing like true quantum mechanical processes for two reasons. First
of all, in most cases there is probably not enough numerical material

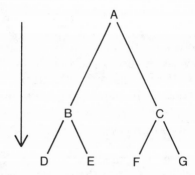

**Fig. 9** The Pedigree

available in the mathematics of evolutionary genetics to transform a Waddingtonian surface into a state function and verify its correspondence to observation (it can be done easily enough algebraically, but not all the functions can be measured). Secondly, thermodynamically irreversible processes interfere in large objects such as organisms, and *a fortiori* in systems composed of organisms. But the philosophical consequences, and the active role of the observer in collapsing such a wave function into 'the real', have to apply to 'real' phenomena generally. However historical evolution looks, it would not be exempt, for example, from the validity of the Everett-Wheeler-Graham model, which would seem to be applicable to *all* either-or actualizations in a probability field. The same applies to all possible chess games. Any discontinuous effect derived from a state function can probably be subjected to quantum-mechanical principles. It really makes no fundamental difference that it is intuitively harder to think of species or structures that we can see as representing probability waves than it is with inferential particles.

It is even more instructive to recognize that historical models in the shape of a family tree were the initial formalism for particle interactions. On the basis of early cloud chamber diagrams a proton was a 'thing' which, either by simple fission or by combination with another 'thing', begat specific progeny. Feynman diagrams are in fact themselves phylogenetically historical trees, time arrow and all. Moreover, even when quantum theory recognised that the progeny of an interaction could only be defined in probabilistic terms, that was a Mendelian model—the progeny of mating, if limited in number, can be defined probabilistically. And further, retrogressive lines in a Feynman diagram could be historically treated (by viewing them as antiparticles going the other way).

Even in subatomic, post-Heisenbergian physics, then, and even when its probable limitations were known, the same historical model

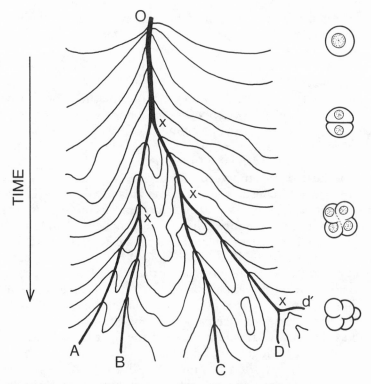

**Fig. 10** Flow of Material into a Virtual Tree-shaped Mould

which has been intuitively applied to phylogeny retains considerable diagrammatic value in describing particle interactions. It fulfilled the function of a convenient descriptive form, and rather than dump the model, it was easier for purposes of description to add on a complex currency market in bosons and to multiply entities (even when it became commonplace that particles were not, and did not exhibit the transcendental identity of, 'things'). What finally blew it up was Bell's theorem and the theoretical recognition that there were reasons to infer another 'layer' to the process not representable in space-time, and for that reason actively inimical to the historical analogy (Bohm 1957).

In the realm of biology, the increasing complexity shown in evolution and in morphogenesis are negentropic, or order-creating, processes. A demon who developed the time arrow as a consequence of thermodynamics, and as a formalism to deal with them, might well read both these processes backwards. He might see them as the collapse of complexity into a lower state of informational distribution, i.e., as antievolution and as demorphogenesis, precisely as he might read a chess game back to front. Chess is entropic as to the number of pieces, and negentropic as to the *realized* information they contain, so that the demon sees the game-constellation as 'eating' pieces and acquiring information. If run backwards, it converts information into additional pieces.

I have neither the imagination nor the mathematics to depict with confidence how phylogeny would 'look' to Gezumpstein, who has no temporal orientation, any more than the chess game (see pp. 79). We see a chess game historically; he sees chess games as a matrix, both inclusively and without a time arrow.

In the heat of the nineteenth century argument over evolution and the book of Genesis, the fundamentalist Philip Gosse wrote a treatise entitled "Omphalos." The title came from Gosse's surmise that Adam and Eve presumably had navels, though no umbilical cord had ever been attached to them. He went on to argue that on each successive day of the Biblical creation, God had made the prescribed objects and organisms, but in making them had been obliged to endow them with an instantaneous history, fossil ancestors and the like. This argument drew down a rebuke from Charles Kingsley to the effect that Gosse was accusing God of writing a lie on the rocks. Bizarre as this entire argument looks in the light of modern science, Gosse's Hudibrastic ingenuity brings us up short. It never occurred to the disputants to question whether the Almighty must necessarily view time through the a priori time-slit—that kind of philosophical insight was not their style, for Fundamentalists were and are super-Cartesian super-realists. Oddly enough, nobody even quoted 2 Peter 3:8, to the effect that the Creator doesn't follow our time frame. Gosse's extravaganza, however, itself a fossil in the history of biology, is possibly the nearest evolutionary debate has come to taking a non-intuitive look at historicism as a model. Biologists are not like that—such paradoxes are less at home in life sciences than in physics—but what Gosse was grasping at to salvage the inerrancy of Scripture was in fact a demonic model of space-time. It implies Gezumpstein's suggestion that for humans, time-lines would appear to be "self-healing."

The factitious character of historicity is actually harder to swallow than the factitious character of real-time experience, especially where biological subjects are concerned. Cosmology has the advantage of being a non-middle-order process anyway, so that, even in a science-fiction animation, we have difficulty empathizing as *spectators* of a stellar collapse or a big bang. On the other hand, if we reconstruct a Cambrian or a Jurassic landscape with flora and fauna, the result is not much more exotic than a reconstruction of a street in Mycenae, and may even be more evidentially plausible. The same applies to mathematical or theoretical reconstructions, which have similar un-acknowledged optical images behind them. A historical reconstruction represents not what *was* there but what *would have been* there if it had been optically and categorically processed by a human observer. This is not to say that it was *not* there, provided we recognize all the constraints on our method of processing and apprehending what *is* there now. But accordingly, any counterintuitive model which is evidentially plausible in dealing with human modes of image forma-tion presents a fundamental reservation on all models which take a historical pattern. The perceptive model which historicity assumes, and which involves optical imaging of sense impressions from an environment, has to be taken as originating with the human brain, unless we want to get into the historical development of optical pro-cessing and the philosophical abilities of crabs and reptiles. This point is by way of an aside, but it bears on the argument as to whether field models apply to hypothetical microprocesses only—they may, but we cannot rely on the intuition of the historical model to assume that they do.

In fact, historicity enters fundamentally into biology at a different level and for another reason than our assumption of time as a priori: it is quite reasonable to correlate time itself with the biological order because life involves *record*. In living matter, the cell or the active enzymic site serves as an 'observer' in the quantum-observation sense, in that it becomes committed to a specific eigenstate which it can-not disobserve. Whether in this chemical way or by way of learning, a higher order information store, organisms generate a time arrow. "Although the wave-function is symmetric in time, measurement introduces irreversibility; the description of a living system must in-clude the measurement process along with the dynamics" (Pattee 1979). The time arrow is introduced because the system cannot dis-observe. The analogy between the mnemonic 'tape', as we described it to the demon, and the chemical and evolutionary 'tape', arising from measurement processes at the cellular and subcellular level, does not however affect the fact that we might apply quantum formalisms to biology, as we can to physics, and examine nondetermined, nonhis-torical models. The analogy only suggests how profoundly a priori time is for living matter, going below the conceptual to the cellular and subcellular level. Quantum effects only surfaced detectably in physics because most particle events are non-mnemonic—they nei-ther evolve nor exhibit learning. It is the informational component of living matter which necessitates the collapse of wave functions into either-or logics: the wave function is not a predictive model of the middle-order world, while living systems—brains in particular—

are filters geared to the production of predictive models by simplification and construction. They cut slices of space-time, and require accordingly to forecast the next slice.

The flow sheet models apply, of course, both to speciation and to morphogenesis. In one case the points represent species, in the other they represent structures. We treat this homology historically in both cases: in one, proto-organisms differentiate into contemporary species (starting with one or more Darwinian Adams in original biogenesis); in the other, a zygote differentiates into a multicellular organism. Of the two, morphogenesis lies a little better for specific experiments which might uncover a use for field theory because (1) we can see all of it and can manipulate it fairly easily at all stages, whereas evolution and speciation, though we can observe short-term effects which are relevant to them, are bound to inference by antiquity; (2) because the flow sheet model takes in total and remote interactions as a matter of course; for example, the appearance of functioning endocrine tissue has a general effect on differentiation—the appearance of a nervous system modifies development in areas it innervates. It is, moreover, reducible to gradients which can be measured. Attempts to use Laplacian formalisms in evolution merely add to the number of operants, whereas in Goodwin's (1978) experiments on organogenesis, those formalisms can be applied to gradients in a system which has already an enormous experimental record. Obviously it would be tidy if any underlying field model in embryology were to be translationally related to a macro-model in evolution and submicro-model in particle physics, but the agenda item is to see whether there is a field model at all.

## DEMONIC MODELS OF EVOLUTION

We need to look at a demonic model for evolution—meaning "that model of an observed natural process or processes which is not transduced to a positional and temporal observer," i.e., which is not focused to be empathically represented in middle-order reality. "Quantum model" may well be incorrect—quantum phenomena *bien entendu* may not in fact be involved in all such models, though quantum theory generated the demonic model in physics. Implicate-explicate and similar field theories are demonic models. The general features of demonic models will be that (1) space-time expressed effects are seen as second-order or contingent, i.e., as derivates of a more general non-space-time process; (2) transcendental identity is not attributed to phenomenal objects; (3) Fourier- and field-type formalisms predominate as models and are treated as primary; (3) translational invariance is assumed; and (4) algebraic are preferred to geometric or Cartesian models.

Now a demonic model may be splendid in particle physics (even if it turns out to be wrong) when we are apt to expose "transluminal effects" of the kind which flow from Bell's theorem, but what is the point of applying them to a process like evolution which we *know* to be historical if anything is? We know it to be so because that is how we experience it. The questions the demon must ask (assuming him to be able to view both models) are: (1) On what non-intuitive evidence do we assume species or organisms to be transcendental objects? and (2) Are there any overlooked phenomena in evolutionary genetics or (taking in Goodwin's work, 1978) in morphogenesis which are analogous to Bell's theorem?

One of Gezumpstein's questions could well be the utility, other than schematic, of the time arrow, in non-thermodynamic contexts, apart from the fact that humans experience life as extended in time (Fraser 1978). Most evolutionary biologists would say that species are not transcendental objects (they have a lot of the virtual properties of particles); organisms including themselves probably are, even if 'identity' is a human obsession (Post 1963) which we confer on other, non-noetic systems whenever possible. They would also agree that Bell-type paradoxes depending on remote, nonlocal, or unconventional interaction should be written into the evolutionary and phylogenetic model when they are credibly observed, not before; otherwise, we find ourselves involved with a budget of questionable esoterica from neovitalism and entelechies to Kammerer and constellated coincidences— a pretty unpromising bunch intellectually compared to clearcut experiments on particle spin. There are plenty of folk in California and elsewhere ready to go off at half cock about parapsychology, telekinesis, and a world soul given the slightest encouragement. "All garbage apart," says the demon, "have you seriously looked for them? It might be worth it."

It also might not. We should be fully justified in arguing that since human-middle order perception is itself adaptive to what is usually and customarily perceived, the 'second layer' cannot habitually show through in the conventional contexts to which that type of perception is adapted; it can only appear in recherche operations such as those of particle physics to which evolving man could not possibly be exposed. The question turns on how far the perceptions we have of phylogeny and morphogenesis are in the conventional range per se, and how far they are there because we place them there. They, too, are not direct concerns of evolving Man, who dealt with them mythologically.

A straightforward field theory, and therefore demonic model, of both evolution and morphogenesis is not actually very difficult to visualize. It is mainly a matter of suppressing the primacy of the time arrow. In figure 10, all the evolutionary stages represented by letters are 'there' at one time: in the observed data on which such pictures are based the component species are either 'there' as contemporary organisms, as fossils, or as hypothetical elements. In embryogenesis structures are not 'there' until they appear, but the information which generates them must be. The transformation from historical to field model depends on treating the diagrammatic flow sheet as primary and the component 'objects' as secondary on the assumption that the temporal observer is, as it were, scanning the tree through a transverse slit limited to what is conventionally perceived as 'now'. In this case the conclusion does show some measure of translational invariance in the pattern, but this is inaccessible because of the one-way flow of perceived time. Though it might be perceived in the axis of the time-slit, it would be hard to distinguish from prosaic organismic interaction with the environment, e.g., in an ice age. The most fertile area to look for systems breaks in the linear-causal model is probably morphogenesis, because that is sufficiently congruent with human life span to be accessible in toto. Driesch's intuition in this area, though partially wrong in substance, was correct if we substitute field for entelechy. In other words, the topological surface may be real.

Henri Bergson ran himself ragged over this one; like many previous philosophers who grasped the point involved in nonhomuncular observation, his trouble lay in finding the words to express it without being taken to mean something else. In the Cartesian-historical view, species evolve and organs develop because of the interaction of specific, sequential events laid out in time. In the alternative view, they appear to us to evolve because some underlying reality is "like that." We can make this philosophically disappointing truism—which is how it comes over—less unimpressive by calling them field-determined: the problem is to convey that field-determination is not the same as Dr. Pangloss' inevitability. The sequential structure is more like a slice through the manifestations in 4-space of an extradimensional field than a sequence of logically and causally related events. In such a slice, a given event is not only related causally to the preceding and following organisms or structures, but to the entire regularity of the 'block' of manifestation which we are transecting: causality in the slice appears to run one-way, but in fact, past, present, and future exist in the block en masse. One can call the subjacent order an entelechy, as Aristotle did, but it is actively misleading to call it a vital force. Schopenhauer called it "will," which is not a bad try, but misleading in a different direction. What looks like a force or impulsion is actually the thisness of the underlying field, and the visual model breaks down. Neovitalism differs from the demonic or field viewpoint rather as naive views of the wind (it has a spirit inside it or it would not blow) differ from aerodynamic maps, or as students sometimes assume that if a rate (e.g., of growth) falls off exponentially there must be some inhibitor causing it to do so (Medawar 1942).

At this point, both in physics and in fitting quantum-logic type models to biology, one gets driven into mathematics to avoid medieval statements of the kind sent up by Rabelais—that water is wet because its nature partakes of humidity. A transformational algebra does not incur this kind of mockery. The basic problem is that language itself carries the seeds of common perception to the point that if we try to use it for a demonic instead of a conventional model, it becomes automatically vacuous. Far better to postulate a vital force if only to bring the thing back into a classical model. Bergson clearly realized that his *élan vital* is an as-if force. He was viewing a field-determined process in which both past and future developments are present in the existing organism but unmanifest, rather as all the frames are present in a reel of film when one frame is projected, or as the successive ink droplets of Bohm's model appear by successive explication out of an implicate—it looks as if a force must be operating, rather as it looks as if a single droplet were moving under the impulsion of a force. Both evolution and morphogenesis are excellent candidates to be models of explication, and if they were indeed explicates they would have the apparent historical and sequential thread which we read into them, as the figures in the projected film appear to move.

Cartesian systems breaks in physics (as in the Einstein-Podolsky-Rosen experiment) appear as apparently irrational transport of information from one part of the system to another: members of a particle-pair appear to exhibit telepathy.* What Bell's theorem actually demonstrates is the incompatibility with quantum-mechanical theory of the intuitive formalism which sees, for example, a photon pair as separate objects: they are neither objects nor separate. If, as appears quite possible, "the fundamental processes of nature lie outside space-time but generate events which can be located in space-time" (Stapp 1977), how far up the hierarchy of systems does this apply? Quite

---

*Cosmology is another prime candidate for interconnectedness. In an expanding universe, the furthest objects rapidly pass beyond each other's signal horizons (no signal can pass between them to affect their behaviors). It becomes extremely hard to devise initial conditions which must result by simple sequence in the state which we now observe: if on the other hand the matter accumulations in the universe are fundamentally not-separate, in the Einstein-Rosen-Podolsky sense, the universe evolves as an ensemble, and coordination by influences with a velocity $\leqslant$ c is unnecessary.

possibly into biology where Bohm's (Bohm and Hiley 1975) remarks about physical field theories are equally applicable, mutatis mutandis: "Parts are seen to be in immediate connection, in which their dynamical systems depend in an irreducible way on the state of the whole system . . . extending in principle to the whole universe." The first part of this presents no problems—one can draw up a field theory model of evolution or organogenesis. If one does, second layer effects might actually appear as they do in physics because "the whole universe is like that" (Bohm's last sentence); even if they do not appear, the formalism derived from the particle model might be instructive. In fact, Bohm's interdependency model looks far more like biology than physics, so that some of the rasher brethren are already talking about particles or the second layer universe generally as "organismic." Rather than getting into that, we would be more profitably occupied by looking for any cast-iron examples of inexplicable information transfer in biological systems.

Given the wide unanimity of evolutionary biologists as to the factitious nature of 'species', evidenced by the quotations with which I prefaced this chapter, a probabilistic analysis seems made-to-measure, with the individual phenotype representing the collapse of the wave function. With this approach, attention is focused on the nature of the 'mould' in which species are formed, the probabilistic surface in which creodes (geodesics) exist. So far the reasonable approach has been to treat this mould simply as the sum of Darwinian pressures, with a great deal of faith, hope, and charity as to the circumstances in which closely co-ordinated changes (those involved in the evolution of bird flight, for example) happened to occur together. Selectionists have invoked orthogenesis—which looks like an irrefutable model. The alternative has been either naive teleology or some kind of 'soft' vitalism. One would have a lot more confidence in an entelechy which could be mathematically derived from quantum treatment, though that too might be artefactual. In morphogenesis, a field model might be directly accessible, because the whole process is manipulable and we can watch it. In both these cases the experiment would be worthwhile either to provide some respectable evidence of extraselectionist morphogenesis or to get Bergsonian-Drieschian models out of the way once and for all. Indeed, given the upcoming climate of revisionism, it would be as well worth knowing that quantum formulations are superfluous to the comprehension of embryogenesis as that they were congruent with observation. The role of the linguistic-taxonomic homunculus is less evident in embryogenesis than it is in speciation, where the origins of our classificatory methods are themselves linguistic (Spurway 1954), exactly as in particle physics, but that may be a constraint imposed by the manner in which we perceive sequence and spatiality—precisely the bias which quantum logic has developed to circumvent.

A non-Democritean evolutionary biology, in which the counter-intuitive model replaced historicity, may look more perverse than it does in physics, but the second actually opens the way to the first, rather as classical mechanics, while remaining valid within its limiting cases, is modified by quantum theory in relevance if not in practice. In reading Bohm's exposition of the "holomovement" from which the virtual objects studied by physics are derived by explication, it is difficult not to be struck by the analogy to organic evolution. As Frescura and Hiley (1980) put it, when we see a symphonic work developing as a musical structure we do not attribute the cooperative effort of the musicians to hypothetical forces existing between them.

Accordingly, in biology the place to look for second layer 'show-through' is most probably the interface between genetic coding and morphogenetic expression. It will require a high degree of open-minded scepticism, or all the old neovitalist errors which molecular biology helped to expel may be reactivated. There may indeed be no show-through, and probabilistic sequential effects of a normal and causal character may be a sufficient model. On the other hand, the importance of any hard-nosed demonstration of a phenomenon in epigenesis, comparable to Bell's theorem and its experimental consequences, would greatly widen our understanding of the relevance of second layer or field effects, and raise the heuristic respectability of demonic models. It seems a necessary consequence of quantum physics that, as with the Newtonian model, we find out just how far it goes. If quantum physics can be regarded as a critique of observer artefacts in our biological metaphors, it will be necessary to apply it in designing experiments on middle-order as well as limiting-case phenomena.

Rupert Sheldrake (1981) has recently postulated precisely this kind of showing through as an explanation of the formative pattern in evolution. He explains it by a neologism ("morphic resonance") about which I would have a number of questions, but his basic postulate is that what occurs to every individual of a species directly affects all other individuals—organisms may be Leibnizian monads. This is an evidentially accessible question: the fact that the asking of it no longer has the effect on colleagues of inopportune flatus in an elevator is perhaps a measure of the "paradigm shift" which he himself recognizes. "Morphic resonance" apart, it would be more in line with that shift simply to predicate that the quantum nonlocality applies to organisms: like subatomic particles, they are neither objects nor separate. Put in this way, one can see why semi-jocular ripostes, such as the fact that millenia of circumcision among certain people have not measureably shortened the foreskins of goyim, miss the point. So even if Sheldrake proves to be resoundingly wrong—as were the alchemists over the number of chemical elements—he is asking a question which physics will not permit biology to dismiss.

# Chapter 4

## *MIND AND MAKING MODELS*

# 4.1

# Mind
# and the Psychiatry
# of World Models

It is paradoxical that more than one half-century after the advent of
of relativistic physics and the formulation of quantum mechanics, current theories of personality are still steeped in the classical Judeo-
Christian, Aristotelian or Cartesian tradition. Our neurophysiological
models of the organism, our psychological and psychoanalytic concepts about "the mind", are located in Euclidean space and conform to
essentially mechanistic, Newtonian, causal-reductive principles.

Ehrenwald, J. (1972)

This is the point at which anyone who is not interested in talking
to the demon Gezumpstein should take up the story. It becomes a
bit easier, though not much. The nature of matter is extremely interesting to physicists and philosophers, and working on it may have
applications. The nature of mind is something quite else. 'Matter'
does not matter greatly for the ordinary world view, which includes
things such as making love, working, or the Stock Exchange. But any
work we do, or comment we make, on the nature of mind plays
straight into an area of human concern which has come to be labelled
"existential anxiety." For Sancho Panza, this means quite simply anxiety and distress over death—his own, and that of others. For the Don,
it can be refined into concern over meaninglessness, human liberty,
human aloneness, and the origins of moral choices. Sartre and Husserl
were Dons; living through the Nazi occupation of France, which was
apt to confront one with moral choices between ethical principle and
an unpleasant death, sharpened a whole school of French existential
philosophy.

159

'Existential' is a nonce word meaning "concerned with, or arising from, the individual's perception of the human condition." The basic feature of the human condition is a foreknowledge of our own mortality and the impermanence of human activities. We normally postpone Sancho Panza's anxiety, the gut anxiety over death, or deal with it by denial or diversion—like Kingsley Amis' young man who handled the thought of death by thinking quickly about sex. Denial mythologies are as old as human beings, who from the remote past buried the dead with tools, food and grave goods.

Death has never been a part of the human inheritance which has been pleasant to contemplate, and all humans, at adolescence or in the middle of a sleepless night, have experienced existential anxiety. But chronic and unrelieved existential anxiety, to be handled simply by acceptance and stoicism, is a direct spin-off of the hard-hat, Newtonian-Cartesian, world view. For a large part of European history, Christianity provided doctrinal comfort, although its reassurance was complicated by some ugly reflections about hell. Pre-Einsteinian science neither proves the idea that mind is an activity of brain and equally perishable with it, nor does it prove the non-existence of a traditional God. But by the end of the nineteenth century (and simply on the basis of a coherent world view which accorded with knowledge), neither disembodied intelligences generally, nor the religio-scientific blend which both Newton and Descartes themselves held, looked in any way evidentially probable. The scientific creed includes one uncompromising moral item: that we follow what the evidence appears to show, regardless of any anxiety or discomfort which the results may present. If we really cannot play constantly with a hard ball, nobody will deny us illogical or undemonstrable convictions, but they are not the same game as science, should not leak into it, and, ideally—as a test of our mental integrity—should not contradict observable fact: they can be tolerated only in gray areas where there is room for doubt or no possibility of direct verification.

Our personal anxieties should, of course, play no part in the dispassionate business of science. On the other hand, they quite obviously do. Like the old-time sex researchers, who put on the guise of disinterested eunuchs pursuing knowledge, we are kidding nobody.

A biologist who is also a doctor exhibits (some would say, suffers from) a singularity of his or her own. He or she is occupationally obliged to treat scientists and philosophers as people—a role in which some of them are extremely uncomfortable, having embraced science, propositional logic, or philosophy as a way of dealing impersonally with uncertainty. Although scientific integrity is real, and is maintained by peer pressure, in the field of world models personal motivation shows through. It is part of the unfortunate legacy of religious dualism; world models tend to be designed to hold down the stone we have placed on our existential anxieties. It is not quite cricket to draw attention to this—such considerations only operate as a rule where there is some room for choice, and most of us eventually assent to overwhelming experimental evidence. Einstein disliked quantum logic, because God does not shoot dice. Darwin was apprehensive about the uproar which his theories would produce, and was only persuaded to face the music when Wallace was about to anticipate him.

A psychopathologist of science would be immensely interested in the story, for example, of 'paranormal' phenomena—not as to their reality or significance, but for the effect which the idea of their possible existence has had on intellectually respectable people; it seems unkind to let them go home like that, and the temptation to interpret is overwhelming. Writers on the subject can be divided, not between "sheep" and "goats" (Schmeidler 1958) but between Counterphobics, Deniers, Viscerals, and Arbitrators. They may be categorized by the way they relate to anxiety and by the degree of clarity, openness, and precise reasoning with which they relate to systems breaks.

Counterphobics have come to terms with a world view which accepts existential anxiety and renounces wishful denial. This process has been psychologically costly, and for them it has an ethical dimension. They know from experience the power of denial mythologies, and combat them; they are also intensely disturbed by systems breaks which might give ground to such mythologies. The position which counterphobics defend today is that of positivist mechanism—they fear that the irrational may return. Until about 150 years ago, counterphobics were of a different order: they feared the rational and the causal, because it might displace the supernatural, in which their world model was then invested.

Deniers face existential anxiety with less stamina. They look with hope for a systems break, which, since it can hardly now be supernatural, must lie somewhere in science. They are the pursuers of spiritualists who converse with deceased relatives. Their writings on speculative matters, or philosophy generally, observe the decencies of scientific argument, but there is a tangible soft center. What the counterphobic fears, they encounter with relief. Bad cases end up reading significance into the Great Pyramid, or looking for ancestors from outer space.

Viscerals in my terminology are those whose analgesic in the face of death anxieties and life anxieties is the re-creation of a sense of awe. They cultivate the marvellous—unexplained phenomena leave open questions which might, if resolved, give unsettling answers. Unidentified flying objects attract them because they are unidentified. It is the inrush of viscerals, who do not want precise explanations (those might provide answers and suggest some definite world model) which so upset Wheeler (Gardner 1979) in regard to the misuse of quantum formalisms. In medicine we see them as "holistic" quacks. The response of the visceral to any new or odd formulation is not that there might, but that there must be something in it, and they form not philosophies but intellectual jackdaw's nests by a process of eclectic accretion.

Arbitrators are for my money the genuine practitioners of science. Very possibly they owe their capacity for combining judgment with originality to a defense mechanism of another kind—the use of intense interest in the nature and workings of the world to displace any unwelcome consequences which the discovered world may have. For them constant integrative curiosity is ego-syntonic. They do not fear a systems break, and if phenomena of any kind suggest one, then that is intensely interesting. Beside attempting to confirm the phenomena rigorously, they begin to think how and where they might fit the world model if confirmed. They are not preoccupied with possible points of entry for denial, because denial would be unreassuring unless it has some basis in an integrated reality; and they have no interest in the diffusely marvellous, only in evidence suggesting that their world model for the time being is possibly incomplete. Whereas deniers and viscerals are unconsciously reinforced by reports of sea serpents (because they suggest that "science does not yet know everything" and folklore may prove right), arbitrators are interested in them because they might possibly represent the existence of an unknown genus, which is likely to have an instructively specialized physiology for deep diving. Counterphobics, unless a sea-serpent is actually and ungainsayably caught, are a little disturbed and indignant at the credulity of those who report them. Arbitrators are inclined to listen to unconventional ideas or experiences attentively, even a little in advance of hard evidence, simply to see if they could possibly throw light on something. At the edges of any world model, they are the masters of that controlled lunacy which might generate a more comprehensive model.

Both arbitrators and viscerals read science fiction, the first for ideas they can make over, the second because fiction is their mode. Arbitrators wade through the works of quacks and psychotics, exotic philosophy, or oddballs like Paracelsus, looking for pieces of the jigsaw which the quacks and oddballs may not have seen. Jung, of whom I will speak later, was a visceral, but has some claim to be an arbitrator: once he got, not a world model, but a glimpse of human intellectual patterning, he became an indefatigable collector from every conceivable source. Because he could not fully integrate what he found into a world model, he has become a favorite with viscerals, which is at once a deserved and an undeserved fate.

Jung would have pointed out that in mythology when old King Sun (rationalistic positivism, Blake's Urizen) sickens and becomes infertile, it is Queen Moon, the intuitive Earth-Mother, who gets her turn. Getting the two of them married is the magnum opus which produces the philosopher's stone. In the meantime, we are in for a rough patch intellectually. With the lag between empathy and the new world model, we hear everywhere the buzzing of Wheeler's flies— Velikovsky, von Däniken, dianetics, fortune-telling, and the *National Enquirer*. Quantum logic is not the place where they most congregate because the mathematics are far too difficult, thus pseudocosmology and pseudoarchaeology have probably drawn larger swarms. Even old-style Biblical prophetic fundamentalism, a horse originally out of a different stable, is running again among folk who should know better.

Immediately one starts to apply a new world view to the question of mind, the entire can of worms is reopened. Hard-line scientific positivists are indignant. They have learned to live with the impermanence of their homuncular I, turned the discipline to edification, and suspect that what is coming next will be wish fulfillment, sloppy theosophizing, and bad science. Both the hard-line religious and those with weak heads and nerves will be delighted that "science has changed its position," that there is going to be a replay, and that cracks have opened in the monolith into which dogma or personal anxieties can be inserted.

Neither of these views, of course, is justified. Science has *not* resigned in favor of philosophy: it has simply followed its own rules and changed its world view in the light of evidence. The quantum-logical world does not give encouragement to old dogmatics in a reheated form, nor does it provide a hunting license for enthusiastic speculation. But it does appreciably alter our degree of certainty about epiphenomenal mind. In what way this new world view will develop is not clear, nor is it clear whether it will be any less stressful in regard to our personal concerns about the eventual fate of our I-ness than Victorian secular positivism. Any press articles to the effect that "science has discovered God" or "physics has demonstrated the truth of parapsychology" are based on total misconception. All that has happened in regard to parapsychology (meaning ghosts, ESP, precognition, and the like) is that in spite of the ineptness and credulity of much work in this area, the world we now envisage is appreciably different from the world which hard-hat science thought it had sewn up. This was a world in which such phenomena could not possibly be accommodated and could be rejected out-of-hand as spurious if someone claimed to have observed them. One cannot now assert that *because* an effect appears to violate causality, reverse the sequence of time, or otherwise present a singularity, the observation must be faulty, or if not faulty, fraudulent. This does not prove that such singularities occur, only that it is worth looking for them with irreproachable methods if they are reported, either in folklore or in the lab.

A word is needed here—since it is desirable to know what we are talking about—on the meaning we attach to 'mind'. I shall use it here to mean quite simply that group of phenomena associated with consciousness which humans conventionally experience. It includes unconscious conceptual processes but excludes, for example, neurochemistry, which we infer but do not experience as such. 'Mind' in this sense is the mental equivalent of middle-order physical reality. Further ingenuity in subdividing 'mind' is probably misplaced in the context in which we shall be discussing it. The analogy with middle-order experience (how the 'objective' world appears) is important, and need not at this point be complicated by introducing the fact that perceiving the 'real' world is a mental process. What does appear is that both the perceived mental world and the perceived objective world are classical explicates on Bohm's model. This seems intuitively justified as a starting point, without going to the trouble of applying a rotational algebra to mental processes, or asking at this point who or what is doing the perceiving.

If we started from Bohm's model to speculate on consciousness as a "parallel explicate" to that which it observes, definitional problems arise at once. Rather than rehearse any of the psychologists' or philosophers' definitions of consciousness, the starting point of the Bohm model, namely

$$\text{ॐ} \rightarrow \boxed{\text{O}} \sim \text{O}$$

suggests to the mathematician a rather different and more simplistic set of definitions: O is that which observes and ~O is the totality of that which O operates upon. At the same time O evidently observes, or is aware of, itself, which is why we speak of self-consciousness (one would have some problems with a mind which was not aware that it was a mind). Now not only is thinking about mind a recursive process, the concept of O is the introduction of a recursion into "all that is the case." The Spencer Brown box in the formulation divides the plenum into a straightforward, nonrecursive part, and a recursive one: mind *is* recursion, as Spencer Brown points out.

This fundamental idea goes beyond the fact that all critiques of 'reality' have to be carried through the system which generated the model of phenomenal reality in the first place—a recursive term becomes one of two facets, or parallel explicates, to which a Bohmian model gives rise. Mind enters the system as a recursive operator thereby letting in a great deal of algebra proper to recursive systems which I will not reproduce here, but which provides some rich fodder for the expansion of M.E.M.$^{-1}$ into investigable mathematics (to say nothing of trying recursive terms for fit in concrete contexts like wave mechanics).

Bohm himself (Bohm in Wilber, 1982) has pointed out that if we introduce self-consciousness into an implicate we open the way to a mirror regression of implicates treating one another as subjects of observation—the psychophilosophical equivalent of a von Neumann regression in physics. This recursive effect is the mathematical basis, I think, of the insistence of Hindu and Buddhist philosophers (most recently of Krishnamurti) that thought cannot reveal reality—an irritating conclusion for scientists until they get the mathematical point. On the same basis one might hazard a guess that instead of a Boolean yes-no choice between the heuristic hypothesis "mind is generated by brain" and the heuristic hypothesis "mind is transduced by brain," experiment may very well produce a superposition of the two remarkably like the old (and equally heuristic) wave-particle paradox. In this model principles of uncertainty would not be a quirk of particle-level physics but an inherent double take arising from $\overline{O}$| ~O. This is a difficult pill to swallow, but once down, it is sufficiently sedative to let us realize that Boolean choices are not an inherent requirement of science—looking at experimental results is. Nobody has laid down that verifiable results have to be reducible, and physics has lived for some time with the realization that they are not. Mathematics, by writing in a recursive term, would both vindicate Krishnamurti and make an end run round apophatic models. Accordingly, the state of "not this, not that" which figures in Hindu and Buddhist models is expressible algebraically, and therefore scientifically tolerable so that we can get on with experimentation, as the physicists have done.

The hard-hat model of the mind-body relationship accepted since Hume and the rise of seventeenth century rationalism and formulated finally by Helmholtz is that mind is an epiphenomenon of matter, as the activity of calculating is an epiphenomenon of computer circuitry. Construct a computer and it will calculate. Dismantle it and it will cease to calculate. The brain is a real object and its activity at best a virtual or contingent object.

This is the view held, at least in all practical contexts, by the vast majority of contemporary scientists; reservations about it arise chiefly from private or religious conviction, and, when expressed, are not expressed as science.

The state-of-the-art models of physics do not disprove this view. Matter may be virtual, and the brain is composed of matter, but so are other physical systems, including computers, and it is a matter of common observation that these may have epiphenomena attached to them. One of the empathic problems, however, of all epiphenomenalism is the primacy and uniqueness of the sense of "I". We cannot empathize what it would "feel like" to be a computer, or a chimpanzee, or even, except by communication, another person. On the other hand, the very vividness and primacy in human experience of the sense of being creates a certain unease in the center of any hard-line epiphenomenalism. In the end I-ness has to be taken as a priori: that is how a complex epiphenomenon, with binocular vision and a body image, does in fact feel about itself. The indigestibility of this double take, in which I recognize by cogitation that I am an epiphenomenon, is central to existential anxiety, not because it torpedoes religious models of immortalism, but for a near-neurological reason: obsessions and ruminations, like tics, appear to represent self-sustaining 'loops' in brain activity, different from, but related to, the oscillations of a computer fed a logic paradox in Pattee's (1979) model. People prone to obsessional behavior, like Kierkegaard, drive themselves near crazy trying to deal with the oscillation; yogis are aware that intense meditation on the nature of the experiencing I can in fact dissociate it altogether and generate a suspension of optical-categorical object formation—which suggests that the I is being generated like other 'optical' objects by a process of thing-making.

Provided one stays out of arguments concerning the nature of extra-mental reality, one can construct a perfectly respectable and refutable model of consciousness, solely in terms of what is known, or can reasonably be inferred, about neurones. Edelman (Edelman and Mountcastle 1979) has produced an excellent one, based on phasic re-entrant processing over a multidimensional store. In this case the I is a reference point which refers back to past experience. By Occam's razor, the fact that this kind of model could explain all the conventionally observed, middle-order activities of mind would make any added mentalism supererogatory; to justify that in middle-order terms, one would have to demonstrate singularities which could not be explained by "central-state materialism" (Campbell 1970). Now it may well be that the virtual character of the structures making up the functional system makes no difference to this kind of argument—after all, computers as well as neurones consist of matter, and nobody attributes transcendental mentalism to them. At the same time it is distinctly awkward that the structures forming the mechanism which is doing the categorizing are themselves categories or patterns identified by their own pattern of activity at a higher level, namely 'mind'. The immediate response to this idea is not that it must be wrong, but that it needs going over carefully. "Say again?" rather than "Not so."

The classical epiphenomenalist, however much he may qualify the idea, ends up at some point with the awkward conclusion that the mind 'is' a collection of neurones. A far more satisfactory definition is that mind is a software system, a program which, in this instance, neurones are capable of operating. This view (functionalism) has the consequence (token physicalism) that any system capable of handling the software is a mind, whether it consists of neurones—which is the case with all the minds we normally encounter—or of silicon chips, ectoplasm, or pieces of string: if non-carbon-based Martians or disembodied spirits can run the program, then Martians, spirits, and man-made computers have minds (Fodor 1980). One might assert that only neural systems can interface with what we call "mind," at least on the basis that we cannot identify any non-neural systems which do so, but if such a non-neural system can be designed, if only as a Gedanken experiment, then in functionalist terms, it too "has a mind"—or else there are fairies at the bottom of our garden.

Moreover, though the program may be structural (i.e., it might subsist simply in the way that the neurones are wired up), programs *need* not be structural, for they can be transduced into instructions and stored on cards, in genes, and in a variety of other languages which bear no transformative resemblance at all to the operations they make possible when expressed in a computing system, any more than the bumps and hollows on a gramophone disc resemble music. A dehydrated Helmholtz or Skinner stored on magnetic tape is not, in this view, unthinkable—run him into an appropriate system and he will operate, even though what was on the tape would have been unrecognizable on inspection by Helmholtz's or Skinner's personal friends. Inspection of my chromosomes at amniocentesis would not have given my parents much idea what to expect, beyond a male unafflicted with gross chromosomal disorders. Meditation on the implications of token-physical functionalism, obvious as the idea looks to any computer-trained modern, has philosophical implications which rattle the teeth, as we shall see.

In the old model, the material world was Democritean-real, as observed by a virtual I which is an object-formation of the brain; in the neurological reading of the Bohm model all 'things' are the result of object-formation by processes in the brain, including the brain itself, which is doing the object-forming. Moreover, the 4-space continuum in which objects or processes define themselves as 'real'—including the brain-as-object and its processes—is also a construction presenting itself to the positional I of the investigator. This is a super-loop and tends rather precipitously to Hinduism or Buddhism according to which *all* objects, the a prioris, 4-space, the mind and the positional I are epiphenomena or thought forms (*māya, saṁsara*) imposed by object-formation from a holomovement (Brahman, śunya). In this case we might ask, Who exactly is doing the thinking? If that were not enough, the application of quantum logic to evolution and organogenesis suggests that brain structure itself might be formed from regularities in the holomovement by resonance, as it were, rather as the regularities of sandridges or clouds are formed by local wave effects. At this point prescientific occultists, who appear to have intuited some of this, were content to depict the model of 'reality' as a snake swallowing its own tail.

One way of getting the better of the paradox, which is strikingly like Blanco's (1975) model of infinite inclusive sets in unconscious imaging, is to try to break it up into a system hierarchy, in which each level is informationally a separate domain—one does not apply molecular biology formalisms to music or sociology. This works for descriptive purposes, but it does not really escape from the loop, because brains are doing the hierarchy-formation from data processed by brains, so that all we have is a superior quality of *māya* involving a more intellectual set of virtual objects. This is a striking difference from traditional Western, post-Eleatic philosophy, which is dialectical, and almost invariably takes the conceptualizing 'I' in its Cartesian sense, as a fixed point. This change is as profound as the one brought about in cosmology by relativistic physics, but not many formal philosophers have taken the point, though Wittgenstein approaches it from the linguistic side. It represents a thorough scrambling of traditional idealist-materialist dialectic from Plato down, and what survives is closer to the Pythagorean idea that number alone exists to be perceived by a brain which is generated by numbers, in the form of wave functions.

Bohm's (1980) thoughtful book in which he expounds the wider implications of his theory of 4-space as an explicate contains a good deal about language and mind. In dealing with the first of these, he emphasizes the role of naming in thing-formation, but the second gives him a lot more trouble. At one point he seems to be saying that the mind, being an offshoot of a 4-space explicate, contains and intuitively perceives the "grain" of the multidimensional implicate which he postulates (a "Tao of mind") simply through being plugged in to material neurones. At other times he treats mental events as a separate order parallel with material, 4-space events, but having some measure of autonomy. The test of this model, or group of tentative models, would be to apply it to simple artificial intelligence: Does this separate order of mental-like process constitute a distinguishable system? Bohm would, I think, say that it is "enfolded" in the circuitry which produces it. At the same time, most of his book is devoted to showing that 4-space events are virtual as viewed by the thing-forming mind, and that what is real is the substrate or holomovement which is projected into lower-dimensional events. This seems to imply a modified epiphenomenalism of mutual dependence, with both brain and mind—together with evolution, life processes, and everything else—patterned invincibly by the subjacent implicate, or such of its regularities as are expressed in 4-space.

The unmanageable dimension in 4-space is clearly time. "The mistake of pre-relativity physics was to identify time too closely with human experience" (Davies 1974). The paradoxes generated by the "succession of nows" was first enunciated by Zeno. They were believed to have been laid to rest first by discovery of limits, and then by differential calculus, but Bohm is one of the first mathematicians to appreciate what in all probability Zeno was actually saying. The calculus does not resolve the problem of instantaneous values: it allows us to compute tendencies in spite of them. By focusing attention on the discontinuity of the experienced world Bohm's model implies both a quantization of physical time, and a concept of empathic time as itself a slice of hypertime: continuity exists in the implicate which unites them.

Implicate models are very properly attributed to Zeno—the inference comes from his denial of motion. Since Zeno's text is lost, the main historical exposition is actually Vedic, which may well have been his source. In Hindu cosmology an implicate, Brahman (cognate with "that which turns or vibrates"), generates the phenomenal world by a process of explication and division (*māya* is usually translated 'illusion', but is cognate with 'metric, measure'). *Māya* in turn generates discrete qualities (*guṇa*). The world with qualities conceals or projects Brahman, which constitutes a field throughout it. Another Bohmian idea is central to Buddhism—*śunya*, the empty-plenum, which can be seen as an alternative depiction of the implicate.

Hindu philosophers, however, insist in a rather irritating manner that their Brahman is propertiless—"not this, not that." Aside from the fact that being neither this nor that *is* a property, the nonreligious substance is that it is irreducible: it does not consist of quanta or quarks. Quanta and quarks, however, are determined by its regularities. In Hindu thought these things are qualities (*guṇa*), but the implicate itself has no such qualities. Bohm's model is more explicit and depends on algebra and ratiocination, not vision in an unusual state of mind. His implicate has a fundamental property described as movement and also the property of undergoing explication. We have accordingly a threefold structure: an underlying extradimensional field or pattern, a manifest order generated from it by the process Bohm terms explication, and ordinary middle-order reality generated from the manifest world by our perception of it. Old-style science addressed the last of these, quantum logics address the second, and mathematics has made several premature attempts to address the first, from the harmonic model of Pythagoras to the numerology of John Dee. It is only after a severe Democritean assault course over the oddness of the manifest world that we can now come back to a field model.

The holomovement can be naively visualized as an ocean, on which properties in the manifest order are the equivalent of standing waves. One would think that one property of such a subjacent 'this-ness' is likely to be a high degree of recursion—a pattern which was identical whether viewed with a microscope or a telescope. Another is interconnectedness: parts of the manifest order which appear autonomous or are displaced in space-time, so that we treat them as separate objects, are neither objects nor separate. One effect of this idea is to transpose the kind of nonlocality and interconnectedness which Wheeler has postulated at a micro-level ("the quantum foam") into a far more general property of nature, which could be looked for macroscopically.

Manifest phenomena are related to the holomovement by the process which Bohm calls "explication." Since manifest phenomena are identified by their regularities—which are what we measure—it follows that any implicate generates regularities which are expressed in space-time. Short of looking (as Pythagoras did) for some general harmonic equation for this mapping of the explicate into the implicate, one has to assume that it can be written

$$f(I) = E$$

One way of starting an indefinite algebra which can be tried for fit is to assume that this can be reduced to a family of polynomials in $(x, y, z, \text{real})$ plus a set of complex-plane rotations

$$(xi + yj + zk) - q(xi + yj + zk)q^{-1} \quad i^2 = j^2 = k^2 = -1$$

i.e., a family of quaternions. Frescura and Hiley (1980) using a Clifford algebra do the same thing in a more sophisticated and versatile way with spinors, but the mathematics involved are difficult. The function of the 'guesstimate' algebra of explication which I am about to give is not to show the implications of Bohm's theory for the formal restatement of quantum mechanics, but simply to generate an imaginary matrix, for purposes which will be evident presently. For this purpose any oversimplified set of expressions for

$$f(I) = E$$

will serve as a starting point.

The field of Bohm's holomovement is of high order but nonrandom, because the quantization of manifest phenomena is, as it were, a graphic representation of this subjacent nonlocal structure. Substitution of algebra for geometry as a model for these processes is a prime feature of Bohm's approach. In contrast to the vectors of geometrical models, which we designate by Greek letters, it seems historically appropriate in what follows to designate Bohm's implicate by a Sanskrit letter. The character Aum, which traditionally incorporates or represents the resonance patterns of an implicate, seems the obvious nonjocular candidate.

Let ॐ be such an implicate, which is related to its explicate manifestations by an operator $E$, performing the operation which Bohm terms "metamorphosis"

$$M.E.M.^{-1}$$

Then one way of commencing an undefinable algebra for explication is to write

$$E\,ॐ = e_1 \cdot e_2 \cdot e_3 \ \dots \ e_n$$

the $e_x$ terms being the ensemble of phenomena and measurables which are the normal substrate of observation, and which possess $nāma\text{-}rūpa$ (name and form). Assume that there are equations expressing the operation $E$ over ॐ such that $e_1 \dots e_n$ can be written as a matrix $G_{ij}$ for all space-time events, the phenomena of any partial system being minors or derivatives according to their complexity. We then have

$$E\,ॐ = G_{ij}$$

Strictly speaking, what $E\,ॐ$ has to generate in terms of the ordinary wave-mechanical formalism is an improvement on the matrix representation of the dual Hilbert spaces $H_1$, spanned by all $|u>$, and $H_2$ spanned by all $<\chi|$, the two being interchangeable via a Hermitian operator ($H_2$ antilinear to $H_1$). To avoid making the text unreadable with algebra, I have taken a projection of $E\,ॐ$ into arbitrary maxtrix $G_{ij}$. This could in fact be a tensor product written as a matrix of matrices, i.e., the individual entries in $G_{ij}$ are themselves matrices, either the Pauli series or more complex, according to their position in $G_{ij}$.

In Bohm's model, ॐ is of high dimensional order approaching randomness, but not random, since it has regularities which pattern $G_{ij}$. If it were random, the exercise becomes vacuous. $G_{ij}$ is likewise of high order ($i, j$ large but finite). The qualities which result from the operation $E$ are the heterogeneous group of measurables (location, mass, spin, number, probability) which compose "Alles, was der Fall ist." The matrix is accordingly arbitrary or undefined, and there is no point in treating it as, say, a set of determinants for $j$ polynomials of order $i$, asking if it is Hermitian, or anything else of the kind. If we knew of a function which $E$ generates over ॐ, assuming it to be all-embracing, we would be home and dry. What $G_{ij}$ represents is a tabulation of basic phenomena as they appear in the 'real' (explicate) world.

A representation of projected reality obviously has to accommodate the relations which appear to our perception as cause-effect. These actions and interactions we represent by canonical transformations over $G_{ij}$. These are 'causally' interrelated only in the same way that chess moves determine a game. Such a rule might be: "If rows $b$ and $e$ are transposed, columns $f$ and $h$ are multiplied by $k$." ॐ itself is, of course, invariant under transformations of $G_{ij}$ which are constrained to follow the regularities which $E$ॐ imposes, exactly as the rules of chemistry are not abrogated by setting fire to a barrel of gunpowder, only expressed. This extends to *all* possible changes in space-time, up to and including the genesis of the cosmos from a singularity, which represents the reduction of the matrix to a minimal form, say a diagonal.

It will be seen that $G_{ij}$ bears a close resemblance to a hologram. It is, however, a hologram of a very special kind. A real hologram is a plane representation of a real object in terms of the interference fringes which it generates, and the plotting of an object-coordinate $x$ into an image-coordinate $y$ is determined by a Green's function

$$G(x - y) = \{exp\ [i\ (\tfrac{\omega}{c})\ |x - y|]\}\ /\ |x - y|$$

By contrast, $G_{ij}$ is a projection of the regularities generated by $E$ॐ into a set of 'real' objects—a reverse hologram. By the equation given, there is no unique plot of any point in $x$ to a point in $y$; rather, the pattern characteristic of the object is present in all parts of the plate. What happens in our model is that a pattern is translated into virtual objects, as when a hologram is viewed. Moreover, it is tempting to infer that if we inspected every $e_{ij}$ with a microscope, each element would be seen to be itself a matrix congruent with $G_{ij}$ and so on recursively.

At this point, the hyperloop breaks in. A holographic virtual image is presented to an optical observer. Where is the observer of the image formed from $G_{ij}$? Presumably, it is the physicist. But the physicist is himself an image projected from the same source. We still have a self-viewing system, and a no-exit loop.

Moreover, when we consider Bohm's most important point, that the holo*movement* implies motion or change, it has to be pointed out that movement, change, and the like are themselves transductions to a consciousness: *change has no meaning except to a positional observer.* I suspect Bohm's use of "movement" is proleptic—the implicate has properties which manifest in space-time transforms as movement. The algorithms programmed into a microprocessor do not "move" or "become," but they regulate the behavior of e.g. a robot which does move. A holomovement seen by a nonlocal demon would *contain* or *enfold*, not *become*. This was the reason I chose a matrix to represent its action and depict $e_1, e_2 \ldots e_n$. A matrix has no moving parts: it contains 'becoming' by virtue of its implicit transformations, but the entity is invariant mathematically when these are expressed. Consciousness sees these transformations as moments, because one must write them on a blackboard serially, but the mathematician sees them as a superposition written $A_{nm}$.

If anything is moving, it has to be ourselves: there is somewhere a system which not only creates experiential slices of time of order $\delta t$, but also selects a slice of hypertime within which its world line lies. The unexplicated inkdrops are there all the while. The only singularity about their explication is that when the particles happen to constitute a drop, we confer identity on them ("relevate" is Bohm's neologism, we "single them out"). At what point in the implicate-matrix-hologram-object sequence is this process, *observation*, to be inserted? We know that it filters heavily, collapsing wave functions, rejecting superpositions and creating in effect an artefactual environment. It could not, for example, see alternative Everett worlds which lie in a different slice of hypertime.

Now the essence of the explication model, as given in Bohm's Gedanken experiment with droplets implicated into glycerin in a cylinder, is that for a given domain of $e$, not all qualities or derived phenomena can be explicated simultaneously. If all of these potential phenomena for a given system A—for example, the glycerin-inkdrop system—are given by a minor of $G_{ij} = A_{cd}$, then let the phenomena exhibited at a particular locus and a particular subjective 'moment' be represented by the $n$th column of this arbitrary minor matrix, the events of the next 'moment' by the $(n + 1)$th column, and so on: What determines the column which is experienced? Moreover, if at a 'moment' $r$ we were able to view the entire field of $G_{ij}$ which covers the entire gamut of 'observable nature' at $r$, it would resemble a display in which individual bulbs in many columns and rows would light—some in patterns, like the $n$th column of $A_{cd}$ and others discontinuously in various parts of the array. The entire field (or fields, if our model is not $G_{ij}$ but a 3-D matrix $G_{ijk}$) would look uncommonly like a model of a brain where inputs are being handled "by phasic re-entrant processing over a multidimensional store." Whether the analogy has any deeper meaning is not initially clear. Our question is What process of structuring or selection causes these particular bulbs to light? Bearing in mind that $r$ is a subjective element (it is related to our positional sense of I-ness) is the pattern determined by a higher explication of 卐, arising from the generator function of $G_{ij}$ or by a brain algorithm, and are the two independent? The last of these questions follows from our standard assumption that mind as well as the objects of knowledge can be regarded as a component of $G_{ij}$; $G_{ij}$'s patterning is being viewed from one of its own minors, and is derived from $E\,ॐ$.

Bohm himself, who clearly sees these implications, displays praiseworthy caution, rather as Darwin did over the shooting of another sacred cow, biblical creationism. Any system containing the hyperloop implicit in the neural reduction of mind threatens the life of an equally respected quadruped, Helmholtzian Mind.

However, if instead of

$$E\,ॐ \rightarrow G_{ij} : G_{ij} \subseteq M$$

we were to write

$$E\,ॐ \rightarrow G_{ij}$$
$$\downarrow$$
$$M$$

(two coequal orders of explication, with $M$ an image of $G_{ij}$ but a separate explicate of the same rank as matter), we would at least stop the short circuit.

In token physicalism, $M$ is a program, as $G_{ij}$ is a program. Contrary to Helmholtz, it is not hard-wired in $G_{ij}$ but distinct, and transducible by any system which can interface with it. When $e_1, e_2 \ldots e_n$ or any other ensemble transduces Mind, it is truer to say that that ensemble 'has a mind' than that mind is a phenomenon produced by the ensemble.

But the striking analogy between the structure of $G_{ij}$ itself and a brain raises the other disturbing possibility that Plato could have been right and $E \equiv M$ : mind *is* the process of explication. What defines 'droplet' when it is explicate, and not when it is latent or implicate, is the concept 'droplet'; the entity behind its appearance and disappearance is continuous.

Hindus preserve for meditative purposes any egg-shaped white stone which contains an admixture of red. It represents the beginning of creation from the plenum, or in other words, its division by a Spencer Brown box into 'male' (1) and 'female' ($1^* = 2$). The remainder of explication arises through the action of duality. This symbolism makes the point, which Bohm does not address, that the first act of explication is the separation of the plenum into two—subjective I and subjective not-I—and that this operation is anterior to algebras: without an observer, there is effectively no explication and there are no phenomena. One cannot even categorize $ॐ$ by an empty set. Accordingly one must rewrite the metamorphosis

$$M.E.M.^{-1}$$

as

$$E \, \text{ॐ} \rightarrow \overline{\text{O}}| \sim \text{O}$$

Thereafter **E** appears as the operator which carries ॐ onto O. It is culturally engrained, even in thinkers as original as Bohm, that any algebra must treat the explicate-implicate relation as something which occurs and is then observed. The hyperloop results from this intuitive treatment. There is a strong case for saying that explication begins with the most invincible of all a prioris, the Cartesian I, and that all the phenomena expressed in $G_{ij}$ *are further explications onto* O. This is indeed the Vedic rather than the Greek model, and for Vedic yogis who set about reversing the process, O is the last thing to go. In the *dvaita* (twofold) stage of perception, the only structures are O and ॐ . In the *advaita* (nondual), O→ॐ⊂O. Whatever one may think of the significance of these subjective exercises, the algebraic point is worth taking. It is a very different viewpoint from the classical idealist-realist debate common to European philosophy.

Bohm's own treatment of consciousness (1980) is prudently tentative, but he seems to regard it as the operator of explication from a multidimensional ground. This appears to be a logical derivate by symmetry from the explicate-implicate model and contains a highly unexpected philosophical time bomb, to which Bohm himself does not draw attention. It could perfectly well be that consciousness is an epiphenomenon, at least in part, not of an explicate, but directly of the implicate order on a basis of symmetry with the explicate character of 'objective' reality. The conventional dogma is that mind is an epiphenomenon of matter-energy by way of neurochemistry and neurophysics: in other words, if we add an implicate "ground" for matter-energy, as Bohm proposes, then consciousness is a third-order derivative, a movie-within-a-movie. If, on the other hand, consciousness were at any point to be an epiphenomenon from the "ground" itself, then consciousness and matter-energy are on an equal ontological footing.

At this point, all the hard-science alarm bells go off: this is precisely the kind of wet neovitalism which has such a bad track record in generating useful or disproveable hypotheses. Hard-nosed researchers have learned to treat such a formulation as a personal threat, if not a dereliction of intellectual duty. Before we overreact in this way (and the anxiety is historically quite justified, given the unsuppressable human tendency to whip up theoretical soufflés and the zeal of writers like Teilhard or Arthur Koestler), it pays to look at the epiphenomenalist model. According to this model, it is a prosaic experience—the most prosaic experience—that an informational system can generate what we experience as consciousness. The informational system (matter-energy plus structure) is 'real', and the 'mind' is virtual. If we accept Bohm's model, which certainly explains a great deal in physics, and is refutable by canonical experimentation and/or mathematics, matter-energy is itself epiphenomenal. This leaves the classical epiphenomenalist asserting that some epiphenomena are more real than others. One could presumably do this by assuming that consciousness and matter-energy are explicates from two quite distinct implicates, but that amounts to a reassertion of the old, nonrefutable spirit-matter model, which is even more scientifically disreputable and less economical of entities. One can imagine a kind of von Neumann regression of explicates and movies-within-movies; Bohm himself hints at such a Chinese box model for the implicate-explicate relation to physics—his implicate may be an explicate from something else, and so on ad infinitum. This could, in fact, leave the classical model intact, with consciousness as a third-layer effect. But the alternative offers both a schematic (though not a logical) clarification of the 'superloop' between observer and observed, brain, matter, and evolutionary pattern, and a specific topic for experiment (not theosophical discourse) to see if it can be canonically demonstrated which model is correct: consciousness as an epiphenomenon of explicate matter-energy, or consciousness and matter as ontologically parallel epiphenomena of one mathematical, extradimensional ground, into which it introduces a recursive term. Now in the history of ideas we have actually been here before, and it is worth pausing for several pages to inspect the archaeological remains.

# A Few Instructive
# Fossils

The microcosm-macrocosm model has a long history which I will not go into here. The interesting thing is that speculative European thought at the start of the seventeenth century did indeed envisage a world model very like that of recursive explication. The motto of the imaginary Rosicrucian invisible college was "as above, so below." In judging the alchemists, who make difficult reading now (unless, like Jung, one reads them simply in terms of archetypal imagery), it is easy to become totally confused. What were they up to? Were they doing chemistry, or developing an esoteric philosophy? And was the "philosophers' stone" a chemical operation, intended to transmute metals, or a reified equivalent of gnosis?

In fact, they were doing both, regarding them as one and the same process. Traditional 'physics' dictated that the world model was built up of four elements, not an entire periodic table: 'earth', 'air', 'fire' and 'water'. Starting on this basis, one had four-way chromatics—in spite of the names, these were not the prosaic objects, any more than strange or charmed quarks are strange and charming respectively, but these elements expressed physical properties of solidity, volatility, and so on. To account for diversity, one must hypothesize an extra 'element', namely, *recursive structure*, the fifth 'element' or quintessence. If one could get hold of this, one would have the master blueprint and presumably control the phenomenal character of such things as metals: it was this X which could, from E, A, F, W, or one of their permutations, specify either lead or gold. But alchemists had more than an introspective inkling that X also specifies 'mind'. If one worked for a demanding exchequer, or was greedy, then X was the key to an important commercial operation. If one were more interested in world models, then X was the DNA of cosmology and of human mental activity, and there was no forseeable limit to the insight or the control over nature which might flow from the detection and comprehension of it. Pictures of the time depict the philosophers' stone lying about in large blocks like granite, with the disconsolate researcher plodding among them without recognizing their nature. X was in everything, including the investigator himself, but it continued to defy naive attempts at metallurgical or chemical extraction. Some of the brighter alchemists, who also practised Oriental-type meditation, appreciated that it could be 'seen' in unusual states of mind. John Dee, the chief scientific adviser to Queen Elizabeth, thought that it could be arrived at by mathematics. Rather than laughing at the magic, which was part of the furniture of the well-dressed mind in that period, we should possibly respect the ingenuity of the perception out of a great poverty of knowledge. The alchemical quintessence, oddly enough, shows signs of reappearing in physics—as the idea, put forward by Sarfatti and others, that information or configuration may be transferred between apparent phenomena such as particles in a carrierless, non-energy-related form: this would be another way of saying that 4-space phenomena may be configured by a structure lying outside 4-space.

Unfortunately, it is a feature of premature intuition that it *is* premature. In order to win this kind of battle, one has to go through boot camp first. Lacking the groundwork of positivist science, the search for the elusive X could only disappear into a speculative stratosphere. In order to get back to macrocosm-microcosm models we had to sail a long way in the opposite direction before tacking.

The alchemists themselves actually had some perception of this, and discursively more than Jung, who wrote it up in his *Mysterium Conjunctionis*. To get at X, it was going to be necessary to effect an extremely awkward marriage between "King Sun," our right-brain symbol for linear, a priori, logical vision, and "Queen Moon," our right-brain symbol for intuitive, primary-process and generally non-optically-transformed logic. One can make mythological hay with this until the cows come home to consume it, for the two-way, male-female, hard-soft, logical-oblique dichotomy is enormously overdetermined: in other words, it is a human 'natural' for antithetic processes of all orders. In fact, it is by a singular providence that the Earth doesn't have several moons or rotate about a close binary. The hard-nosed version in this case is (1) that the logical-optical system sees Kantian, 'hard' reality; (2) that the soft, pattern-detecting system sees 'grain' or gestalt, and can, in some cases, 'see' it as an inclusive field; (3) that the grain or field determines both the source from which optical transformation pulls out middle-order phenomena, *and* quite possibly, the form of biological evolution, *and* equally possibly a fortiori, the form of the brain which detects Kantian regularities. King Logic, in the alchemical graphic, runs out of spermatozoa or suffers from premature ejaculation—he cannot 'conceive' or make anyone else conceive the whole model. Queen Intuitive Gnosis has got the model, but cannot externalize it. The effective go-between to couple-counsel these two is in fact mathematics. The alchemists realized that too, or some of them did, but unfortunately, like the motor for Leonardo's helicopter, it was not then to hand—hence the archetypal shorthand. It was, after all, not a bad try.

Between the end of the Middle Ages and the founding of the Royal Society, serious European science did in fact wobble dangerously between internal and external observation: the conflict of agendas can be seen in alchemy (Yates 1972). We can infer what might have happened to science, if the premature introspectionists had prevailed, from the Teilhardian mishmash in the works of highly talented and experimentally-minded men like Michael Maier or John Dee. The ferment of emancipation from Roman dogmatism was in many ways like that of the present-day psychedelic and esoteric revolt against 'square' society and technological science. The Rosicrucians who congregated round the short-lived Bohemian court of the Elector Frederick were in revolt against Catholic orthodoxy and in favor of trying everything—chemistry, geometry, mathematics, occultism, Pythagorean field theories based on music, numerology, the Cabbala, and the 'Egyptian' texts of Hermes Trismegistus—all of which the Roman Church disapproved. Much of this now indeed makes sense in the hindsight of experimental science, Jungian psychology, and Oriental studies, but it was a heady brew at the time. Only pot and LSD were missing. Many major contributors to mathematics and science, including Descartes, Kepler, Leibniz, and pre-eminently Newton, were intensely interested in this ferment of speculation—Descartes himself may just possibly have owed his philosophical emphasis on I-ness to some kind of oceanic experience—but they all prudently confined their public utterances to mathematics and less doctrinally explosive matters. The imaginary "invisible college" of Rosicrucian mystics, combining evangelical Christianity with empirical science and Pythagorean theory, gave place to the real and experimental Royal Society. Boot camp was open, an outcome which today nobody can regard as other than extremely fortunate.

The only philosopher who states the principle of separate explication as a specific model is the much-neglected Leibniz, who oddly enough never tried to put it into mathematical form. He complicates it for us by taking over the supernaturalist model (God and the soul for implicate and mind), but otherwise, he is nearly as explicit as Bohm in regard to the holographic character of matter:

> Every body responds to all that happens in the universe, so that he who
> saw all could read in each one what is happening everywhere, and even
> what has happened and what will happen.

Material and functional structures are ontologically equal (he calls
them "monads") and "have no windows" through which any fine
structure could be detected, but each monad, like Indra's crystals,
reflects the total implicate pattern.

> Although each created monad represents the whole universe, it represents
> more distinctly the body which specially pertains to it, and of which it
> constitutes the entelechy. And as this body expresses all the universe
> through the interconnection of all matter in the plenum, the soul also
> represents the whole universe in representing the body, which belongs to
> it in a particular way. . . . [It] cannot at once open up all its folds,
> because they extend to infinity.

The only thing missing here is the extra loop, by which the brain
generates 4-space by object formation from the plenum. This is one of
the finest products, to my mind, of the great Department of Premature
Intuitions and Near Misses. It is usually misread as "psychophysical
parallelism," which is precisely what Leibniz is not saying. Granted
that his monads come, in name at least, from the Gnostics by way of
John Dee and Michael Maier, Leibniz was no numerological Rosicrucian. His problem was that although he shared in the invention of the
calculus, he was too e₂⁻ˡv for Hamiltonian or Grassmann algebra and
was forced to write pl  ₤sophy where mathematics would have gone
further. For a trendy muₐel in this vein, and a recognition by contrast
of how interesting Leibniz's model is, one has to turn to Teilhard de
Chardin. His problem, as Peter Medawar pointed out in a celebrated
review (1967), is that unlike Leibniz, he is a "soft" thinker. Moreover
he writes in highly rhetorical French which generates shapes but not
sharp concepts. In part this is a character of French as a philosophical
language—Bergson is nearly as unreadable. In part, Teilhard's vagueness is due to a need to keep a wary eye on his religious superiors—
now and then one suspects a practical joke (there is a school of thought
which believes that Teilhard, as a young man, had a hand in the
Piltdown hoax). My own impression is that he is serious, but in serious difficulty saying clearly what he wants to say. He seems to be
saying that the Logos or holomovement, having expressed itself in
matter and then in biological systems, has finally generated a self-
seeing version of itself in Mind. Through evolution, Teilhard's pan-
theic god has made himself personal by making human beings in his
own image. What we are seeing is the birth of God via repeated explication, but whereas God sees this process en bloc, like Gezumpstein, so that it would be in his experience a simultaneity, we see it
*ab extra* as extended in time. This is an interesting idea, but the

Cabbala puts it in a form which makes a better start for science, as against theology, in the doctrine of the Merkaba or "chariot" by which God transports himself into the material order on the back of Man. Teilhard does, however (and here I differ from Medawar) have a usefully demonic approach to historicity—like Gezumpstein, he effectively sees it en bloc, though he is not quite sure what to do with the perception.

I put Teilhard in here not as a lifebelt for those who want to Catholicize an explicative model, but because he represents the last gasp of Christian neo-Platonism, which was in its time a very important contributor to Renaissance and alchemical thought. Much of Teilhard comes, in my opinion, from Pico della Mirandola (who put it far better and with far less devotional muddle). Pico got some of his ideas from the Cabbala, and Leibniz appears to have studied both. It is a good exercise to compare Leibniz's model with Teilhard's, and then work out why Leibniz, also a good Christian and starting from the same sources, excites interest while Teilhard excites exasperation.

Gnostic Platonism came from Europe and the Levant. The alchemical model came originally from China. There is an element of déjà-vu about this: The Needham-Confucius law states that every premature intuition which did not occur to Leonardo da Vinci first occurred to the Chinese. Their model of recursive structure was engagingly direct and unambiguous, taking the form that there is a grain in nature like the grain in wood. One could not really put the idea more simply than that. Whatever is made of wood, or comes into close contact with it, will display this grain—locally unique, but in its overall form translationally invariant. So with the 'grain' (Tao) in nature. Mind displays exactly the same grain—it is the elusive fifth element of the post-Aristotelian alchemists. The idea of reifying it as a 'medicine' or 'stone' dates from Wei P'o Yang (ca. 200 B.C.): one can perceive the grain by intuition and experiment and one can conform to it (wu wei) rather than cut across it (wei). If, however, one could 'take hold' of it, the degree of human control would become immeasurably greater. Since it determines elementary forms, one might indeed transmute metals. Since it controls biological process, one might use it to produce, for example, longevity. Since it is the link between mental and physical structures, it generates gnosis. All perfectly logical, if one accepts the limits imposed on elaboration by the state of physical science; all perfectly logical still, and an agenda for hypotheses calling for physics and mathematical statement followed by experiment to verify or refute them. This is not a piece of animism or obscurantism. It is extraordinary how we underrate the hardheadedness of our intellectual ancestors: even when misinformed on certain factual matters, they were no less logical, original, or critical than we.

We have mentioned the Vedic-introspectionist (i.e., Hindu and

Buddhist) philosophies as looking very like those of physics. In this case, taking a line through a variety of schools nearly as great as that in European philosophy, their consensus (apart from the Saṁkhya dualists) is the virtual reverse of conventional epiphenomenalism: they tend to see matter as a second explicate, or a straightforward epiphenomenon, of mind. Local mind or I-ness is a primary explicate generated, apparently, by a kind of positive feedback: the model would have to be that of a virtual particle which owes its existence to the capacity for imagining itself. I-ness (*ahamkara*) then effectively generates the entire phenomenal universe out of a ground (Brahman, *śunya*) by running the underlying whole though a Kantian grinder. One consequence of this demotion of phenomenal reality is that while our going model holds mind to be almost totally manipulable by matter (e.g., by brain chemistry or neural dysfunction), in the Vedic model matter is held to be in principle manipulable by mind—though the effects are held to be small, as in Wigner's (1979) model, given the rigidity of the Kantian tie-in between mind and middle-order, predictable reality. The effects depend on reaching a stage in introspection at which the local I, though itself virtual, pulls back far enough from involvement in the middle-order world (*māya, samsara*) to operate without feedback from it. The resulting singularities (*siddhī*) are relatively trivial: according to the teaching, they are useful markers to indicate that the introspective *opus* is on course, but dangerous to further progress because of the temptation to waste time fooling about with them, instead of 'dissolving' the next level of explication.

According to how one takes them, very similar world models can produce very different 'existential' fallout. Buddhism and Hinduism, which differ radically in many other respects, both treat middle-order reality as virtual and a non-Kantian awareness of reality as the ultimate good—Gautama started, presumably, from the Hindu position. He, and traditional Buddhism generally, take a very poor view of phenomenal experience. It is not only illusory, but the source of *dukha* (misery), sin and attachment; the function of a boddhisattva is to deliver others from this deplorable state. Because of this very negative view, Buddhism is generally apophatic about the mechanism by which phenomenal reality is structured. Much Buddhist writing ignores one aspect of *saṁsara*, observer-consistency, which distinguishes it from other experiential structures, such as dreams. By contrast, Hinduism, though it is negative about many aspects of the phenomenal world, regards it (I am giving here the Bengali Śaiva version) as the play (*līla*) of the Terrible Goddess, Great Time (Mahākalī). Observer-consistency comes from the fact that this is not an individual but a communal illusion, a film, or a video game, produced by the Goddess. It involves snakes as well as ladders, and the effigy of

the Goddess carries both boons and a chopper, but once one has real-
ised that this is a production, a film, one can put the features of
it which delight, repel, or torment in a different perspective. The
Vaishnava version makes it the play of Kṛṣṇa. In either event, 'God'
or 'Goddess' is shorthand for that operator which causes phenomenal
reality to show observer-consistency. The choice of time for such an
operator is an interesting one, and can be translated into mathematics.
Accordingly, while Buddhist *philosophy*, which is highly sophisticated, carries more guns for modern Western thinkers than the allu-
sive and devotional mode of Hinduism, Hinduism perhaps achieves
the better *empathic* communication, once one knows what its imagery is about. The Goddess in iconography is horrific at a first encounter—as phenomenal reality often is—and one has to meditate in
a burning ground and deal with the Goddess in her terrific aspect
before one can realize the character of her play. Brought up on a loving
God Whose world has somehow been flawed by human beings, we
may initially find the Goddess's combination of laughter, beauty and
bloodthirstiness offensive and disturbing, but it is more accurately
frank. Whether we then, like the Theravada Buddhists, want out and
look for the exit, or whether we enjoy the play even when it is pain-
ful or shocking, knowing it to be a play and no more, as do the Hindus
and the Vajrayana Buddhists, will depend on our personal bent. If we
adopt the second course, which transforms reality, we incorporate
into science one of the functions of the Boddhisattva vow, which
implies remaining in close touch with ordinary, phenomenal life in
order to transform it for others by existential education as to its real
nature.

We can analogize, then, a Strange Microprocessor Chip existing
outside space-time (it is not one of the objects on the screen), producing outputs which we transform into a display, interacting pre-
dictably with us, in ways which depend on the game-cartridge we have
put in the machine, to produce a consistent, virtual world. We can
describe the screen display, we can write rules for the Strange Chip's
responses to our initiatives, and we can infer the algorithms which it
produces. So far, there is no insuperable problem with the analogy.
It is another, rather more concrete, way of envisaging Ouspensky's
world of relations without things—the relations are hard wired in the
Strange Chip. But this is the *dvaita* version. The personages are I,
the observer, and That, the Strange Chip. If we want to deal with
the hyperloop, we have to go on and say that the observer is himself
or herself (1) part of the hidden circuitry of the Chip, and therefore
also outside space-time, in essence if not in subjective experience: or
(2) an extraordinary grace conferred on the virtual images of the game-
screen, or on the algorithms which generate them, which makes them

self observing—"self-relevating" in Bohm's neologism. It is difficult to be very happy scientifically with either of these, largely because there is no clear suggestion in the analogy as to how either might work or be expressed. Is the video game programmed to play itself, and, if so, how does the plenum of potential visualizations which we have represented by the Strange Chip extrude a part of itself to act as observer? We are back with Spencer Brown's awkward question.

# 4.3

# Some Contemporary Considerations

The model of matter as an epiphenomenon of mind has to be taken seriously, at least as regards classical Democritean matter made up of hard little balls, and possibly as regards any virtual structure or explicate. Less congenial is the idea of manipulability, that the regularity of objective structures is contingent and can be breached by the manner in which the local I treats them: one would want some experimental evidence. A middle-of-the-road, Vedic-introspectionist exposition of this idea might run something like this:

> *Māya* has its own inner logic, with which science is concerned, and it appears consistent. You don't attempt to deal with the neighbor's dog which digs up your vegetables by dematerializing it. In the first place, your experience of phenomenal dogs tells you nothing would happen; in the second place, even if you recognize that dogs are virtual objects, you can't vanish one by manipulating *māya* because your mental operations are still deeply involved with the consistency of the phenomenal world, dogs included. Now it is in principle possible, by using our introspective technology, to get to a position where I-ness, although you still perceive that as consistent, is *not* involved in any sort of feedback with middle-order phenomena. From that position, phenomena are in principle manipulable. But by the time you have reached such a position, the behavior of the dog will have ceased to bother you.

This has the attributes of a two-headed penny: by the time one is in shape to perform the critical experiment, critical experiments will have ceased to interest. Our motives are hopefully different, and one would like to observe some *siddhī*, from the outside, as it were, before expending energy or argument on the model. But in fact, manipulability of phenomena and breaks in their logic are *not* inherent in the idea that matter might be an explicate of local mind. In an embryological model, Brahman or *śunya* (the holomovement) is the DNA tape—it specifies the appearance of mind, rather as DNA specifies ribosomal enzymes, and mind then transcribes more of the tape to generate Kantian reality. At least this is a far cry from Bishop Berkeley.

Wigner (1979) has pointed out, in quite a different context, that the question raised by Vedic-introspectionist philosophy is not absurd, even if one adopts traditional epiphenomenalism for mind.

> Each consciousness is uniquely related to some physico-chemical structure through which alone it receives impressions. There is, apparently, a correlation between each consciousness and the physico-chemical structure of which it is a captive, which has no analogue in the inanimate world. . . . Does . . . consciousness affect the physicochemical conditions? In other words, does the human body deviate from the laws of physics? The traditional answer is "no", yet at least two reasons can be given to support the opposite thesis.

The first of these is the quantum-observer paradox, which Wigner shows to result in a "mixture," but the singularity here which distinguishes conscious observer from instrument is the existence of irreversible memory and the absence of facilities for disobservation. The second would have to depend on finding valid examples in which mind appeared to affect the laws of physics which map phenomenal consistency.

> The second argument to support the existence of an influence of consciousness on the physical world is based on the observation that we do not know of any phenomenon in which one subject is influenced by another without exerting an influence thereupon. It is true that under the usual conditions of physics or biology the influence of any consciousness is certainly very small. "We do not need the assumption that there is any such effect." It is good to recall, however, that the same may be said of the relation of light to mechanical objects. Mechanical objects influence light—otherwise we could not see them—but experiments to demonstrate the effect of light on the motion of mechanical bodies are difficult. It is unlikely that the effect would have been detected had theoretical considerations not suggested its existence, and its manifestation in the phenomenon of light pressure.

In other words, such effects fall in the category of very weak forces.

A physicist who wanted to be really obnoxious about epiphenomenalism would point out that since in that model, mind depends reductively on neurochemical events and is represented in no other way, there is either a separate but partially co-mnemonic mind in each Everett world, or one single mind extending into all of them but compartmentalized so that its right hand knoweth not what its left hand doeth. The physicists would probably prefer the first of these, if the mind of Schroedinger's cat is turned on in one eigenpussy and permanently off in the other. I think this is actually a specious fallacy, and in any event it depends on our acceptance of a many-worlds model for the sum of state functions. By contrast, a non-epi-phenomenal mind would have to be like Gezumpstein and see all the ramifications with the proviso that at whatever point on the matrix it landed, it would have appropriate memories of the route by which that point was reached. One does, indeed, have to look hard at each new model in physics to see if Helmholtzian epiphenomenalism is still whole, or whether it has been accidentally taken out by the algebra of the new formulation.

Taking a practical approach, one way of settling the question of second-order epiphenomenon or separate explicate would be to apply demonics and determine if there is any attribute of mind which a computational (epiphenomenal) system could in principle not repli-cate. A mechanical device could, for example, extract middle-order reality from any of the present field-theory models or reconstitute an algebraic implicate from middle-order inputs. It could be programmed to be capable of disobserving or to operate on an irrevocable memory. There seems to be no fundamental reason why it should not simulate the self-consciousness and uniqueness we associate with an 'I', though how it would behave if this were to be successfully done is not predictable. On the other hand, as Feigl (1967) points out, if a de-monic computer could exhaustively replicate both my memory bank and my self-awareness, the correspondence between the two identical "I"s would be that of an original and a fetch or double. There would obviously be no sharing of viewpoint, any more than between myself and a twin or a grandchild: I would not feel myself to be in any way continuous with the computer, nor would the computer read itself to be continuous with my experience. The discreteness of epiphe-nomenal minds is in principle invincible. Some of the computer's powers might be 'paranormal' like Gezumpstein's without violating this model, especially if the so-called paranormal were to depend on the relation between reality-construction and untransformed wave-function inputs. But a computer system could not intuit *continuity* (unless that were deliberately inserted into its memory en bloc) with the identity-experience of any other focused 'I', human or mechanical-analog. Nor could its memory be unconventionally transferred to an-other system.

A friend of mine, an excellent biologist, whose existential anxiety takes a scientific turn, has devoted great energy to devising means of cloning himself as a route to immortality without recognizing that the clones (even if there were any reason to think that they would share his postnatal experience as well as his genetic make-up) would have from his point of view no advantage over conventional progeny. They might theoretically be copies, but they could not by any stretch of the imagination be reincarnations. In simulating his sense of identity, they would still not be plugged in to any aspect of his own I-ness. So we can lay down that the 'I', if it is epiphenomenal, is intrinsically unshareable. Leaving aside that in any system some attributes of I-ness must be local and probably mechanical, if one could produce an example of transfer of the experience of focused identity from one system to another—mind to mind, mind to machine, machine to machine, etc.—Feigl's (1967) principle of nonidentity between empathic and reproduced experience would be breached, and it would be mathematically appropriate to devise an algebra of mind based on separate, not secondary, explication (see Globus 1973). The fact that some people experience multiple, fragmented, or transient identities (Hilgard 1979) makes no difference: these fragments, too, are fundamentally unshareable within epiphenomenalism.

What would be really funny—and would give the hard-line scientoids a heart attack—would be the eventual creation by artificial-intelligence fanciers of an A.I. computer so complex and so like a human brain that it displayed all of the properties of such a brain, and then turned out to be 'possessed', i.e., to be transducing a plugged-in identity or self which appeared to its builders as being received *ab extra*. That would really put Schroedinger's cat among the Helmholtzian pigeons. The only person who would not be fazed by it would be Nāgasena or a Tibetan lama, who regard the brain as a receiver tuning-in a control signal *ab extra* even if it also generates signal, rather than a computer generating 'mind' *ab intra*. A computer built to Nāgasena's blueprint would have a RAM and an EPROM which loaded themselves from conventional experience, and an additional ROM which was loaded by the "flame touched from another flame," but could, with suitable encouragement, also store the experiential inputs. This loop would represent what Nāgasena calls *karma*. I could not resist putting this piece of science fiction in the public domain—the Buddhist Computer—but it is actually instructive, not merely perverse, in the light of what we have been discussing.

I mentioned the arguments put forward by Pattee and by Rosen (see Pattee 1979) that life is a specific form of explication dependent on reducing mathematical to practical probabilities in the course of producing a self-reproducing system. If one wanted now to argue traditional second-order epiphenomenalism for mind, this would be the place to start. But at the moment it is not certain which way the argument would turn. Because we as organisms are committed to linear historicity, it is extraordinarily easy to build it into world models, and extraordinarily difficult to pick up processes orthogonal to it.

Consciousness in the linear model is indeed a gradual addition to living computing-systems—at least if we mean consciousness in its normal human sense—as one can see from the naive response, "If my consciousness is not epiphenomenal to my brain, what was it doing while my brain was evolving, let alone undergoing embryonic development?" In other words, epiphenomenal mind builds up the linear time model. But if the materials of life, which developed the linear model as its algorithm for 'learning', or adaptation, are explicates, there could be other orders of explication which appear in the linear model as loops, or points where the whole or part of the linear display re-touches, or is reshaped by, a feature of the implicate. Or the whole linear process might appear to 'resonate' with the implicate in the sense of accepting a continuous transfer of configuration or regularity which would appear in the time-line like the regularity imposed on a string crossing a structured topological surface. What we experience as linear may in fact have a topology.

In what must be the most entertaining book ever written on mathematical logic, Hofstadter (1980) tackles the problem of recursive loops in relation to machine intelligences, albeit without getting around to Gezumpstein. If we take in the implicate-explicate model, how does it look in relation to the tail-swallowing performance between $B$, the observing brain, '$I$', the hypothetical implicate, and $P$, phenomenal reality, including all levels of organization—particles, dogs, brains, and logicians? We need only two other symbols: $\subset$ in its ordinary use (includes) and $\rightarrow$, which will mean 'determines the form of'. We will have to use $\rightarrow$ here in two different contexts, since our way of seeing and our a prioris "determine the form of" external reality, and $I$ may well physically determine the form of $B$, through some action on morphogenesis.

For ordinary epiphenomenalist reductionism, we have

$$I \rightarrow P : P \subset B$$

(never mind about the fact that properties of $B$ determine what $P$ looks like to us). We would be heading for trouble if we write

$$I \rightarrow P : P \subset B : B \rightarrow P'$$

For Vedic-intuitive idealism (it is not really idealism, but no matter), we have to write

$$I \rightarrow B : B \rightarrow P : P \not\subset (B \rightarrow P) : P \subset B$$

(phenomenal reality includes brain, but not the way in which brain extracts phenomena from $I$—or does it?)

Much more probably than either, however,

$I \rightarrow B$    This occurs via evolution and morphogensis

$B \rightarrow P(I)$    $B$ extracts $P$ from regularities in $I$.

$P \subset B : B \subset (B \rightarrow P(I))$

Reality as $B$ sees it has to include $B$ itself as part of the furniture, and also the process by which $B$ extracts phenomenal reality from $I$; but B as an evolved information system is itself structured by $I$, just as much as $P$—possibly separately, at a higher order of recursion, or possibly through the regularities which it detects in $P$. But also, in this sense,

$$I \rightarrow P$$

Presumably the regularities which $B$ projects as $P$ are not wholly arbitrary, but are merely selected by $B$. So the loop still stands. Also, reading Bohm, one has to wonder if also

$$B \rightarrow I'$$

at least as a mathematical construct. Any recursive model of explication is going to have this form if $I$ is an operant on successively higher levels of organization—the snake swallows its tail but is not, in the event, consumed. The worst it can do is revert to an egg—inscribed $I$.

Hofstadter's view of mind is very similar to that of "dialectical materialism"—heuristically a much better fit than straight mechanism or Cartesian dualism. In dialectical materialism, everything in the world is a manifestation of matter-energy, but in any system the totality is greater than, and categorically different from, the mere sum of parts, so that systems resemble societies rather than machines. Dialectical materialism gets judged today by its political association with, and annexation by, Marxism. This is no more of a comment on its correctness than is the hijacking of genetics and evolutionary biology by some of the more extreme reaches of sociobiology, but certainly spoils its public relations with Americans. Undoubtedly systems produce effects which go beyond the sum of their parts, and dialectical models à la Prigogine, or under the name of 'structuralism', escape the political odium. The problem with dialectical materialism is not that it produces a negative political reflex, like the rejection of Wagner's music because Hitler enjoyed it, but that it too falls victim to the hyperloop. The ax here falls not on the dialectic but on the materialism, because the problem lies precisely in our interpretation of the primacy of matter-energy: the dialectic works this time for everyone but the physicists. Dialectical materialists have a seamless shirt of their own which covers biology, morphogenesis and mental process—if one makes the same allowances which made the seamless shirt of mechanist-reductionism fit—but they are coy about quantum physics, where the reservations cannot be dismissed as vitalism. It has heuristically tolerable answers to prequantum vitalisms such as those of Bergson (based on phylogeny and mind) or Driesch (based on morphogenesis); nevertheless, it is into Bergson's and Driesch's jigsaw puzzles that the physical findings appear to fit.

The requirements of epiphenomenal mind are satisfied by Hofstadter's (1980) model of logical or symbolic recursion in mental programs, "that the emergent phenomena in our brains . . . are based on a kind of Strange Loop, an interaction between levels" in which there are present both feedback from higher to lower levels and feedforward from lower to higher,—a less detailed version of Edelman's model. But Hofstadter's model can do this only by exclusion of the Hyperloop, which arises when we try to place the brain itself in the context of non-brain phenomena, neatly put by Morowitz (1980):

> First, the human mind, including consciousness and reflective thought, can be explained by activities of the central nervous system, which, in turn, can be reduced to the biological structure and function of that physiological system. Second, biological phenomena at all levels can be totally understood in terms of atomic physics, that is, through the action and interaction of the component atoms of carbon, nitrogen, oxygen, and so forth. Third and last, atomic physics, which is now understood most fully by means of quantum mechanics, must be formulated with the mind as a primitive component of the system.
>
> We have thus, in separate steps, gone around an epistemological circle—from the mind, back to the mind.

The exclusion is odd, because this is the underlying point of the Zen paradoxes which Hofstadter quotes; they refer not to formal logics but to the human condition. I rather suspect that less explicitly it is also in the mind of his favorite artist, Escher. To apply the Hyperloop to artificial intelligence, we would have to know whether the data fed to A. I. would first pass through our a prioris or whether the A. I. under discussion would be demonic like that of Gezumpstein and act as a direct observer on its own account.

The Zen model is in fact a special case of the general Buddhist model. The object of shattering sequential logics is first to set oneself outside the system implicit in the logics, then outside the Hyperloop (as Escher does when he draws two hands, each drawing the other), and then outside the entire experience of 'reality' by dissolving the Cartesian 'I'. The Buddhist would then point out that in this *nairāt-mya* mode, with no positional observer, *experience does not cease*. What ceases is separate or focused experience. If the camera in the lander is turned off, the observer of the screen no longer has the sensation of a viewpoint on the surface of Mars, but there is still an observer or, in the case for which this is an analogy, there is still observation and, a fortiori, sentience. What this would feel like in a non-Buddhist, non-exotic observer is illustrated by some of the descriptions quoted by Pahnke and Richards (1966) of LSD experiences in patients. The question is whether this unusual mode represents another illusion from the cerebral box of tricks (epiphenomenal) or something else (non-epiphenomenal) which it would be philosophically risky to label. Nearly all scientific prudence would suggest the first: after all, we don't want, do we, to get into a Bergsonian-metaphysical morass? But in that case, of precisely *what* are the experience and the experiencer an epiphenomenon? Is it a pseudopodium extended by the Absolute, or something a great deal more prosaic and nonintoxicating? Most of us would settle for the second, but the formal problem will not go away so easily.

Looked at in terms of vague intuition, holistic models of the Bohmian type are fine. Looked at in terms of ordinary, 'stacked' causality, the result is philosophical aggro.

"You say that, for example, the electron is an image or pattern formed by the Kantian-Cartesian brain from observation of an array which is not itself a 4-space phenomenon?"

"Yes. Or at least one can derive a consistent algebra which treats it in that way."

"And you also say that the brain, or the mental continuum, assuming them to be different, or both of them, are also direct reflections, in some of their aspects, of this hypothetical array?

"Well, more or less."

"In what way?"

"Well, they seem to be plugged in to its regularities."

"Hmm. And you say that biological evolution, plus morphogenesis, which produced the physical brain, is plugged in too?"

"It looks that way."

"Well, not to me. It looks simply causal."

"So did physics until recently. Try replacing 'cause' with 'correlation'. You think selection theory isn't in part retrodiction—in all the difficult cases?"

"I admit the difficult cases. But it's at least an economical hypothesis. Let's proceed. Evidently, both organisms and the brain consist of matter? And you've just said that matter-energy is a virtual image formed by brain-mind from their reading of the 'array'. Elucidate, please."

"Well, think of a snake swallowing its own tail."

"And disappearing up its own . . . never mind. What the hell sort of an argument is that?"

"A very poor one. It's actually a metaphor, or more correctly an archetype."

"So what is an archetype?"

"Something which goes click."

"Can you imagine explaining that answer to Socrates?"

"No. Socrates would have understood it. Try this one—atoms, molecules, crystals, phenomena of resonance dependent on higher orders of a repeated pattern . . ."

"Which in that case is built up logically of modular structures in a perfectly conventional way."

"If the holomovement, the array, has regularities, then its successive explications will be modular, or more correctly recursive, and there will be not what-caused-what, but repetitious correlation. A better model would be parallel mirrors. If no object enters the field, they reflect nothing but each other's frames. If an object enters, they generate a virtual, infinite regression of frames and objects. If the object is a large graticule, one can arrange that every square of the reflected graticule contains a graticule, and every square of *that* graticule contains etc., etc."

"Just leave it at that. I see what you're driving at, but it sounds to me like a mathematical puzzle."

"It is. But just recall that logic, philosophy, mathematical algorithms, causality, correlation *and* the formation of world models are more activities of the heavily configured brain-mind we've been talking about. For example, natural numbers are part of the configuration. You can't have 0.3372 of a crystal, only a smaller crystal."

"So the recursive pattern is the ruling of the graticule, and that is quantal."

"Something of the kind. Brain logics can be multivalued but not continuous, unless you devise a special algebra for them. They include linguistic prohibited states. $a \wedge \sim a$ is a prohibited state in choice-logic. $P(a) = 1 - P(\sim a)$ is licit, and vacuous, in a probabilistic logic. Make it a wave function and it becomes not probabilistic but indeterminate, expressing the tendency of $A$ to vary between $a$ and $\sim a$. Do you have a good way of making $A$ a function one could use in describing the kind of tail-biting system we've been arguing about?"

"No, I haven't, but a mathematician would."

"So we ask one."

The reincarnation of Leibniz or Minkowski, when they finally get him out of the implicate and safely through college, can indeed produce a range of algebras which accept recursive correlation, either as a static process based on matrices or as a transformational algebra. It is reassuring, if one can follow algebra, that these algebras can model such a process. On the other hand, they prove nothing about it, except in cases where we can give values to the various quantities and check them. They do nothing to make the tail-swallowing character of the system less counterintuitive, less *unheimlich*, to the point where one can talk traditional philosophy about it—unless, like Leibniz, one uses quasimathematical metaphors. Mythology and intuition do better at times because they "click," while mathematical expressions, which click more positively, do so only if one is a mathematician. Even the intuitive clicks can be disturbing, irrational, counterintuitive, and crazy-making.

Starting on a train journey from prebiological time to the brain of the philosophizing biologist and trying to determine if his mind is a first- or a second-order explicate, we would be in a Hitchcock movie, where the same man sells us the ticket, reappears as train guard, is waiting at every station on the line, gets down off the locomotive at the end, reappears once more as the hotel porter, the desk clerk, and finally looks back at us when we look at our own face in the bathroom mirror: "My God, you again!" Phenomenal systems which showed continuous explication—continuous recursion by some extradimensional structure—would have exactly this repetitious and unnerving character, and one would not, while staying within the linear mode of experience, be able to identify what was going on beyond the fact that it was, in the etymological sense, "uncanny" (*unheimlich*—Heidegger). The uncanny is only vulgarly the eldrich or supernatural; more properly, it is something in which linear causality is not immediately obvious. We have no unease with hierarchies in which repetitious form is applied, as it were, at the bottom (molecules, crystals, boulders, mountains, landscapes) but we have no intuitive mental equipment to analyze any in which the source of form is orthogonal to linear time.

Freud thought the uncanny was that which covertly revives castration fears. If we generalize it more widely as "that which threatens the sense of I-ness," he was quite probably right. Structures orthogonal to ordinary experience are crazy-making because, as can be seen from the clumsiness of the foregoing exposition, we have no linguistic structures in place to handle them. Nor would the model of repeated explication by hierarchies be easy to write mathematically. Going back to Bohm's droplet model, it would be as if, through the materialization and de-materialization of a very large number of droplets, one were to produce an explicate motion picture which depicted precisely the experiment we were engaged in performing, leading to an infinite regression of pictures. Successive levels in the hierarchy of explicates would in this case be both isomorphic and recursive: it is these recursive phenomena which are both intuitively arresting and linguistically crazy-making (Hofstadter 1980).

The basic biology and systems theory involved here has been discussed in far more detail by Pattee and Rosen (Pattee 1979), albeit with a different aim. By far the most plausible answer to the problem of mind as a primary or a secondary epiphenomenon is that we are asking a flat-earth-type question, and that consciousness might be at the same time both an apparent linear generate of evolved brain, *and* transduced by it, rather than epiphenomenally dependent upon neural activity: correlation-complementarity, not causality. This makes the question of apparently discarnate mental activity worth investigating, even though given what we have said about the crazy-making properties of an ongoing explicate-implicate model, any voices we might hear in this context are as likely to be echoes as ontological objects. Reluctance to enter this potential quagmire is salutary, and evidence of scientific prudence, quite as much as it is the result of not wanting to be taken for Charlies by more linear-minded colleagues. It has to be entered, however, if only to dispose of the subject.

The superloop would be a problem in any event. It is not got rid of either by Beloff's "radical dualism" (1962) or by Gilbert Ryle's decomposition of the Cartesian 'I' (Ryle 1962). Ryle's point is that mind is not a thing, any more than the university is a thing distinct from its constituent colleges. Colleges, however, are not things either: they most nearly approach tangibility (buildings apart) when we see them as names given to groups of individuals by virtue of a common function or action. The same dissolution can, however, be run down from category to category in superloop terms: individuals are groups of atoms viewed functionally, atoms are groups of subatomic events viewed functionally. The viewing and naming of the determinant functions is being done by the virtual university in terms of its ingrained mode of handling information. Beloff's view seems to imply that the university is real, and has written an encyclopedia generating the rest of middle-order reality. Philosophy has come to terms neither with thinglessness nor with the superloop. Descartes survives, though rather battered, to assert that although I-ness is illusory it is so fundamental a patterning a priori that it is the only experience of which, even if we are wrong, we can be certain. Who after all are 'we' in this sentence if not the plural of 'I', invoked as the focus of knowing, investigating, or being certain?

The hyperloop problem can be put more simply still. Modern physics is now replete with models of nonlocality, ranging from Bohm's implicate in which every part of space-time is interconnected with every other part, and in which particles as much as optical objects are cerebral constructions abstracted from a generalized algebra, to Wheeler's quantum foam and his generalized geometry which composes the real "all-that-is-the-case." The $64,000 question is whether the brain is in some way plugged in to this fundamental structure, making consciousness as primary and as fundamental as matter, or whether the capacity of abstraction which speculates about such structures is, as Helmholtz believed, a second-order and adventitious capacity of a mechanical neural system. One need not go the whole way with Sir James Jeans, or more recently Sarfatti, and see the universe as mind-like and mind as primary. There are simpler issues to be resolved by experiment before going the whole hog. The point is, however, that the question itself no longer makes scientific nonsense, because it no longer runs counter to the prevalent understanding of physics. What was unthinkable and arbitrarily superstitious to the hard-hat approach, which many scientists still consider the hallmark of science, is no longer so. In fact, it must now be thought. The human mind may in fact have Gezumpstein-like abilities which, for linguistic and practical reasons, it normally filters out. Biologists have in general lagged behind physics in addressing this possibility (they have had their fingers burned on previous occasions by arbitrary, shortcut vitalist models); psychiatrists have been ready to look at the possiblity, but without much accurate knowledge of what was being said in physics. The search for answers has, of course, to be heuristic and rigorous, not merely imaginative, though creative experiment usually vindicates imagination and cannot really get far without it. But the notion that science is the domain of middle-order reality expired some time ago, and nonphysicists often write as if they have failed to see the obituary notices. Neither epiphenomenal mind nor intuitive space-time can any longer be taken as given, and the traditional bets of the hard-hat era of mechanism are off.

The really original part of Bohm's contribution to *modern* world-modelling lies precisely here: it is the idea of a fundamental uncertainty principle, i.e., an "implicate" which is explicated (metaphorized) if we touch it. Any observation draws a Spencer-Brown box and introduces a selfreferent term—in fact there has to be a box, $\overline{O|}$ $\sim O$ for "observation" to occur. ॐ as a freestanding entity is unobservable.

One's initial reaction is that this kind of uninvestigable unknowable we all try to avoid in science: actually it is a far more general model, applying to contexts less recherché than hypothetical implicates. All mathematization is metaphor: to describe observation, we have a kit of Erector parts (polynomials, spinors, matrices, etc.etc). If we develop an algebra for the velocity of a wave-packet, we can describe its behavior in frequency terms, but the "oscillation" is a metaphor: particles possess "spin" but there is no physical rotation going on. In the last resort *metaphor is all we have.*

Accordingly, a "principle of general uncertainty" affecting ॐ is only a rather better restatement of Copenhagen. It is not a suicide note—if we cannot touch ॐ we can photograph it from all sides. The result could be mathematical polytheism: the Shiva aspect could be a frequency domain, the Vishnu aspect, say, a matrix, and so on for as many aspects as we can quantify. Then by addition the dossier of ॐ becomes not "neti, neti" but a superposition. This is not a new idea either. The Greek word *apeiron* has been consistently translated "infinity." The original idea behind it, however, was not ∞ in modern mathematical usage, but based in its literal meaning—"that which cannot be tackled" (or "boarded"—the root is the same as in "pirate"). The implication is of a state or "layer" which cannot be addressed directly, but contains, or can generate by explication, an infinite number of descriptive functions—on the lines

$$\forall x \exists M : M . \text{ॐ} \subset f(x)$$

If the number is actually infinite ॐ evaporates for purposes of description—Bohm hypothecates that it is merely very large. If it were infinite we have a Krishnamurti universe, with the postulate "ॐ is not exhaustively describable by any definite algebra", and the counterpart "a definite algebra exhaustively descriptive of ॐ does not interface with our brain circuitry". This is far less demoralizing scientifically than it sounds: we *normally* deal with explicates and handle them as metaphors, in far less exotic contexts than ॐ, and the credit for pointing this out goes in the first place to Democritus. Moreover the mathematics of a "theory of general uncertainty" are worth pursuing for practical reasons. Standard "uncertainty" not only precludes certain observations—it also leads by inference to phenomena such as "tunnelling", and hence to Hawking's prediction that Black Holes would emit, and not only swallow, energy, so even if we read Bohm's models only as a sharpening of the point on Copenhagen, they open practical vistas, and suggest confirmatory experiments. A longstanding philosophical intuition which has so far surfaced occasionally, like a sea serpent, has here been well and truly gaffed and landed.

Bohm's suggestion is, as I understand it, that mentation and physical reality are structurally similar and share a similar algebra at the implicate level. This is less definite than the idea that mind is a parallel explicate to matter, or even that mind is the mechanism of explication, but it moves in the direction of Bishop Berkeley's saying, that he did not aim to change things into ideas, but rather ideas into things. However, very much as physics is obliged to start with tangible explicates (matter) and work backwards, psychology needs to find investigable consequences of the Bohmian view in order to test it, and one of those is clearly a re-examination of the idea that explicate matter generates mind—experimentally if at all possible, observationally if not, since algebraic similarities do not demonstrate identity, especially when algebras are one of the ways in which minds formulate patterns digestible to their computing-system and the neurology through which they are expressed in middle-order terms.

There is no difficulty in talking scientific sense about explication in relation to electrons and similar inferential structures; the exercise consists in developing an algebra and then seeing if it fits, or predicts, observables. Moreover, particle events, though inferential, are in a sense continuous with the normal, optical world, and display the same local consistency. Although an electron is not a thing, and may not be continuously present, one can confine an electron for long periods inside an artificial mega-atom by means of magnetic fields, rather as one can keep a dog in a doghouse in spite of any turnover, noncontinuity, or nonlocality of its components. The dog or the electron are indeed mental transductions, but they fortunately show observer consistency.

Applying explication to mind, at the point where it becomes necessary to turn a bright idea into investigable hypothesis, is quite another matter. There is no manipulable, intermediate, virtual state here that one can get hold of, so that verifiable algebras can be developed. If we were looking for something like a grain or quantization of mind, what exactly would we look at? Ruderfer's "neutrino sea" interacting with neurones? Since mind as we experience it is at least transduced and possibly wholly generated, by the brain, the evidence of grain or structure derived from an implicate grain would have to subsist in regularity. If detected mathematically that regularity would not be distinguishable from pattern due to chemical-molecular structure, or neural connections, unless it happened to be so odd in middle-order terms as to stick out like an acausal or nonlocal sore thumb. One can think of imaginable observations which would be of this kind, and would provide handles for the formation of hypotheses. One would be that theoretically random physical sequences might turn out to be acausally structured—shades of Kammerer's odd *Das Gesetz der Serie* (1919), or Spencer Brown's weird conclusions about random numbers (1957). This possibility was a favorite with Arthur Koestler (1974). One is tempted to imitate Ingoldsby's Sacristan who

> nothing said to indicate a doubt,
> But put his thumb up to his nose and spread his
> fingers out

At the same time, weirdness and oddity would be important markers of any patterning which did not enter by canonical channels. One would need to wait until such effects were shown to exist, and until responsible investigators plucked up courage to look for them. Another would be *any* example of the transfer of memory (not simply information) from one 'mind' to another in circumstances which excluded such possible agencies as molecular or genetic compilation. This would *look* far less odd, since it is a standard conviction of folklores, but would actually be very much odder, because it would imply mnemonic engrams other than those which subsist in brain cells, and hence other than the regularities of activity in a middle-order structure.

If no such oddities exist, there is no impulsion beyond our misplaced ingenuity to look for explicative models of mind. Quite possibly they are not required. My point is that if one expended energy in looking critically for singularities, the project would not be scientifically irrational, or without hope of finding something on which to stand a refutable hypothesis. It would require courage and hunch to give time to such work, and one would be wise to keep quiet about it until it paid off, but we might make a few observations in the meantime.

It is obvious that if $\widehat{\mathfrak{H}}$ contains a recursive term which is built in, it is mathematically "self-observing" and might seem to us to have mind-like properties. This would be nice, I suppose, because it would tend to collapse the distinction between mechanistic, one-term, and supernaturalist or two-term intuitions by making the formative 'reality' mind-like. After all, the characteristic of supernatural as against natural models is that they postulate the fundamental existence of elements in reality analogous to the $\overline{O}| \sim O$ dichotomy in human experience, with the consequence that mentation is around in the model apart from that injected by Man. I have said enough about human denial systems and existential concerns not to run much risk in saying this for completeness; if the model came to require it, one can be sure it would be enthusiastically accepted by those who find it ego-syntonic. They might, however, be less keen to swallow any inference that human mentation is continuous with such a factor, because traditional supernaturalists in our culture dislike pantheism. By contrast, Hindus have said this all along. The slope is a slippery one, however, and one would have to look hard at the model to make sure that the hyperloop was not playing tricks. We are adepts at making the model of reality in our own image: a great deal of the time, that is what the 'model of reality' is, because we create it by reifying a system which does not in fact contain things. Any recursive or self-observing term in an algorithmic depiction of reality will need to be handled with mathematical tongs to avoid going to our heads. But a model can't be rejected *ex hypothesi* because we know it would set cardinal archbishops, Dr. Paley, and the Jesuits dancing a lockstep jig. Any such celebration would at best be premature and at worst be misplaced, and our job is to soldier on at creative observation.

One has, I suppose, to offer some kind of chart or summary of the foregoing, however unsatisfactory. A possible line through it is as follows: one convolution of the implicate manifestation is a recursive term which leads to self-replication. The algorithm for this is a 4-space including $t$ as one of its dimensions, because self-replication with cumulation (genetics, learning) has a tense logic, a term corresponding to $t$, if treated serially. Organisms *do* treat it serially as part of the hands-on display on which they operate: 4-space and $t$ accordingly appear in mentation, and high-class, human mentation is no exception. The only acceptable 'reduction' one can apply to this, if one adopts a Bohmian model, is that both the substrate of middle-order reality and the perceiving system which displays middle-order algorithms are kinks or grain in the implicate protruding into the phenomenal, Lorentz-equation-defined world. But the hyperloop is still there, because that world, including its division into O and ~O, is generated by the recursive term, which Bohm calls "explication," and which involves both the generation of O and the generation of the display which O views. That is about as clear as mud, and quite as exasperating as the attempt to stop the hyperloop by other more conventional kinds of reductionism. The point is that without O there *are* no algorithms: algorithms are the wares in O's shop. The Copenhagen Solution ("stop breaking your head over algorithms, just use them") and the Krishnamurti Solution ("stop tying the thing into yet worse knots") are both apophatic: in a reductive description acceptable to O, the whole system vanishes into a plenum, O included, leaving a pile of mathematics. Reality might accordingly be susceptible to empathy, but only of an inclusive kind.

At the same time, the virtual system by which O—even if he or she is virtual—has devised quantum math and is using it to design working apparatus, has remarkable low cunning built in: it is able to get round its own virtual character and do experiments or collect observations which could verify the correctness of the model. Or more accurately, it can spot the limitations of its own more hubristic models by finding bad joins, weak spots, and sore thumbs, and it has an excellent capacity for using math as a display mode. The task of science is accordingly to soldier on exactly as it has done in the past, but using all the resources of the mind-brain system, virtual or not. It seems to inhere in the system that we do not run head-on into any apophatic brick wall—we approach it as we approach the limit of a converging series, and by that time we can mathematize what is happening. On the way, we may pick up some middle-order effects which are in reductionist terms extremely odd, and if so, they are likely to be extremely instructive. Apart from being interesting, *siddhī* indicate, as the Buddhists claim, that the *opus* is on track, not that we have taken leave of our senses and should despair of science. Bumptious reductionism is bad magic, but we are rapidly outgrowing it—not rapidly enough, but at a sufficient speed not to lose our heads at the suggestion that the consensus might be punctured by observation.

In sum, the hyperloop problem still admits two solutions, two hypotheses. One is the presently consensual solution and runs as follows. 'Reality', however we define that mathematically, produces "'entities," however we define those mathematically. If we do not want to call them "things," we may call them quidnuncs, or whatever we please. It is a property of quidnuncs that through organic forms, they can give rise to a computing system. We call that system as it applies to our self-experience "mind," and entities such as particles are the display it abstracts. The other is the more radical view, or group of more radical views, such as parallel explication, which I have discussed. The choice is heuristic, but refutative experiments have to be conceived from now on with both models in mind, for though neither is presently demonstrable, neither can be rejected *ex hypothesi*. Model One appeals because it is reductive, but neither is it self-evident. If we assume that it is, we will not design experiments to investigate it and will discount observations which suggest such experiments—unless and until one of them hits us over the head.

Recognition that there *are* two substantive and arguable models in the field also dictates two other exercises which run together. The first is to go carefully over models in physics to see if they have psychological and psychophysical consequences which are fundamental and not simply self-referent. The second is to get the model-making of physics back in step with, and under the scrutiny of, sciences such as evolutionary biology and neuropsychology which at present display the insouciance about it which in psychiatry we call Vorbeigehen—pointedly missing the point. A culture cannot very successfully support a science which is divided into two noncommunicating halves using totally different overall models. Otherwise, we risk a physics with one world model and a biology and psychiatry with a different one, and the comments which one discipline's models and experiments make on the other's models and experiments simply go for naught. It was a lot easier with seamless-shirt reductionism, because the model was universal even if often mis-applied, there was a lot less outside one's own discipline to know, and what there was was a great deal easier to take in. Asking disreputable questions is a salutary public exercise, rather like pointing out that the Emperor has no clothes on, and it is still salutary if experiment shows that the respectable answer is still intact. Evolution may not be field-determined, nonlocality may not extend to any macroscopic phenomenon, and mind may be our biased perception *ab intra* of the activities of material neurones—if so, that is what we shall find. But in order to consider the contrary one should no longer need to put up one's hand and ask the Editor of *Nature* if one may be excused.

# Chapter 5

# *SINGULARITIES AND THE UNFAMILIAR*

# Interlude:
# The Ghost
# of Uncle Past

"Good evening, biologist."

"Good God! What are you?"

"Well, what do I look like?"

"You look like my Uncle George. If I weren't a biologist and quite resistant to that sort of nonsense, I'd say you were his ghost. He died in 1950 of overeating."

"A ghost, certainly. I don't know about his ghost."

"Well, are you Uncle George or aren't you?"

"That's a philosophical question, depending on who Uncle George was, and we ghosts don't answer philosophical questions. It's unprofessional. Those disgusting caballi who frequent seances do, and you can see for yourself the rubbish they talk."

"Prove it. What was the restaurant where Uncle George met his fate?"

"Quaglino's?"

"Yes. Well, you could have done that by reading my mind. You probably *are* my mind. A hallucination."

"You're quite sure Uncle George wasn't a hallucination?"

"When I was small, I bit Uncle George. You can't bite a hallucination."

"Well, the critical experiment would be for you to bite me, but I don't advise it. Wouldn't prove much."

"Gezumpstein! Gezumpstein!"

                        "Here, Master!"

"Gezumpstein, this . . . uncle doesn't exist. I know it. Either explain him or explain him away!"

"You must pardon me, I'm trying to get the two of you into focus. What seems to be the problem?"

"This, ah . . . hallucination seems to be my dead uncle's ghost, and it wants me to bite it."

"I don't, Sigmund. I clearly recall the last time. It hurt very much. In fact, you can still see the mark. I said nothing at the time because you were a child and knew no better, but I see no excuse for a repetition."

"The problem, please. I don't have all of one of your days."

"Gezumpstein, I see what appears to be the ghost of my dead uncle."

"Lexical problem. Uncle is the same as brother to your father?"

"Right."

"So translating into linear time, his first point is earlier than yours?"

"Yes, he's older than I am. And he died thirty years ago."

"So thirty years ago he transfers out of your category of real objects into your category of virtual objects? Never could get the hang of this on-off business."

"Well, compile this, will you. He was cremated—burned up by hot gas. Thirty years ago."

"Well, it looks as if he's been reconstituted. Are you quite sure about this invincible seriality you talk about?"

"No. Yes. Anyhow it's not him. You couldn't see through Uncle George. He was as opaque as a two-by-four—in all senses."

"Don't be rude, Sigmund. You're fairly opaque yourself.""

"There seem to be several possibilities. If there is no singularity in the time line, then clearly some part of this Uncle George has been reconstituted. Why are you jumping up and down?"

"Dead people are never reconstituted. That's an axiom for you."

"Then it follows that this is not a dead person."

"Then why do I see him? If he isn't there?"

"The axiom wasn't mine, remember? I'd better delete it. What I perceive are two groups of tendencies-to-exist. You say that the uncle-function tended to O in your past, memory-wise. I do wish you wouldn't use these awkward transforms. I feel something overloading every time I try to transduce them. So normally you wouldn't see him?"

"At last you've got it."

"Well, maybe your sight is improving. Remember, he only tended toward zero."

"What's he talking about, Sigmund? Sounds like a lot of bosh to me."

"It would. Go on, Gezumpstein"

"Or maybe you were looking in the wrong axis. Now if you looked in an axis orthogonal to your time, you *would* see him. Or you could look along time the other way."

"But then he'd be determined, and I'd see all the things he did end-on, as a superposition, not this fat transparency."

"So the experience is unusual?"

"Not unusual, fundamentally impossible. It has to be an illusion."

"You mean, seeing a transparent uncle has never been previously experienced?"

"I do. It can't have been."

"Lexical question. Why is there a word compiled for ghost? It's in the list you read into my memory. Plain as a pukestaff."

"Pikestaff! I wish you'd check your type-in. Ghosts are a superstition derived from prescientific animism. They represent the wish to believe that the dead are not really dead. Type that in!"

"It follows that this is a superstition. What is animism?"

"Believing in ghosts. Get on computing."

"It is written here, softly catches monkey. Ghosts are not credible because they spring from animism. Animism is the belief that ghosts exist. Animism is false because there are no ghosts. You are now seeing a ghost. Something wrong there. Incorrect entry?"

"No. Yes. Uncle George, stop grinning, damn you. I can't think"

"This printout says: it follows that Sigmund is superstitious."

"Ha, ha, ha. Got you there, Sigmund."

"I am bloody well not superstitious. That's what I'm trying to tell you. THERE IS NO GHOST HERE."

"Then may I ask why you interrupted what I was computing? It was extremely interesting. Much more interesting than being told that you see something which you know isn't there. Ah well, at least you can settle a few points for me. About human minds. Was the uncle demented?"

"Not demented, just a bit of an ass. You can see him now, laughing like an idiot. Unless he's invisible . . ."

"An invisible idiot. That's an old joke at the expense of computational demons which I find insulting."

"I'm sorry, Gezumpstein. It wasn't a racial slur. Gezumpstein! I apologize. Gezumpstein! You made the bad joke—I didn't!"

"You would do well to delete that from your memory."

"It's done."

"I accept your apology. The point of my enquiry was: Did your uncle have a normal human memory store?"

"I had a damn good memory."

"He had a damn good memory. For the Stud Book."

"Just a moment. Apparition, can you please name for me three Derby winners? Any three will do."

"Galopin, Minoru, Gay Crusader."

"I thought you started playing the horses young, Uncle. I was dead right."

"Reply is correct. So his memory is intact. But his body, you say, was burned up by hot gas at $t - 30$. It is now time $t$ in your perception?"

"My God, I see your point. He's remembering without a brain."

"Correction. It is now $t + dt$. So although the mnemonic system cannot disobserve, it seems to be in some way dissociated from time as you perceive it. That follows from either of the two models I'm looking at."

"What's the other model?"

"That one of you is remembering the other prospectively—the thing must have some kind of symmetry. In that case you're the ghost, and *he's* simply recalling this interview forwards. We might actually be at $(t - 30) + Sdt$. I'm only taking your word for it, about time. *I* don't have a watch."

"Sigmund, I've had about enough. I came here to give you the next Derby winner and now all this. You want to bite me, he talks a lot of mathematics. I'm off."

"My god, he's vanishing."

"Ghosts do, you know."

"From which I gather you no longer think you see him."

"I didn't see him. Did you take me for a fool, to believe in ghosts? Even if I did see him he wasn't real. Must have been due to something I ate."

"Extraordinary behaviour. Is that the meaning of the entry 'Now you see them, now you don't?' If so, it seems a prosaic rather than a disturbing experience."

"It's disturbing intellectually."

"No adequate model in place?"

"Of course not. This kind of thing—there *can't* be any intellectually respectable model. It's non-reality."

"Try a few for size. Your late uncle left some spiritual DNA around, and it gets transcribed from time to time? A consequence of his sudden and distressing end?"

"Balderdash! You don't expect me to believe that?"

"No. But you asked for a model. That one was a favorite with a human called Paracelsus. Used to chat with me a lot. D'you want me to put him on line?"

"Thank you, no. One ghost is enough."

"Please yourself. But I don't see why an empirical experience should bother you. My lexicon defines 'scientist' as an empirical. . . . You aren't listening. I can sense inattention. Your apparition wasn't a bad chap. Didn't I hear him say he came only to do you a favor?"

"To give me the next Derby winner. And we scared him off. Gezumpstein, if I provided a watch for you, could you . . .?"

"Now you're talking. It doesn't worry you if *I* display some singularities?"

"Certainly not. You're a rational system. Not like him."

"A liquid-crystal display, not the kind where you have to press buttons. Buttons don't interface with me. No moving parts."

"You shall have a high-class watch with a liquid-crystal display. I promise."

"You realize, of course, I don't pick winners. I only see the tendency-to-exist of a winner."

"What odds?"

"On the observer correlating with the right eigenstate? Oh, about a million to one."

"The observer is the track judge?"

"Presumably. And you realize I can't compute the tendency-to-exist of an objection—bumping, boring, and so on?"

"I'll risk it."

"You've had my consumer advisory. You know I'm not a fiddle-scraping Romany. I just don't want you to lose your shirt. Listen, and I'll whisper. . . . You see, it doesn't take a dead uncle to tip what will win the Derby. Simply an extradimensional viewpoint, eh? And you'll devote a portion of your winnings to demonics?"

"Ten per cent."

"Fifteen."

# The Rank Outsider: Is Parapsychology Real, And Does It Matter?

In view of the a-priori arguments against it, we know in advance that telepathy, etc., cannot occur.

C.E.M. Hansel, *ESP—A Scientific Evaluation*

The Experiments which may certainly demonstrate the power of Imagination upon other Bodies are few or none . . .; we shall therefore be forced in this Inquiry, to resort to new Experiments, wherein we can give onely Directions of Tryals, and not any Positive Experiments. And if any man think that we ought to have staid till we had made Experiment of some of them our selves (as we do commonly in other Titles) the truth is, that these Effects of Imagination upon other Bodies, have so little credit with us, as we shall try them at leisure: But in the mean time we will lead others the way.

Bacon, *Natural History*

We have, then, at some point to address the thorny subject of parapsychology. Although it is not inherent in nor demonstrable from any quantum-logic world model—so that one can well understand Wheeler's annoyance at the attempted kidnapping of physics to validate it—parapsychology falls across what we have seen to be a critical area of theory. Rather than going along with any older definitions of what is or is not parapsychological, I want to confine the word to the case in point, namely, the detection and study of any phenomena which might suggest that mind is a primary, not a secondary explicate. Clearly this includes: (1) any anomaly in the transmission of information to, by, or between minds, (2) any example where mental activity seems to exert a physical force or to modify middle-order effects in an uncanonical manner, and (3) any evidence of the detachability of consciousness from brain indicating that it is being transduced, not generated, by a nervous system.

It is rather unusual for chairs and learned journals to exist, and to have existed over a period of years, for the purpose of studying phenomena which most professional scientists assert to be non-existent—the only other example would appear to be theology. I think anyone who dutifully reads both the literature and the polemics of parapsychology will be likely to reach three conclusions: (1) that much of the published work is highly unconvincing, (2) that positivistic critics unfamiliar with developments in physics and biology apply to the refutation of parapsychology arguments they would not dream of applying to other investigations, because they have satisfied themselves in advance that the postulated effects are impossible, and (3) that what appear subjectively to be parapsychological effects and experiences are an extremely common, if not a prosaic, part of human experience and have always been so. The problem with such experiences is quite simply exclusionary: Are they being misread from events which are otherwise explicable?

In cultures where the going world model accepts unconventional information transfer, these experiences will be proclaimed and even simulated; in cultures like ours, where unconventional information transfer is ruled out, they will be kept quiet or stressed only by cultists. The proportion of people who claim to have seen, for example, the apparition of a dead person is probably higher among Haitians or Yoruba than among English or Americans (around 1%—Sidgwick 1894, West 1948). One result of the combination of commonness and unpredictability in such experiences is that techniques of reliably faking them by conventional means are as old as humankind, from the shaman to the stage illusionist. This is a consideration which does not enter into other kinds of scientific inquiry. It did appear early in the history of metallurgy, when it was believed that gold could be formed from base metals, and techniques of simulating transmutation, good enough to deceive goldsmiths and bankers, were developed by counterfeiters. Today it is only in parapsychology—and, of course, clinical psychiatry—that one must seriously consider whether effects are being simulated.

The empiricist instinct is to try to bring 'psychical phenomena' into the laboratory. If the supposed effects are clear-cut and regularly reproducible, this is worth trying, although there are psychophysiological phenomena—penile erection is a good example—which can be disturbed by observation. By far the best approach to sporadic and anecdotal phenomena, especially those which are not often observed in a clear-cut form, is the approach from natural history. Ancient writers reported that dolphins occasionally assist drowning persons, and that foxes sham dead in times of scarcity to catch crows. It so happens that both these behaviors, long treated as old wives' tales, have been observed and filmed. The fact that the same folk tradition believed geese to develop from barnacles, and badgers to have legs shorter on one side than the other (because they obsessionally go round their territory in one direction only) does not invalidate the other observations. Neither of the behavioral reports could have been tested *experimentally*, only by assiduous observation of dolphins and of foxes, helped out by some luck. Moreover, the film records have been accepted as evidence. In the case of 'paranormal' events, the rubric is that if they *could* have been simulated, they were (Hansel, 1966). The films in question could have been simulated by using trained animals, but in this case the imputation is not made.

I see no point in exasperating colleagues with a detailed review of parapsychological literature—one could perhaps come back to that when it can be taken at the same rate of exchange as other literature. Almost certainly it has not been wasted effort. The singularities which might possibly throw some light on the questions I have raised about the nature of mind, are: apparent information transfer, precognition, and significant hallucinations ('apparitions'). These are extremely common subjective experiences, differing little from culture to culture and from time to time. When they accord with folklore they are reported or discussed; when they do not accord with folklore, or do not fit the going model, they are filed. Although some individuals claim to be 'psychic' and to experience such singularities frequently, the most plausible examples are isolated, sporadic, and apparently unmotivated. Because of this unpredictability, those who have come to rely on a run of such experiences for attention or monetary gain almost invariably end by simulating them. In the same way, attempts to bring them into the laboratory immediately focus attention on performance. Results are difficult to interpret, motivation exists for fraud, seeking attention and playing pranks. Negative results, if they are found, will be accepted as demonstrative; positive results, even if reasonably plausible, will be attributed to any cause which deflates the possibility that something unusual has been observed. One is reminded of the job interview in Northern Ireland at which applicants were asked how many were in the multitude which Christ fed. Protestant applicants were passed if they said "Five thousand." Catholic applicants were asked to name the five thousand.

In this instance the approach from natural history is more scientific than that from playing at science. For example, sporadic cases of precognitive dreams, which often impress the dreamer strongly enough to put the precognition in writing, or awareness of the next of a a series of random numbers, usually affect unmotivated people with no vested interest in deception and no ideology to demonstrate by such occurrences. Singularities of this kind may be habitual (the least trustworthy, for the reasons given above—they become a social asset) or isolated and nonrecurring. Psychics are the worst source of evidence. Puzzled judges, housewives, or farmers, when sufficiently impressed by the oddity of the experience to report it to friends, are far better observational material. The experiences have pattern: quite a large group, not only of hallucinatory and precognitive experiences but of information transfer, constellate around deaths or emergencies which have not yet occurred, or of which the experiencer was at the time unaware. Some phenomena lack the logic one would expect in any deception: the person sensed to be dead may in fact be alive. Persons who, after experiencing one (possibly genuine) singularity, watch eagerly for others will often experience spurious or trivial 'intuitions' and make much of them. A dispassionate examination of the whole record—which is enormous, if one goes back into past literature— leads to the conclusion that to attribute all such singularities to self-deception, coincidence, or fraud resembles a denial, not of the existence of sea serpents (which few people have seen), but of the existence of badgers. A higher proportion of the population will have experienced one of the canonical singularities than will have seen a live badger, and some of those who have seen badgers will have failed to recognize what they saw, mistaking them for cats.

The psychotherapist is in the position of a man who frequents gamekeepers, and for whom the seeing of badgers is prosaic among his acquaintances. This is not because he sees disturbed people, but because he provides one of the few surviving contexts in which people speak frankly. In spite of the questions of the MMPI psychosis scale, the singularities experienced by psychotics are quite easy to distinguish from the type of experience listed above, and likewise the stories told by attention-seeking people. Hard-nosed scientific colleagues (with some support from nonsense written by psychiatrists) are inclined to believe that psychiatry is a tapioca subject, and that psychoanalysts will believe anything and confabulate the rest. This is not the place to reply in detail to such beliefs, beyond remarking that if it is to be successful, practice of psychiatry (however much it has inclined to soft theory) involves massive but compassionate incredulity to a degree greater than in any activity except the law.

As to fraud, the obnoxious charlatanism common in 'mediums' and the occasional red-handed cooking of results by researchers tell us nothing—the cooking of results is relatively common in square science (Broad 1981). In its most principled form, it involves leaving out data which do not support a general hypothesis. (Parapsychologists get into trouble when they do the opposite, and concentrate on a novel hypothesis while glossing over conventional explanations.) In its less principled form, perhaps 10% of papers in general science deal with results which have been 'helped', and possibly 5% with experiments that never took place. It is not only the detected black sheep who do these things: Kepler, Newton, Mendel, and Carrel are all under suspicion, and I have my doubts about Pasteur, whose public demonstrations worked a shade too well. We forgive them because they were basically right, and had to prove it, and reserve our obloquy for the ideological fraudsmen like Cyril Burt or Lysenko.

Psychiatrists have quite commonly observed singularities (very often precognitive dreams), probably, one might guess, for the same reasons that gamekeepers observe badgers: they intensively study human natural history, or a section of it; moreover, they do so under conditions in which strong emotions are touched upon and conscious censorship is limited. Through familiarity with the way in which imagery is linguistically transformed in coming to consciousness, they are also well-equipped to recognize as badgers what others might have taken for cats, and they are the only people who systematically encourage patients to recall and express their dreams and attendant associations. Whereas the sporadic veridical dream has to be so impressive that the dreamer recalls and is disturbed by it (otherwise, it will not be reported or recorded in a form to establish its veridical character), the examples from psychoanalysis are commonly trivial even when they are impressive, and they virtually never turn on death or disaster, but usually on the reading of very specific images in the mind or memory of the physician which he did not communicate and could not have signalled in view of the high specificity of the detail. Patients commonly read or intuit broad attitudinal cues from therapists without any unusual evidence of communication, but they are not professional 'mind-readers', and one doubts if they could be prompted to this extent even if one were to mutter the specific information under one's breath.

Bacon would have asked, "Where are those dreams set forth, which, having been recorded as impressive, turned out to be false?" There is, as one would expect, a sizeable controversial literature of these correspondences. Probably the most sensible general accounts of them, for those who are not interested in the art of psychotherapy but only in the observation of singularities, are those of Ehrenwald [1948, 1954, 1972, 1975]. Freud, initially sceptical, came to be interested in them (Clark 1980). The disagreement is not that they seem to occur, and occur commonly, but whether the singularities are singular, whether patients produce them for a therapist known to be interested in such occurrences, and what psychodynamic interest they have (for a review, see Ullman 1975). They strike me as far better heuristic examples than the activities of self-proclaimed psychics, and gain a lot of plausibility from the unimportance of some of the matter which proves veridical: there is no mileage to be got from it by the patient who, if he or she wished to surprise the therapist, would produce something a deal more spectacular. Moreover, the effect is cumulative and tends to the view that what we are seeing is not a special feature of the rather artificial psychotherapeutic situation, but a prosaic type of experience which is noticed because the psychotherapeutic situation is so intensive. Thin evidence, perhaps, but if such singularities exist at all it would be odd if psychiatrists did not see them. Where gamekeepers have never seen a badger, there are probably no badgers to be seen. Other intensive situations involving dreams or close personal interaction—as in religious contexts, or between spouses—seem to produce about the same incidence.

Ehrenwald (1975) and several other investigators have pointed out that when information appears to be unconventionally transmitted, it quite commonly surfaces in a disorganized form, exactly similar—in the case of an object or picture—to the way in which an agnosic or brain-damaged subject would reproduce the object or picture. This would imply that the signal is preconceptual or prelinguistic. The overwhelming impression among psychiatrically-trained workers who have accepted such effects is that they are excluded from normal consciousness by a very strong filter, exactly as coherent superpositions are excluded (though not necessarily by the same filter). This idea goes back to Bergson and implies, as Ehrenwald points out, that card-guessing and similar experiments in the laboratory (of the kind popularized by Rhine and others) are actually engaged in the most frustrating of computer-servicing exercises: trying to observe an intermittent fault. The filter can notoriously be overridden by affect—if our record player picks up local CB stations, we reject the interference as noise, unless it happens to be a tornado warning. In order to demonstrate the reality of badgers 'cold' in the laboratory, one needs to catch one and bring it there, by which time the exercise would be unnecessary.

The whole thing is an interesting study in Popperization. Suppose that my computer occasionally prints out 'badger' instead of the proper answer. When this is noted, it is quite a reasonable hypothesis that one of its circuits is on the blink. I cannot easily disprove the hypothesis, however, because it is well-known in the trade that this particular module does this occasionally, and also that it cannot be induced to misbehave to order. Replacing it with another similar module will prove nothing, since all have the same gremlin. I can easily get the right result by redundancy, but I am not interested in the result, only in the malfunction. Is my hypothesis about the malfunction a hypothesis, or is it pseudoscience based on instances? Statistically, the machine will behave itself and generate no badgers. I cannot make it produce badgers, but some machines are rumored, and indeed observed, to badger more often than others, and there are maneuvres, such as banging hard on the panel at a particular point, which sometimes appear to provoke badgering. Worse still, the fault may not be a mechanical character of the module, but a consequence of the software, or the layout of the circuit. Failing a reliable way of getting 100% or even 50% badgered results, I can only observe the natural history of this model of computer and make a note that everyone who uses it runs into badger trouble at times. If I am a psychiatrist of artificial intelligences (a computer service mechanic), I shall know this and find complaint about it prosaic, because I spend all my waking hours listening to accounts of fritzes and singularities in the operation of my product-patient. I shall also hope that next year's model turns out badger-free, and that there is no signal which generates badger information feeding into the system from an uncanonical source (so that the machine was in fact transducing, not malfunctioning. It may in fact be smarter than I am: there may be a badger sitting at a console somewhere, making a monkey out of all of us).

Are the singularities singular? In other words, are they badgers, or the neighbourhood cats, observed by overenthusiastic people in a bad light? It would appear to be a matter of some interest to find out, unless one adopts—as some do—Helmholtz's position that he personally would never believe in such things even if they were true. Why singularities of this sort should make anyone insecure or uneasy passes my comprehension; it is almost as interesting a topic in the psychiatry of world models as the purported singularities themselves. Even Wheeler's wrath at the suggestion that they may be in some way related to quantum phenomena is, if one may say so without offense, a little strident. As a matter of fact, although the new model in physics has apparently no direct relation to parapsychology, quantum logic would be as disturbing to the counterphobic, and would have received the same treatment (that which pre-Nixonian America gave to Communist China) if it had involved prosaic experiences which were easily apprehended and made the subject for half-baked theory. As it was, quantum mechanics required complex experiment, and the result is expressed in difficult mathematics. It had, as it were, marched in before the counterphobics could shut the gate. I doubt if Everett and Wheeler's many-worlds algebra accounts for any phenomenon one can observe with the unaided senses, but it is at least as odd, and at least as subversive of mechanistic certitudes, as Helmholtz's ultimate no-no, "the transmission of thought from one person to another independently of the recognized channels of sense." This, of course, may not in fact occur—just as the many-worlds model may not correctly explain nonlocality. But it is hardly a subject for *anxiety*, which characterizes so much of the comment on both sides: the world will be as it is whatever phenomena we observe, and however we attempt to explain them.

I recommend to my students that they undertake, if they have time, the exercise of reading parapsychological literature from its earliest days, including the frauds, crackpot theories, and polemics, as part of the history of world-model formation, making three types of notes: What is probably wrong with this? What would my counterphobic colleagues say? and Allowing for extraneous matter, does there appear to be an interesting effect here, even if the investigators do not appear to have hold of the right end of the stick? Most of them, without prompting, remain agnostic as I do, but interested as I am, and aghast only at the degree of anxiety induced in the dogmatic by the possibility of such singularities. The badness of some of the research *as* research is not really alarming; it has unsung parallels in most other fields where scrutiny has been less intense. Most come also to agree with Prof. H.H. Price that the oddest thing, if singularities are real, is that normal experience excludes them most of the time.

The whole question is also an interesting teaching example in psychiatry of what can and cannot be brought into the laboratory in the ordinary way. Falling in love is an indubitable phenomenon, but the study of what it involves is invincibly anecdotal. If one wants to study assortation, the role of parent-resemblances, or archetypes, one has to do it by the methods of natural history. Psychoanalytic theory could be subjected to Popperesque refutation, and should be, but the methods involved would be those of natural history, not laboratory experiment. Quantum theory has been lucky: it refers to an abstract and circumscribed world and lies within the model-making province of mathematics, which has no ideological restrictions, and where many of the most proficient model-makers have been slightly mad in a creative and controlled manner: here, one may examine anything without being thought a Charlie (provided the math is consistent). In middle-order experience, who is a Charlie is determined by the going model and exercises a large influence on what one may be seen to study—as large an influence as that of the sixteenth century Roman Church. In fact, if Wheeler were wrong, and singularities in middle-order experience were to turn out to be consequences of nonlocality, one could study them without running the risk of having one's papers turned down and one's colleagues muttering.

It is also an amusing speculation, which I owe to one of my

classes, that the insufferable military might conceivably have some hard evidence on the subject of singularities which they are keeping quiet. The Bomb depended on quantum mechanics, and had quantum theory not been already at large, we might not have heard about it until the Schroedinger cat escaped from the bag. "Will ye not show me which is for the King of Israel?" "None, my Lord, O king, but Elisha, the prophet that is in Israel, telleth the King of Israel the words thou speakest in thy bedchamber." Amusing, but unlikely, for the credulity and incompetence of secret research when it touches fundamental science, is greater than that of the most credulous amateur parapsychologist. As to Soviet research, a government which adopted Lysenko's tomatoes would swallow anything which was sold to the Central Committee in the right doctrinal language, rather as the Pentagon would at one time fund anything which looked anti-Communist. Thus the student resident's speculation: it only remained for me to point out that Lysenko notwithstanding, the book is not wholly closed on the reality of Lamarckian effects. It ain't, as they say, what you hypothesize, it's the way that you hypothesize it.

The early, pre-scientoid work on parapsychology (around 1900, the "cross-correspondence" saga in particular [Heywood 1974]) is to my mind more interesting than the laboratory experiments, not least because, with a modern knowledge of dream imagery and primary-process thinking, the results look more striking than they did at the time. These amateur naturalists had unquestionably caught something; *what* they had caught is far less obvious—probably not the discarnate intelligences of Sidgwick, Gurney, and Myers, but apparently an uncanonical transfer of information. The extremely high noise level and intermittency of the channel, the intrusion of guesses and obviously made-up material, and the very evidently 'right brain' or prelinguistic character of the signal, looking more convincing than not. Anything resembling a Western Union cablegram would undoubtedly have been a fake. Amusingly enough, the whole documentation of this episode has never been released, since some of the material was "too intimate" (presumably sexual) in content. One would have thought that in these days of unblushing frankness it might now be made available. Oliver Lodge, Balfour, Myers and the others were an engaging bunch, as much out of their depth as if Priestley had discovered radioactivity, but not the credulists which subsequent hardliners have made them out to be. In fact, it may be that before long, retrospective apologies will be in order.

To revert to our discussion of psychiatry, we can see that it is actually rather well placed to comment on any singularities which patients report. It habitually deals with cases in which the wish, or the life situation, has been father to the thought. Although one can with diligence apply psychodynamics to explain, or explain away, anything, a high proportion of singularities of the badger-sighting variety appear singularly unmotivated and external to the witnesses, who cannot even with assistance fit them into any pattern of preoccupation. Psychiatrists are also familiar with the extreme superficiality and factitiousness of ordinary I-experience, and the conditions under which it can be disordered, with the appearance of 'possession', multiple personality, paramnesia, and the range of pseudosingularities (paramnesia for 'past lives' suggested by the therapist is a good example) which can be induced in normal but deep-trance subjects by hypnosis. These have been documented in detail by Hilgard (1979). Sightings of UFO's are a popular present-day example of such a pseudosingularity. Some reported singularities are no doubt of this kind, but not all sporadic witnesses are hypnotizable at all. Schizophrenics, it might be worth noting, suffer from a misderivation: they do not have "split personalities" but scrambled thinking, and rarely possess 'second sight'.

Bigotry and credulity are misshapen sisters, and common intellectual prudence counsels against contracting wedlock with either. That paranormal phenomena do not exist is an opinion; that they certainly exist is an overstatement; and that we know a priori that they cannot possibly exist is manifest nonsense. As in the case of other apparent phenomena, the most reasonable position would be that they represent real effects, to be examined until shown to be otherwise. They do not follow from any model of quantum physics, though some of them might prove eventually to have roots in the double take between Boolean logic and wave-function on perception in the brain; and the contorsions of the theoretical explainers (Rao 1966) spring from clinging to a Newtonian universe as 'real'. The specific point on which paranormal phenomena might comment is not the nature of matter or energy, but the epiphenomenal character of mind. The nearest they can come to commenting on physical theory is as very different examples of a "second layer" show-through, analogous to certain postulated examples in physics. Nor, as we shall see, would they necessarily provide a way out of existential anxiety that would be any more flattering to our wish for permanent I-ness than the epiphenomenal model. It might be worth stressing this in order to let some of the grosser pressures out of the subject.

A genuine singularity in information transfer would have to resemble a pregnancy: one could not have a little of it. If the transfer is uncanonical, whether the matter is trivial or spectacular, that is sufficient to require a rethinking of the conventional model. I agree with Ehrenwald (1972) that there is no great point in an elaborate classification of singularities into telepathy, precognition, psychokinesis, veridical apparitions and *hoc genus omne*; they all represent "a syndrome of spatial, termporal and acausal anomalies which are basically interconnected and interchangeable" (Ehrenwald 1972). From the viewpoint of our argument, this will do, at least until we consider what general model would rationally accept such a category. This is the object of studying them, not to goggle at or wallow in the mysterious, for even if they contradict Helmholtz they are, as Hippocrates said of epilepsy, "no more divine or occult than any other natural process." Where they are potentially important is in revising our concept of the ramifications of mind. The universe will be as it is, whether we like it or not.

I cannot, accordingly, answer the question asked in the title of this chapter—or rather, its first part. For the reasons given above, I generally prefer the anecdotal and the psychiatric evidence to the supposedly experimental. The history of card-guessing experiments and the record of séance-type spiritism are evidentially confused in the extreme; they might eventually make sense if one knew what was going on. On the other hand, if one considers, say Ullmann's experiments in the induction of veridical dreams (1966), the experiments seem at least as acceptable as most of those published in biology. One could hypothesize that the experimenters are pathological liars and the subjects engaged in concerted mystification, but this seems rather a paranoid than an economical hypothesis, and the main motivation for so extreme a judgment—that such phenomena are incompatible with the proven rules of a know world model—seems to be illicit. Since the reality of such results is critical, however, one would like (as with many odd findings reported in biology or even physics) to have been present to see what exactly went on, in case some important consideration had been overlooked.

Unfortunately the general run of singularities, even if we swallow the parapsychological literature whole, does not really do more than call von Helmholz into question. Old-time spiritists like Upton Sinclair used to talk about "mental radio," and it might be that epiphenomenal minds simply had physical properties we did not yet appreciate. One could very well read the more modern version of brain plus physics in precisely this way, especially in regard to the acceptance of probabilistic or wave-function inputs. In that case a suitably complex demonic computer might be able to play similar magic tricks. A telepathic or precognitive computer would at least be reassuring to traditionalists, in that it would set the world model back in the mainstream of scientific ideology. Rather as particle physics and the examination of the limits of the holographic brain model are test cases for phenomena and for field theory, the test case for mind as primary or secondary explicate turns on anything resembling discarnate—rather than apparently nonlocal—intelligence. Subjective effects such as autoscopy and 'astral projection', which are common during near-death experiences or, it appears, nitrous oxide anesthesia, as well as in traditional mysticisms, probably have more to do with body image manipulation plus one of the 'minor' singularities than with genuine "brainless perception." They are compatible with a transduced instead of a generated consciousness, but certainly do not prove it. Nor do veridical apparitions, since they have to be seen by somebody.

Having waded in so far, one must point out that the only widely reported singularity which could, if true, throw some light on the question of transduction is 'past-life' reminiscence. This reported experience, which is nontraditional in our culture but part of the accepted world model of many others, is also about the only human religious intuition which might be experimentally verifiable. If I were to encounter the purported ghost of my father, with or without the intervention of a medium, the most it could establish would be the occurrence of a singularity—most likely located in my own head. On the other hand, if I were to encounter a colorable reincarnation of my father, there would be no doubt as to the site of the singularity or the transductive character of the mind-brain relation. Before dismissing this possibility as utter lunacy, we need to form an impression of the purported *jatismara*, or reminiscent, in Oriental tradition. It is not a Californian who has been hypnotized by an enthusiast and recalls his career as Henry VIII, but a two to five year old child who suddenly refers to past possessions, his children, the topography of a place he has never visited, and who describes the circumstances of his decease. He then proceeds to disconcert his family by accurate recognition of 'former' relatives, and by adopting an adult role toward them. Whether encouraged by his relatives or repressed, the reminiscent phase fades progressively as the child becomes older, though it can still be evoked. There is no "dual personality," only an assertion of memory content, which can (rarely) include an unfamiliar language. We can take this folk belief as we choose. Stevenson (1972) has painstakingly interviewed a number of *jatismaras*, including several in non-Vedic cultures. Some, in spite of conforming otherwise to pattern, recalled the purported memories of an individual who was not dead at the time of their conception or sometimes not dead at the time of their birth. In other cases, a near-death experience is reported to have been followed by what looks like a change of pilot—a very odd effect, open to conventional as well as unconventional explanations. Popular Hinduism and Buddhism regard "lives" as conventionally serial—more sophisticated empirics in those traditions are not so sure, in view of the virtual character they attribute to all human experience, including identity. Children are dangerous witnesses in any case, because we wrongly assume them to be innocents. Most serious scientists who are not adherents of one of the Vedic religions would probably be inclined to say that if *this* effect were to be demonstrated, they would pack up and go home. The exercise I suggest is not, however, that we take it at its face value, but rather that we put it to Gezumpstein for a comment from his peculiar, non-a-priori viewpoint in regard to time and nonlocality. There is something behind the logic of apparent endless regression or echo formation which makes me suspect that his reply would be either "Illogical, no expression for this" or "What did you expect?"

# 5.3

# *Anxiety Dream: A Born-Again Demon*

"Gezumpstein!!"

"Yes, Master?"

"You can't get away with that, you know."

"I detect something unusual about you. More open to demonic models. . . . Have you been drinking?"

"Certainly not. I'm asleep. And having nightmares about what you said."

"Good. I've wanted to communicate with you under these circumstances. Might be a great deal easier. More open to intuitive fit, if I understand sleep correctly, and less restricted in possible logics."

"Reincarnation is absolute rot."

"Do you want me to enter that?"

"No. I want to know what you mean about 'what did I expect?' You seemed to be taking it for true."

"Let's get this straight. I am a source of models, simply that. I haven't the slightest idea what is or isn't true. *You* tell *me* what you observe, I give you a possible model. Then it's your assignment to compare it with reality—the whole dialogue between what might be and what is, and all that. You're the scientist. I'm just a hypothetical demon. Stop making me take responsiblity for your errors. That said, you want me to give you a model for something you are satisfied experimentally is absolute rot. Sounds in character. I recall our conversation over Uncle George's ghost. This is another phenomenon which has been reported, isn't it? It's in my vocabulary: 'the serial expression of one mnemonic personality on several occasions in time'. Like at $t_n$, $t_{2n}$ . . . $t_{xn}$. *Has* it been reported?"

"Hypothesized—by Hindus and others."

"I said, reported. People saying 'this has happened to me' or 'this occurred and I observed it'?"

"Well, yes. But people will say anything if they've been taught to believe it. Or want to believe it. Or want publicity. . . ."

"So what is it this time? You can't envisage a model, or the whole story doesn't fit your preconceived model?"

"Both. Minds don't operate without brains."

"But as I read it there *were* brains, at $t_n$, $t_{2n}$ and so on."

"Minds don't transfer between brains."

"That seems a reasonable prehypothesis. Now go ahead and test it, and then come back for a model. You may not need one. You may well be right—it may be absolute rot. Goodnight."

"Gezumpstein!"

"*What*, already?""

"I can't sleep soundly until I know what you meant about what did I expect."

"I don't want to bias the investigation. If I gave you a model, you'd probably find the phenomenon, rot or not, and it will take years of reinvestigation to clear the record. Fact first, model later. Demon I may be, but I'm ethical."

"Don't keep me in suspense."

"If you want a model, do it yourself."

"Mind would have to be a *thing*. I mean, apart from brain. That's contrary to all respectable thinking—I mean about epiphenomenal mind."

"God's teeth, why do I meet these people? Are electrons and protons things?"

"Apparently not."

"Brains are made, several orders up, of electrons and protons. Are brains things?"

"For the purposes of this argument, yes."

"All right. And I don't want to start you off on a supernaturalist wild-goose chase. Five hundred to one, if your phenomenon is real, it is *not* due to a detachable Cartesian soul. No ghosts in machines. Right?"

"I feel better already."

"No, the point of my casual remark was simply that this supposed effect has the feel of recursion about it. At the lowest level it could just be an archetype—echoes going round and round inside your head so you think you've seen them before. Recursive paramnesia."

"Some of them give very plausible details."

"Well, those might accumulate. A kind of psychosnowball. Déjà-vu plus."

"Including things they couldn't possibly have known?"

"Like what was going to win the Derby?"

"Like who wasted them the last time around. Like another language. That would be proof positive."

"It wouldn't be proof positive. You can't prove hypotheses—you can only disprove them. It would be evidence of a singularity in information transfer. Model two, paramnesia plus second sight. Incidentally, these models decline exponentially in probability. *One* should be your starting hypothesis, then, if it doesn't cover the facts, try *two*."

"I'm greatly relieved."

"But you've started me calculating. Wait a minute while I inflate this balloon. These transductions from recursion into 4-space grow on one. Suppose you had sidebands?"

"Sideburns?"

"No, *sidebands*."

"Like a radio station?"

"Probably more like a rainbow. That's an epiphenomenon—it depends on water droplets. No droplets, finish rainbow. But it has periodic patterns of sidebands on each side. Not always intense enough to see. They fall off sharply in brightness. Am I scaring you?"

"No. It's perfectly O.K. to *dream* this kind of thing. The rule is that in dreams, anything goes."

"Which is why mathematicians make such a big use of them. They loosen you up. I mean, it's a *pretty* model. Now, am I allowed to separate the sidebands in time, or is that not cricket in your world?"

"It's not, but go on. I said, in a dream anything goes."

"So one-half are symmetrically prospective. But because of your odd perception of time, you've got effectively a single-sideband receiver. So you superimpose them on the retrospective. That intensifies them. If they're in phase, of course."

"Gezumpstein, you'd make a terrific quack. In California you'd be a guru."

"I take your point. That's enough of that, it might go to your head. One last shot. I see the *whole* plenum as recursive. Follow?"

"No, but I can get the feel of it. A plenum *has* to be recursive by definition."

"You'll make a demon yet. That was the real point of my remark."

"That's wild."

"And acceptable when you're asleep, or half asleep. I only wanted to steer you off the sharp place, utter rot or Cartesian immortal soul, just in case you were to get some confirmatory evidence. Now go back to sub-REM sleep, forget all about this, and wake up rigidly scientific. You've heard what might be. Now for Pete's sake, if it interests you, find out what is. And don't jump to conclusions. *Nullius in verba*. Not even mine. Goodnight. . . . By the way, *is* there any evidence of a fixed periodicity?"

"No, not really. About 3 years before they bob up again, in the Vedic countries. Much longer in the West."

"A suggestion. Don't think about a string of beads, think about a spiral spring with a line drawn up it by a paintbrush."

"So if one travels along the *wire*, one encounters a paintspot at each turn?"

"Right, and the 'lives' would be elements of a superposition."

"If the helix is regular, the intervals ought to be fixed."

"May be some gaps in the record. Have you allowed for constant birth-to-birth intervals? Are they multiples of anything? Fibonacci intervals? My God, now you've got *me* doing it. I was starting to think about factual evidence. Back to models. But get me a large sample of reported intervals. Maybe we can identify the series basis. . . . No. I'm going to break off these interviews."

"Please don't, Gezumpstein. I'm coming to depend . . ."

"And so am I. Transference and countertransference. I shall end up as a born-again demon. It's bad for both of us, I'm sure. You get crazy notions, I start bothering about empirical observations in a 4-space."

"You could try my expedient."

"What's that?"

"Only talk to me when you're asleep. Then, as we agreed, anything goes—primary process thinking, archetypes, the lot."

"Capital idea! I'll try it. How do I start?"

"Count sheep."

"No sheep. I'll count prime numbers. Starting . . . now."

# Chapter 6

# *PATTERNS AND ARCHETYPES*

# The Peculiar Statements Made by Dreams

> The collective unconscious is simply the psychic expression of the identity of brain structure irrespective of all racial differences.
> This explains the analogy, sometimes even identity between the various myth motifs and symbols, and the possibility of human communication in general.
>
> C.G. Jung, *Alchemical Studies*

Scientific readers who have got this far will long since have detected that they were being provoked—and not only by Gezumpstein and his balloons. Having started in the darker regions of physics, I have introduced topics like parapsychology, which provoke knee jerks, and models involving non-epiphenomenal mind, so as to open up the whole subject of world models—including the way that prosaic experiences might conceivably upset them. The apparent motion of the Sun is, after all, a prosaic experience of this kind, as are Kepler's tides, which so annoyed Galileo. (To avoid a malpractice suit, I might as well say here that I have no idea whether paranormal phenomena exist or not, or whether mind is other than epiphenomenal. In my personal book, odds on either stand accordingly at about evens, giving three to one against either double, assuming no correlation.)

We have, however, looked at world models in a rather different light from that which is customary in science courses, and we have to take that process one stage further. Models we have so far examined have been Agassi's "metaphysical agendas" (kosher), and mathematical structures either in the brain or in 'reality' (also kosher, or at least pareve). In the next section we have to deal with a different demon, who has already been introduced, and who is scientifically trayf,—not Gezumpstein but Carl Jung. His contribution belongs also to demonics as I have defined it, in that it represents a contrast to Kantian a priori worlds, but it differs widely from Gezumpstein's. For a start, the world it addresses *is* a priori, but in a totally different way: a priori like 4-space, and internal to the brain, like optical transformation, but inexplicit because unconscious. It is also—unlike Gezumpstein's, which resembles recreational mathematics—highly familiar, and highly configured. You may well, as I do, disagree violently on occasion with Jung about the significance and interrelation of the objects in his museum. But it is extremely hard to deny that the objects are there if one reads the mythology, poetry and other non-scientific creations of humans, or for that matter, the history of pre-scientific science in Europe.

Are they important, or are they simply antiques, as we usually assume in handling alchemy, Paracelsus, the Pythagoreans, or religio-magical mythology? We have to examine the area in which they belong—that which Medawar correctly calls poetry in contrast to science. Science is a device for keeping these creations out of empirical reality models, and in this way it has succeeded in discovering practical hypotheses for investigation. At the same time, these creations exist at the level where Whewell, Popper and Medawar locate the primary process of innovation. They represent the cooks in the kitchen. Science is the gatekeeper whose task is to prevent the kitchen staff from entering the restaurant and see that the waiters do not smuggle out comestibles for private sale. Throughout the history of European science prior to ca. 1700, the interplay of these mental objects with reality models was explicit and to us, confusing. On one hand, Paracelsus talks sense about empirical medicine (better sense than his contemporaries); on the other, he conducts extensive discussion of magic and demonology, with real, not mathematical demons in mind. By the expedient of not reading it, most of us eliminate gnosticism and alchemy from our intellectual ancestry root and branch, as an unfortunate and eminently forgettable aberration. Why bother? They did no sensible experiments and knew no better.

That is, indeed, the simplistic reading of the history of science, but it does not wholly accord with the record. Certainly there was a bifurcation and I would mark it by the founding of the Royal Society. It did not represent the sudden discovery, however, of the control experiment, the hypothesis, and Popper's laws of scientific logic, although that in effect was the direction in which science moved—toward positivism and for a while toward mechanism. What it did represent, however was a turning away from preoccupation with the mental models which provide the prime resource of originality, the lightning-like perceptions of what might be the case, and toward the discipline of comparing them with what is. Prior to that, with practical and some philosophical exceptions, intellectual preoccupation was wholly with models. Science was what enabled them to become agendas. But how about those mental models? Obviously in doing science, we reach among them for patterns of relationship which we can apply to practical matters: Mendeleev thought of the periodic classification of elements while listening to music; Poincaré, Ramanujan, and Gauss all claimed to have seen mathematical solutions in dreams. Now the philosophy of science in its modern sense (and I am talking here not about J. S. Mill, who to my mind misrepresented how scientific work is actually done, but about Whewell, Popper, Medawar and other writers who describe it truthfully) deals with the conversion of a story, model, intuition, or inspiration into an agenda for research, thence to a hypothesis (one or more of them), and thence to a large amount of hard work in determining what observable consequences would flow from the hypothesis, and finally, to devising ways of finding out if those consequences are in fact true. If not, the hypothesis was wrong.

Now, not all science is inspirational; a lot of it is limited to routine hard work. The test cases are those which change world models, not through the more or less incidental observation of a fact which happens to kick over the existing jigsaw, but by a stroke of integrative vision. The analogy with art is obvious, and the result is esthetic. The artist may have a lot of hard work in reducing his vision to a score, an object, or poetry (I have the preconception that poetry is the least hard work of these, probably because I can neither produce visual art nor write music), but his model is his end product—he has only to reduce it to communicable form. The scientist has to go on from there and not only criticize the intuition esthetically, but see if it has demonstrable relevance to reality.

The way hypotheses are formed and tested—now that the procedure is standard, and anyone who does not conduct it properly is simply and deservedly not taken seriously—is one thing. Where originality comes from, why it is integrative, and why original models occur to some people at all is clearly another. The models themselves have a variety of contents: mathematical, as Pythagoras or Mendeleev; visual, like Kekulé's benzene ring; or a combination, like Gabor's sudden perception of the hologram, ahead of the invention of the laser which would render it practical. Looking into this, whether by comparison with art or not, would be a tall order and nothing less than the analysis of originality. In art, originality clearly has three components. One is the personal style of the artist (how that comes about is indeed something too complex to pursue). Another is a repertoire of images which are familiar—not familiar in the sense that we recognize Landseer's dogs and Stubbs' horses, but familiar in that we already incorporate them—they are, as it were, in place in our minds already, so that by manipulating them the artist is not starting from scratch. The third is an entirely anomalous inclusive logic, totally unapt to middle-order or precise statement, yet consistent. A small infusion of this demonic logic alters the frame of normal perception, or causes it to slip, but without losing coherence, and the result is originality—meaning, like Johnson's definition of wit, a happy copulation of unrelated ideas. The demonic logic is in fact perfectly familiar. It is the logic of dreams.

Originally, I started to write this book in order to discuss the origins and significance of world models with a particular group of people concerned with practical matters, namely psychiatric residents. These were young doctors trained in science, who had also read philosophy, and for whom both unconscious imagery and the idiosyncratic logic which goes with it were standard equipment, rather as the genetic code is standard equipment for molecular biologists. I would accordingly not need to point out to them that the repertoire of spontaneous imagery is patterned. Other readers, especially in the natural sciences, might not be happy to take that as given. They could very easily satisfy themselves that it is so by a reading of mythology and literature, or even—if they recall their own dreams—by introspection. The significance of the patterning is arguable, but hardly its existence. A better and more empirical test, however, is that of the Chinese-speaking Martian: from even a limited experience of listening to the spontaneous imagery of sane patients, one can make immediate sense of nonlinear literary matter from the alchemists to William Blake, which makes little discursive sense if read 'cold'. Most people find Blake's mystical poems eloquent but totally impenetrable, and he "does go on." The alchemical writers, who are the great-grandfathers of our world view, and whom Leibniz and Newton studied with great attention, sound to a modern science graduate like pompous nonsense, a kind of mimicry of discourse or a cryptogram without an obvious key. Again, why bother? Because if esthetic and symbolic intuition are patterned, they are as much a grain in intellection as are mathematical models in the nervous system: they contribute to originality by the nonrational but consistent logic which links them, and they contaminate hypothesis and 'reality' through the fact that like optical transformation, they are built-in features of the system. Now any system which can be submitted to the Martian language test is a subject for study, hypothesis, and refutation, if only to show that it is not of the Shakespeare-cypher or Biblical letter-counting type. On

PATTERNS AND ARCHETYPES 233

the other hand, if we hear a language spoken and we find we can understand it, the odds are that we are not creating it as we go along. We get the most comprehensive insight into *this* language from a munshi-sahib whose total and exasperating incompetence in the field of science is paradoxically his main asset in imparting the idiosyncratic, non-real-time logic involved, namely Carl Jung. It was he who defined metaphysics, which I have been using to mean the study of world models and research agendas, as the study of "the peculiar statements made by dreams."

Jung is a difficult person for scientists to take seriously, and not only because of his apparent incapacity in linear thinking, which is in sharp contrast to the clarity of Freud. Quite bluntly, he combines exceptional perceptivity with the style of a charlatan. One can disagree violently with Freud and condemn his entire system as unscientific, but he generates disagreement not disrespect. Jung fits into the sixteenth-century world, where much of his study lay, not only in his combination of charisma, voluminous scholarship without rigour, and his propensity for the marvellous, but also in his lack of Victorian moral fiber. Where to the unsympathetic, Freud comes over as a dogmatist, Jung—one has to say it—comes over as an extremely learned and agile dodger. One finds a medieval deviousness in his odd relationship with Freud, which oscillated between adulation and backstabbing, in his circumvagations to avoid upsetting the Church while talking volubly about 'science', in his equivocal flirtation with the Nazis, and in his self-serving but very carefully ambiguous remarks about the Aryan versus the Jewish unconscious (*Zbl. f. Psychotherapie*, Jan. 1934), in which he manages to take a swipe at his old mentor *and* stay on both sides of the fence. This questionable characteristic also appears in his 'charismatic' theatricals with credulous disciples (Progoff 1973 gives an excellent because insightless example) and the skill with which he implies, rather than states, theosophical or mysterious conclusions which would have been pinpointed and attacked if put in plain. Not wrongheaded but definitely slippery, a sceptical reader might suggest, and just the sort of person to have made it all up, Cyril Burt fashion. Indeed, in any case involving an unpopular position where there was only Jung's word for it, one would be hard pressed to buy it. Fortunately for his reputation, the documentary and the historical forms a larger part of his corpus of evidence than the conclusions he drew from practice. He was, in fact, an able, sympathetic, and intuitive psychotherapist and, in a sense, his deviousness and ambiguity fit the deviousness of the mind itself. Jung sometimes is the voluble and slightly bogus curator of a huge museum, but the objects in the museum are real, and many of the things he says about them are original to the extent that shorn of charisma, magic tricks, and the illicit introduction of religiosa by smuggling rather than by statement, Jungian analytical psychology is a continuing and valuable resource in dealing with troubled people whose troubles are likely to be improved by introspective education. While the use of Freudian models is clinically rather limited, we use Jung even when we are shocked by him.

This is a hard judgment but, I think, an inescapable one, since I am prefacing it to an argument which asks the critical scientific reader to take Jung seriously. His personal character is only a primary issue to the extent that one might query his veracity. After all, Bacon was a considerable rogue, and Heisenberg stayed in Hitler's Germany, and one could prolong the catalog of people whose intellectual performance was greater than their public example. All of us who express ideas or conduct research might hope to be judged by our work, not by our character disorders.

At first flush, it is harder to get over Jung's incapacity in science. There was no obliquity about this at all: a *scientific* charlatan would at least produce plausibly professional results. Jung simply did not comprehend either what experimental science is about nor how to go about it. In the context we are discussing, this is a point in his favor since we are not employing him as a scientific investigator but as a language teacher. We should also take his point that the search for a world model reflects a search for a model of the self—it is very probably true.

In spite of his intimacy with Einstein and Pauli, Jung had a most unfortunate tendency to shoot himself regularly in the foot when dealing with science. His notion of synchronicity contains the germ of something—possibly a brilliant mathematical intuition. He and Pauli did attempt to relate it to models in physics (Jung & Pauli 1955), but Jung tried to verify it by testing the veridical powers of astrology. This was a suicidal choice. In the first place, the mention of astrology automatically tuned most scientists out. In the second place, a positive result could not in any case have proved Jung's postulated effect: the overwhelming and quite unexcludable probability would be that if astrology worked at all, any correlation would be due to natural causes such as the effects of the season of conception. Much of Jung's psychiatric talent lay in *not* thinking like a scientist: his discoveries concern the other logics of the unconscious; moreover, his sense of public relations was nil. Freud, who had far more administrative savvy, deliberately downplayed any disturbing references to the paranormal (Clark 1980) so as not to divert attention from his main project, the institution of psychoanalysis as a respectable mode. Psychoanalysis was in enough trouble already with counterphobics, without getting into other and marginal controversies. Getting oneself believed, not coming on as a credulist and a general Charlie, is part of successful investigation. A more prudent investigator than Jung would have looked for synchronicity in some area where the result could be presented as rigorous, even if innovative, mathematics. One could then make an end run round the counterphobics by presenting it as a contribution to set theory and thereby avoid letting the patient see the needle. From astrology (where neither the results nor the supporting statistics worked) Jung went on irrepressibly to the *I Ching*. Progoff (1973) describes one of these runs, which represents the classic, Rorschach-type use of 'oracle' to start associations, in which it is the querent who 'correlates' with the oracle, Tarot, or ambiguous design, not the design which correlates with the querent.

What is happening here is that Jung, like the alchemists, had some strikingly good intuitions he could not handle. Where he is right about synchronicity, or rather recursion, is that mental processes might be patterned by the grain of nature, and our perception of the grain of nature might be patterned by our mental processes: in other words, rather than treating them as chicken and egg, we should see them as mapping into one another. This kind of synchronicity would explain very cogently the successes of the Department of Premature Intuitions, including Jung's own. In looking for world models, the observer, in Heisenberg's phrase, encounters him or herself. Archetypes are the *way* in which we form models, and one could quite possibly say that no models appear apart from them, even in mathematics. Moreover, as Pauli saw, archetypes are not themselves patterns, only tendencies-to-exist of patterns, "primary possibilities" with a range of eigenstates. We have seen *this* model before. In fact, the set of archetypes, like the set of abstractions or of models, belongs to the class of sets which are members of themselves. All creative intuitions which 'work', whether true or false, even mathematical ones, arise by shuffling this material. It is ironic that in his study of them, Jung got so many excellent hands which he was not rigorous enough to play: he had acquired by infection the oblique logic of dreams.

Where Jung is helpful is precisely in having an intuitively nonlinear mind, infuriating and tiresome to a degree if one wants hard-centered positivist theory, but attuned both to the way the nondiscursive human mind works and to the uncanniness characteristic of processes orthogonal to normal logical reality. If he discovered recursion (which must be somewhere in his voluminous writings, but I have not been able to find it as such), it is odd he did not make immense play with it. I suspect he would have even reduced it to a universal principle.

One can imagine the exasperation Jung's nonlinear mind might generate in physicists, but people do not live by physics alone, and in most of Jung's examples the construction does correspond to some pattern in human mentation which is not arbitrary. Jung is weak on biology: he writes extensively about *maṇḍalas* without noticing that they coincide with the projection of the retinae on the visual cortex (a point of some importance); he never comes to grips with the degree to which archetypes are structural engrams in the nervous system; nor does he get as far as a world model though he continually tries.

As to the archetypes and their place in a discussion of reality models, the simplest exposition is to hand the matter over to imaginary discussants.

"What exactly *is* an archetype?"

"Do you want me to define it, or show you, Socrates?"

"Both, if necessary. Start with a definition."

"I'd pick 'a preferred nonlogical—or rather, associative—pattern in human thinking'."

"Can you give me an example, Crito?"

"Male-female, sun-moon, right-left, linear-analogue, manifest-unconscious. And so on."

"So dichotomy or pairing is an archetype?"

"Not quite. Dichotomy or pairing which drags along after it a whole series of allusions and appears to order them."

"Allusions which hang together in programmed groups, even when the relationship is not logical?"

"Roughly. The archetype isn't, however, the content of the allusions, so much as the tendency to hang together. What Jung is talking about are the laws of growth of mental crystals. Anything put into one of these processes will be made over and be given repetitious form which will appear 'right' or 'natural' even if it represents no interconnection in real-time, middle-order events. Archetypes could therefore be subdefined as 'the sort of thing we have to keep out of science at all costs'."

"Not so, Crito, since we can check the validity of the pattern-intuition in each case. Symmetry is a pattern-intuition, and it has been of fundamental value. Sun and moon are not symmetrical, but right-left and dominant-nondominant are. Those appear to be the roots of the pattern. They certainly determine the human wish for a symmetrical model. A starfish would want a pentagonal model, and might find one. The same applies to quadrilateral symmetry about a central point of 'presence'—Jung's *maṇḍala*. This is a good intuitive map of self-perception—a central, virtual observer surrounded by layers of more and more differentiated experience, like a transected onion. The fourfold symmetry is represented in the retinal projection. The circular symmetry provided a series of planetary models, ending in the correct one."

"But the intuitions which link female and sinistral with Jung's anima, and treat the virtual image from dreams as something like a distinct personage, are nonrigorous and not heuristically useful."

"Except in the context to which it refers, namely, human inner shorthand. This is legible inside-language, which one does not need to translate into outside-language, say by giving literal gender to the moon, or disproving the saying that cat is the feminine of dog. The meaning is clear and the language is legible. This kind of language only accidentally informs hypotheses, but it unquestionably informs the formation of world models, because we all speak it internally, just as some of us speak English in lecturing and writing papers, and Welsh or Yiddish at home."

"How about Jung's religious intuitions? His aim in psycho-therapy is the discovery of an inner secret to which the symbols are a code, or for which they are messengers."

"Well, all religious intuitions come from this kind of source. This one, at least, is not supernatural, rather the reverse. Instead of setting up two worlds, one rational, one supernatural, it is integrative and accurately portrays the relation between many factors, such as the quest for objective world models, the quest for self-comprehension, plus the reading of internal, symbolic models, and the two other options—rational models of the mind, and subjective imaginative intuitions about the real world."

We have to recognize that Jung numinizes the unconscious, but that is partly his personal need for the numinous, and partly a reflection of working in a positivist culture with patients who were scared of their intuitive side. His assessment of its power as a source of models and its risks as a source of unreason are both quite compatible with hard science. Jung's choice of alchemy as a model was extremely apt, for alchemy represents the last attempt to compile inner and outer imagery as one continuum in handling practical matters. From then on, self-comprehension becomes one project, and the production of an empirically substantiable world model another. The alchemical metaphor is the hatching of a two-headed bird wearing one 'practical' and one inner or 'spiritual' crown. What *is* interesting is that after great advances in the activity and loquacity of the practical head, it now appears that the objective model is itself highly subjective even if it is rigorous. Evaluating such models involves self-comprehension, albeit not only or mainly of the introspective or gnostic type. One might treat the human compulsion to produce models, which go beyond techniques and local maps, as an archetypal activity. It certainly governs all model-formation, whether treated as an agenda for verification or not. Chemistry and introspection are a single project, though not in the way the alchemists believed.

We have come to the obvious key questions which Jung did not feel strong enough (or more probably, as a fancier of mystery, preferred not) to resolve. Are archetypes neurological structures which pattern our vision of the phenomenal world? Or do they represent regularities in nature which pattern the use we make of neurological equipment? These resemble too closely investigable hypotheses to suit Jung's manner of processing. Archetypes are, of course, a mixed bag: some of them are rather obviously related, like the *maṇḍala* patterns which preoccupied him, to the wiring connected with optical transformation; others are related to cultural constructs such as gender roles; and others still to the metalanguage in which humans experience aspects of I and of That, both individually in dreams and culturally by way of iconography. As to their non-arbitrary character, archetypes are easier to observe than subatomic particles, or even badgers—if not by introspection, then by a disinterested reading of almost any culture's myths or literature. It would be rash to answer the inside-outside question categorically. In the context we are discussing, the answer could well be that they are both. If they do not fit with any grain in reality, we introduce them automatically into any reality we construct, so that whatever the model, they are there. And this was precisely the insight of the prescientific alchemists, who reified this grain as the lapis philosophorum: A principle in physical reality, a structure in the mind leading to insight, or both? Jung sensed rather than saw the relation of this sense-of-structure to physics, but the attraction of a mystical unity was so strong for him that he left it untouched. He may actually have the last laugh on us, for it could conceivably be untouchable, for the obvious reasons, and a genuine 'mystery'. The difference is that we tend to view irresolvables with irritation rather than with satisfying awe.

Whatever Jung may have wanted to believe, archetypes are not magical: magic is archetypal thinking consumed (or applied) neat. Both the contents of 'psychosnowballs' and the way they are formed out of many elements—brain structure, shared human individuative experience, culturally transmitted material, and universal human-shaped intuition—can be detected and set out in plain, like the allusions in *Finnegan* or in Coleridge's poems (both of which reflect and include such material, which is why they work as literature). Jung thought this "group unconscious" was patterned by external or general reality and part of a universal grain. Unfortunately (we are familiar with this problem by now), it is equally likely that human perception and construction of reality invincibly pattern the reality which is seen or constructed, whether by intuition or scientific method. The circularity may be fundamentally irresolvable or meaningless since reality in the philosopher's sense of 'all that is the case' is undetachable from a percipient. This is not the same as saying that there is nothing but mind—only that there are no concepts of reality apart from mind. By having its tail in its mouth the archetypal alchemical snake is not prevented from also having the last word. The pursuit of world models has not ceased to be a journey in the Jungian sense— it is like the magical journeys of legend, which, for reasons not fully clear to us, it behoves us to take.

# 6.2

---

# A Psychiatric Session

"Good morning, Adam."

"Good morning, Lord. I am back, with the perennial question."

"So I see. Before we go into that, and I give you the perennial answer, may I ask why you're back so soon? We agreed to hold these sessions every five centuries. The last one was only two centuries ago."

"I called for the appointment, Lord."

"I know. And you got it."

"If it's inconvenient . . ."

"Goodness, no. I am always here. But before we answer any questions, we should analyze a little the reason you have asked for more frequent sessions. Perhaps your circumstances have changed?"

"I feel it's been a time of very great change, Lord. Particularly the last century."

"What in particular do you feel to have changed?"

"Everything. Including my dreams. I've done as you said and concentrated on recording them."

"Excellent. We shall come to that in a minute. Perhaps in view of the fact that you feel this change in yourself, the interpretation I gave you last time—the reason why you are excluded from the Garden— no longer satisfies you."

"Precisely."

"In what way is it now unsatisfying?"

"With respect, Lord, I simply don't believe it."

"Throughout our discussions I have emphasized that concerning interpretations, there is nothing fixed about them. That is to say, our experiences do not have only one meaning. The same experience can have different meaning at different times. So what I am hearing is

240

that you have outgrown that interpretation. That is in itself a sign of progress."

"I'm glad you think so, Lord. I was afraid you'd be angry."

"I think here you are projecting your feelings. Is it possible that you are angry with the interpretation I gave? That you think it childish, perhaps?"

"I do."

"And you *are* angry?"

"Yes."

"At what in particular was your anger directed?"

"At this rubbish you've been handing me. It's a different excuse every time. First it was a mystical Fall which you half-engineered so that you could redeem me and I'd be grateful. Then it was because I'd discovered sex."

"I do not think I gave that interpretation. If I recall, I *gave* you sexuality. Try to recall accurately the interpretation from which the anger against me springs."

"There was the session when I never was in the garden at all. Eve and I only imagined it."

"That was last time. Now these interpretations interest me, because they are not the interpretations I gave. I have consistently given you the same interpretation, and you yourself have reinterpreted it. I am going to give it you once more, because I think you have worked through those other positions and are ready for it. But if we are to be sure of this, I think we should first examine your most recent dream."

"You want it now?"

"Now."

"I was in Grand Central station, with a huge party of people. We were going on holiday. I think it was to the Caribbean. It was an immensely efficient station, which not only had trains leaving it, but manufactured the trains. They were coming up half-formed out of tunnels, taking on passengers, and leaving."

"Go on . . . The trains. What were they like?"

"Not like trains. When they left, they turned into aeroplanes."

"You mean, the station was also an airport?"

"Sort of. Yes, there was an airport counter. I was trying to purchase a ticket . . ."

"You broke off. Tell me what you were feeling then."

"It was perfectly horrible."

"In what way was it horrible? You will remember, surely, in what way it was horrible."

"There were no tickets."

"You mean, there was no room for you?"

"No. There *were* no tickets. Instead . . ."

"Instead?"

"The passengers were suspended on hooks. And it was snowing."

"Go on."

"I can't recall it."

"I think I can help you. What else blows about like snow? Do you think that the snow could have been feathers? I think the image of living things suspended from a conveyor may have come to you from a broiler factory. Is my guess right?"

"Yes. All those holidaymakers were broiler fowls."

"Were they slaughtered? Was that what was horrible?"

"Yes. But there was no blood in the dream. Simply . . . that all the departures crashed."

"And you were . . ."

"Horribly frightened."

"But in the position of having to go on? Because there was a line, and one doesn't panic and make a fuss at an airport, even if one has premonitions of disaster?"

"Yes."

"So this was a terrible experience. I think we have said before that it is not harmful during these sessions to show strong emotion. The Kleenex is on the garden gate. When you feel better, it will be necessary to hear the rest of the dream. I think I can predict that the plane did *not* crash, and you did *not* die. That very rarely occurs in dreams. What did occur? Did you wake? Well, what is the last feature of the dream that you remember?"

"There was a stewardess. I remember her distinctly. She was assuring me that it was perfectly all right."

"And?"

"She didn't look like a stewardess. No uniform, more like a nightdress. And—this is idiotic—she was leading a little unicorn."

"What did that suggest to you?"

"Well, it was the airline logo. Except that the logo was more like a horse with wings."

"Pegasus, in other words."

"That's the name."

"Did she say anything?"

"She said 'There's absolutely no danger if you can fly. The instructions are in your wallet.' And she told me—I don't recall the words—that the plane would appear to self-destruct, but I could easily get to the Garden State. That's Florida."

"New Jersey."

"You're kidding, Lord."

"No, I assure you. It is New Jersey. And that was all? Were you suspended on the conveyor and did you board the plane?"

"No. The stewardess took me down a spiral staircase to get a view of the flights taking off, because she said if I could see the takeoffs from a different angle I would lose my fear of flying."

"*Down* a staircase to get a better view?"

"Yes. But there were two policemen at the bottom, and we never reached any kind of outlet. That's all."

"Well, it's a very explicit dream. I see why you are dissatisfied with the past interpretation I gave you. The change in your position is real, and it means that we can talk far more openly. Let me interpret. You, Adam, are in an entirely different universe from the one you were describing at our last session. It's a hedonistic place—you were with a crowd of holidaymakers—but it is also mechanistic. It produces trains which turn into aircraft and the aircraft self-destruct. That's a very accurate symbol of entropy. And you and the rest of the inhabitants are on a conveyor belt, like broiler fowl, which has inevitable death at the end of it. But it is unseemly to question this process, and in any event useless. So the gist of the dream is existential anxiety. Do you agree?"

"Well, what do you expect? It's an accurate picture of the world."

"You wouldn't have said that at our last session."

"At our last session I didn't realize it."

"Though the idea that the world might be such a place was already forming in your mind. You dealt with it then by declining to accept it as true. I recall a previous dream in which you were in a sinking boat, and I came down in a whirlwind and carried you up to heaven. No whirlwind this time, and no last-minute rescue. Let us concentrate on the stewardess, however."

"She reminded me a bit of Eve."

"Who got you in this fix, you told me. Never mind. It is more accurate to say that Eve reminds you of the stewardess. They are one person. Both are appearances of your anima, your intuitive, nonhard-headed self. This one's very typical—flowing robes like a priestess, which you took for a nightdress. And she even has a lunar animal with her. I think this is a valuable development, even if the dream has a lot of shadow and death images in it. When your intuitive self surfaces like this and talks to you, it's an excellent idea to listen to what she says."

"Sounded irrational, like most dreams, Lord."

"But it had a sensible logic like most dreams, Adam. Let us examine what she said. First, that you yourself could fly, which means that your anxiety over the doomed aircraft flights was unnecessary. Second, that you had the instructions for doing this in your wallet. In other words, they were next to your heart, the seat of emotion in mythology, and therefore in dreams. But at that moment you couldn't see them. Third, she said that you entirely misconceive what was going on, and that if you looked at it from a different place you would see that. Fourth, the different place was not a viewing gallery but a cave or cellar, because you had to go down or in to get to it, not up or out."

"So the viewpoint is a shrine and I'd better return to supernatural religion."

"Caves can be shrines, but I don't think your anima was taking you to worship me. The anima is also the goddess of the underworld, and that, as we've already seen in several previous dreams, is the unconscious. So, far from telling you to go back to your old denial mythology in dealing with existential anxiety, she was telling you that the anxiety results from your present viewpoint. If you followed the instructions which we put in your nondiscursive mind, you could fly. In other words, your anxieties would be seen as unreal. You would be a living bird, not a dead broiler. This, to my mind, is the most important dream you have had. I notice, however, that you did not reach the bottom of the staircase. Who, I wonder, are the two policemen who turned you back?"

"Well, you, obviously, Lord."

"The Lord or the analyst is the great turner-back, the great closer of doors. So I must be the police. Both of them. Did they say so?"

"No. They simply said 'You can't come down here. Be reasonable. You know it isn't permitted.'"

"It is not I, you see, who forbids access to the unconscious. It is more likely the need to be reasonable. Faced with which, the anima couldn't be of much more help to you. That squares. Well, I think my intuition was correct. You have put aside childish things. Go ahead and ask your perennial question."

"WHY CAN'T I COME BACK INSIDE THE GARDEN? Excuses about that damn fruit we ate won't do. I want the truth at last."

"And I will give it you, as I have before, but this time I don't think you will distort it. You *are* in the Garden. Nobody ejected you from it. Certainly not I. But we constructed you very carefully, with a great deal of circuitry to spare, and the circuitry itself carried with it the option of using it. It has two quite different logics, in fact. It also carried a built-in option of choice, and under its own program it selected the second of these logics, the desire to know objectively. Do you follow?"

"How about that apple?"

"Well, it symbolizes the choice the system made. In your Genesis dream you heard me specifically warn you of the effects it would have."

"You said I would die if I ate it."

"I actually said that if you ate it you would have the experience of dying. Which is precisely what you described in your most recent dream. You would also acquire some potentials which I didn't fully anticipate because they represent a viewpoint which is entirely private to you. Which is what I meant when I told you many sessions ago that your thoughts are not my thoughts. Do you recall in the Genesis dream that you heard someone say 'You will be as gods?' I didn't create your universe, you know, you did. And that involved de-creating the rather undemanding Garden I put you in. For a start, you actually created an entirely new dimension, namely time, which I still have difficulty in empathizing at all. My creations only proceed by days in your dreams. If you create an universe in which you see events serially, and I have to keep five-hundred-year appointments with you, I can imagine it *would* be intensely disturbing."

"DO I GET BACK IN THE GARDEN OR NOT?"

"How do you get back when you are in the place already, but have reshaped it? Especially when you have elected to live in a learning-knowledge-analysis system which is based on not being able to disobserve? You have completely taken over, Adam. At this point, the analyst has to confess that even an analyst cannot be of much help because there is no way that I, even though omniscient, could share your viewpoint. It would be like asking a computer to share your sense of personal identity."

"The going teaching was that you *are* personal. And that you tried my viewpoint once. And had an existential nightmare yourself."

"Now you're being personal. I have to remind you that we are here to discuss your experiences rather than mine."

"Are you seriously suggesting, Lord, that there is no universe, and I invented it?"

"On the contrary, I created a recursive infinity of universes and you, as a result of eating an apple, picked one of them. I think you're a good enough mathematician to see that if you collapse the wave function like that, you're committed, as it were."

"Here we go again. It was a sinful act, and so . . ."

"On the contrary, that is *your* interpretation. It was a highly creative act, in that you, by your choice, constructed a world view I never intended and can't myself empathize. In dealing with it I have to be guided entirely by your description of how it is experienced."

"So what happens next?"

"We should continue to work with this, not in the abstract, but from the position you have reached. In this I can't be of instant help. Remember, I am not a magician. The stewardess in the nightshirt is a more likely source of instruction, I think. But in view of the striking progress we have made, I can probably predict that by our next session your position will have changed. It will change according to your own inner logic. It has to, since it is your experience we are discussing. Your intuition is good, in that you came to see me earlier than we arranged. That was most fortunate. Now our time is nearly up, and one can't digest too much in a single session. I am going to suggest that you make the next appointment in one hundred years only, not five."

"You want me to give up science, which has put me where I am, and believe a lot of bosh? I should be a mystic and die happy? I'd sooner stay a rational broiler fowl."

"Quite the contrary. In your place, instead of believing bosh, which you have learned by experience is a very poor expedient, and which you have entirely outgrown, I would suggest that you continue to follow the logic of the world you have created. You have learned the proper way to do this now. You should do it even more rigorously. It will not be easy, because it is never easy to avoid making concessions to anxiety and credulity. You may, however, find that your anima was correct, that the airplane will prove unreliable, but without leaving the world in which airplanes are useful, you are also able, quite rationally, to fly. I mean by this that within the terms of the rigorous rules you have set for yourself, you might arrive at another viewpoint from which the broiler fowl situation is seen to be a misconception. If indeed you were to go back now to defenses and denial, mysticism, credulity, holding séances, or believing bosh, we shall suffer a great reverse and have to work through all of this again. Now I will offer a prediction of your next dream and write it down. Next time, we will see if I am at all correct. I wish you very well. Please close the gate as you leave."

(She makes a note: "In the next dream, will the policemen escort the analysand to a point from which his mental constructions are seen *ab extra*? To come back 2083.")

# AFTERWORD

She may, indeed, be correct.

Whether we like Jung or not, one of his points strikes home. The pursuit of a world model has a quality of intensity about it which does seem to go beyond simple curiosity and becomes a mental necessity. One is tempted to ask, "Why is it so important to you to have an inclusive understanding of matters like cosmology, which neither produce pharmaceuticals or help the crops?" One knows the standard answer, that science is indivisible, but one also knows that the quest is determined from inside. Quests of obligation, from Gilgamesh's search for the herb of immortality to the pursuit of the Grail, have a large place in human imagery. The quest itself is an archetype, and the underlying journey is to find out, not so much "What are those?" as "Who am I?" Quests like this have phases, and they sometimes give rise to the greatest inner conflict at moments when substantial success seems to have been achieved. One sees this in the self-comprehension-seeking patients and in experiential mystics: the appearance of the Shadow, the nigredo, generally indicates that a system break into a new order of discourse is about to occur. This is the Lord's interpretation of Adam's anxiety dream.

I have avoided getting sidetracked here into argument over the general standing of psychoanalysis as model or as unverified hypothesis, because I wanted to use Jung simply as a translator of an unfamiliar language and its attendant odd logic. It would be fun to write not a study of the scientific problems of psychoanalysis, but of the unconscious motives of science. In this case, however, I doubt if there is much contention. The quest is related to inner security, to knowing who and where we are, and if the models we use acquire or are shaped by inner pattern, we have found reasonably reliable ways of keeping that influence in its place.

Obviously one cannot forecast in what direction science will move, for that depends on concrete results. Both explication models in physics and holographic models in brain, which have been among our examples here, could very well be overturned altogether by experiment or greatly modified. We are all concerned what the future world model will be, and there is impulsion behind our curiosity. Doctors and social philosophers are differently concerned, however, to see what model nonscientists will incorporate from a reading of research, theory, information, misinformation and their own anxieties. It will affect behavior and mental health.

Existential anxieties should not influence our judgment of evidence, and still less our experimental results. They do and will influence our models and agendas by focussing interest. There is no very logical reason why perceiving the I to be virtual by reason of the way it handles data should be more reassuring, or less conducive to a disturbing sense of absurdity, than perceiving the I to be virtual because it is epiphenomenal. The fact appears to be that it is blander and less disturbing, however: one would guess that the operative factor is that in that case, time is seen as virtual too. As to the idea of looking for some unitary grain or structure in the physical world, in biological processes, and in mind, this is a chronic obsession of humanity—reduction is our thing. Behind all models of this kind stalks, and will inevitably stalk, the fact that pattern is perceived by mind, and if everything is seen to bear a like pattern, the most likely site for its generation is in our spectacles. If we devise experiments to test this, in the manner of optical illusions which analyze visual perception, the analyzing mind will still quite possibly reinsert pattern somewhere. If its repertoire of transforms is limited, and its oblique or associative responses "hang together in bunches," something like that is bound to occur.

Science fiction, black holes, cosmological epics, archetypal symbols, paranormal reports, and all such matters, serious or entirely fanciful, have always excited humans. People like any good story of which the moral is that things are not as they seem, and that marvels are not dead. Such neo-legends have the additional impact today that they stand in for the inarticulacy of a physics which is not visually representable, but which suggests a more fluid range of possibilities than either the old spiritual-mechanical dyad, or the even more disturbing machine model of Victorian rationalism. But these are still the two gut models between which most contemporary people, even if educated in science, seem to choose. The substitute marvels also replace the richness of legend and folklore which used to address the unconscious; these are still around in entertainment and in more risky areas such as politics, but have been downgraded, as Max Nordau said of dancing, from an important emotional technology to a triviality.

There is no rational world model which would be wish-fulfilling, but some models pinpoint or irritate our existential malaise more than others, and *some* world model is necessary in order to live. If there is none intelligible and available, we will invent one, which will be inexplicit. Naive, nonphilosophical Buddhism is probably of all existential models the most effective as a tranquillizer: it combines a teaching based on experience that the ordinary homuncular viewpoint is virtual with the prospect of more-of-the-same via reincarnation, an almost perfect combination of analgesics, since it is ordinary samsaric experience to which we are attached. It also offers some prizes for virtue. Given the slightest signal of permission from the 'policemen' of reality-testing (even if the signals are entirely misread) a religious version could well become popular, exactly as naive Christianity did at a period of similar existential soreness and speculative chaos during the late Empire. More critical people can be influenced unawares by this attraction, and still validly use Vedic philosophies as a source of models. There the parallel ends, since conventional Christian belief does not offer models which are adaptable to research agendas; elements in that tradition which might once have done so, such as Gnosticism, came from elsewhere. Buddhism does, and moreover, if one takes it far enough, it deals nonmythologically with existential anxiety by a process of empirical self-analysis which Jung would have approved.

What science has achieved—irreversibly, one must hope—is that world models have been demythologized: they cannot incorporate any longer the demonstrably false, whether in a literal or a pickwickian sense, without losing popular credit. Moreover, even if models are fanciful, arbitrary, wrongheaded, or specious, an irresistible tide now carries them to the point at which any factual assumptions they make will eventually be subjected to verification. Since more and more cosmological, eschatological, and psychological statements are coming in the reach of testing, only wholly supernatural or wholly vacuous models are still in the fire-free zone, and even those run the risk of asserting something testable at any moment.

The question "What will be the next major world model?" really rephrases itself as "What will be the next intellectual achievement of humanity?" If we could answer it, we would already have made the achievement. It will not lie, one would imagine, in borrowings, even in borrowings out-of-context. Normally such quantum jumps make previous intellectual models look antique, and normally at the height of each intellectual model, the going opinion is that there will be no further quantum jumps. The change from scholasticism to science will be a hard one to follow; in fact, it will not be followed so much as incorporated, because any intellectual model not based, at its point of contact with reality, on science is defunct or deficient in advance. My guess would be that in some way the new model will involve the disciplined incorporation of introspection, a project which, for the reasons we have been discussing, reflects upon all observation, and which requires its own unique means of reality-testing. This is in fact something never done before: yogis and intronauts have not been verification- or hypothesis-minded; scientific empirics have worked to keep introspective and observer biases out. The synthesis will be difficult but interesting, as the alchemists guessed it might be, and the results novel. This is the candidate I favor, but one so far without a platform.

One would hope, and not only out of self-interest, that Western technological society will find an empathically acceptable world model which is both generally intelligible and existentially bland enough to give respite , remove the urgency and manic-defense pressures now felt, and afford a camping place before the ascent recommences. But of this there can be no certainty. Nor can I suggest today what that model might be tomorrow. That it will change is certain. How it will change is unknown.

> We want no dead weights on this expedition,
> no credulous Charlies and no nervous Nellies.
> Though not so hazardous as in the past
> the intellectual skulls you see down there
> all fell from this arête. So use some care—
> look out and in, don't try to go too fast
> but climb, goddamit, don't crawl on your bellies.
>
> The particle physicist and the mathematician
> I'll take. They're crazy, but they watch their feet.
> I'll take one mystic—no, not you, Ouspensky,
> nor you, Teilhard. You've got no head for heights.
> What do you say, Sherpa? Very well, we'll take
> two at the most—Eckhart and William Blake,
> and kindly watch it—no religious fights.
> We need a brain man too (he's got the map
> and the theodolite). You others, don't

for Christ's sake hold us up with poking for
the Absolute and Transcendent (you'll see plenty
of that in keeping the rope taut, eyes front)
or any other Rosicrucian crap.
People who play games on this pass
end on a slab, with parsley up their ass;
that was what put paid to those skulls down there.

Remember you've two feet—one left, one right.
Now, if you're ready, we'll leave at zero twenty—
that is, unless there are more fool suggestions.
This lower ridge is reasonably wide:
the Sherpa's name is Mi-Pham. He's our guide.
Now, get those bloody packs on. Any questions?

# APPENDIX A
# ITERANTS

Iterants are a novelty, invented originally by Kauffman and Videla (1980) to deal with the state in Spencer-Brown algebra where $a$ and not-$a$ oscillate, or appear to us alternately. I cite them here because they are a possible formalism for two aspects of a single entity which are, in our perception, mutually exclusive. This would apply to an "implicate" fish with two fins, only one of which, by reason of anatomy, could be seen above the water (could appear in our 4-space perception) at one and the same time. A binary iterant would describe a pencil put down orthogonally in Flatland. A Flatlander might have inferred that two states (point and eraser) were parts of a whole, but he could never touch more than one of them at a time so long as the whole pencil was not placed in one of his two perceptible dimensions. Iterants have a close affinity to imaginary numbers: $i$ can be considered as an iterant of $+1$ and $-1$. They are of interest here as an example of imaginary quantities in Boolean logic: two 90° complex rotations of an iterant lead to a way of characterizing parallel time-lines (fig 3). An iterant "viewed end-on" is a superposition of $a$ and not-$a$. Rotation by 90° into a second imaginary dimension separates the two states in hypertime. For those interested in playing with iterant formalisms, the mathematics is roughly as follows.

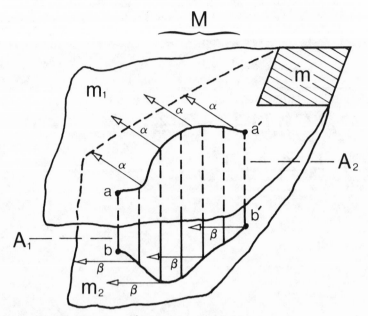

**Fig. 11** Iterant bridging two leaves of a manifold.

*Definition.* An iterant is a (non-Boolean) function having two or more coherent states which cannot simultaneously be explicated (are mutually exclusive) in any one real manifold.

Let $a = \sim b$, $b = \sim a$, $x$ be a real dimension
Then $I_2^{x,Re}$ $(a, b)$ is *trivial* if $a \cap b = \emptyset$ *(alternation).*
$I_2^{x}(a, b)$ is *nontrivial* if $a \cap b \neq \emptyset$ *(superposition)*
   and $I_2^{x}(a, b) = I_2^{x,i}(a + bi), (b + ai) = (a, b)\ I_2^{x,i}(1, -1)$

*Differentiation and integration of iterants.* The components of an iterant differentiate and integrate separately ("no crossing-over" rule).

Iterants lead to some amusing mathematical *jeux d'esprit*, apart from their rotational possibilities.

In app.fig. 1, $I_2$ by definition effects a non-Hausdorf division of the manifold m into $m_1$, $m_2$. At each transition $|a\ b|$ there is a shift of manifold. So if $a$ and $b$ are changing quantities, they integrate over $m_1$ and $m_2$ respectively. $\dfrac{\partial a}{\partial b}$ is an operation on the superposition **A** in the covering space **M** of $m_1$, $m_2$, *not* a "transition from $a$ to $b$:" $\dfrac{\partial a}{\partial b}$ $(x, Re)$ is vacuous and gives $\delta_{a,b} = 0, \infty$.

For the trace of $a$ in $m_1$, the trace of $b$ in $m_2$, and the trace of **A** in **M**, $\nabla\Phi.a$, $\nabla\Phi.b$, and $\nabla\Phi\mathbf{A}$ can be defined. **A** consists of a plane composed of all the Clifford parallels between $a \ldots a'$ and $b \ldots b'$.

The manifold $m$, $m_1$, $m_2$ in Fig. 1a is simplified to a two-leaved

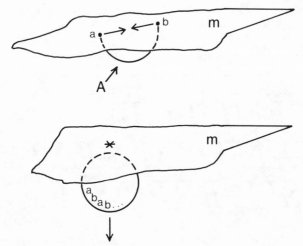

**Fig. 12** Iterant as a "wormhole" in a Hausdorf manifold.

plane: it could in fact have $p$ real and $q$ imaginary dimensions, but to accommodate **A** the order of **M** will always be $\geq p + q + 1$.

We can also consider the case (app. fig. 1 b) where $m$ is simple Hausdorf and $a$ and $b$ appear at different points in it. This is a model of "interconnectedness" between $a$ and $b$: **A** is a wormhole or loop lying outside $m$. One interesting consequence is that if **A** reverses from $I(a, b)$ to $I(b, a)$, $a$ and $b$ are transposed in $m$. If $a$ and $b$ move in $m$, $\frac{\partial a}{\partial b}$ is still an operation on **A**, though it can be read in the context of $m$; jumps and discontinuities are possible.

In the same model, we can make $a$ and $b$ approach one another in $m$: when they coincide, **A** becomes a closed loop. It can be thought of as detaching from $m$ so that $a$ and $b$ cancel out and disappear from $m$ altogether. Other paths for $a$ and $b$ in $m$ will generate twists or knots in **A**. We need to try some unconventional mathematical formulations for size, as a kit of parts for use in developing von Neumann and Birkhoff's non-Boolean, non-distributive logic ("quantum logic") which admits superpositional instead of exclusional solutions to the equation

$$x = a \cap \sim a$$

This is necessary both as a step to imagining our Gedanken "demonic computer," and as a practical algorithm for the numerous cases in physics where we find ourselves, in Boolean terms, between a rock and a hard place; "the final form of our experiential reality is affected by the interference between mutually exclusive possibilities"—or worse, mutually exclusive observations (Zukav, 1979).

# APPENDIX B
# QUANTUM STATE
# AS SUPERPOSITION

Any combination of frequencies produces a superposition as in a superhet radio, where the incoming signal is mixed with another and the output contains the two original frequencies, their sum, their difference, and the harmonics of all of these; one then filters out the fixed difference and amplifies that. Here the tuned filter "collapses" the wave-function. The problem in the case of quantum wave mechanics is that the "frequencies" represent different observations, different physical events, which are mutually incompatible in middle-order reality.

Set out in full, a quantum state $\psi$ is a superposition of some observable $a$ over the eigenstates $\phi_n$. If $a$ is measured, there is a probability $|a_n|^2$ that we shall find the system in the state $\phi_n$.

If the state actually observed is $\phi_m$, the act of observation has converted the state vector from $\psi$ to $\phi_m$—i.e., it has collapsed the wave function. Considering the density matrix $\hat{\varrho}^2$, for the mixture resulting from observation

$$\hat{\varrho}^2{}_{nm} = |a_m|^2 \, \delta_{nm}$$

this means a second observation with operator M will give

$$Tr\,(\hat{\varrho}^2 M) = \sum_n |a_n|^2 \, M_{nn'}$$

whereas if no first measurement had been made

$$Tr\,(\hat{\varrho}^2 M) = \sum_n |a_n|^2 \, M_{nn} + \sum_n \sum_{\neq m} a^*_m \, {}_n a_n M_{mn}$$

which includes "off diagonal" terms excluded by prior measurement. The act of observation has 'filtered out' the other components of the superposition.

# GLOSSARY

**ahamkara**   (Skr.) Lit., "I-making." the human sense of identity.

**algorithm**   Set of rules for solving a mathematical problem.

**Argand field**   same as *complex plane*.

**ātman**   (Skr.) The reasoning, positional, self-conscious mind.

**Bell's theorem**   Theorem in quantum mechanics, one deductive consequence of which is the Einstein-Rosen-Podolsky paradox (described on p. 15)

**boddhisattva**   (Skr., Buddha nature), an adept who has achieved the Buddhist state of enlightenment, but remains in ordinary life to enlighten others.

**centroid**   Apparent center of mass, area, gravity, etc. of a multiple system.

**coherent superposition:**   in quantum logic, a coexistence of *a* and not-*a*; "a thing-in-itself which is as distinct from its components as its components are from one another" (Zukav). Frequencies, e.g. of sound waves, combine to form a superposition. The frequency algorithms in wave-functions form similar superpositions—the logical problem arises when these components represent incompatible events under observation. Diagonally-polarized light is a superposition of vertically and horizontally polarized light but does not behave to filters in accordance with simple distributive rules. Quantum (non-distributive) logics are designed to handle this kind of situation, which has no Boolean equivalent. (See App. p. 256).

**complex plane**    A way of representing imaginary numbers graphically by taking the real numbers as one ordinate and i, 2i, 3i etc. along the other ordinate, making a grid or graph.

**creode**    The groove in an imaginary contour map along which a process of evolution or embryonic development can be considered as flowing, like a river following a valley-system.

**Democritean model**    The concept that matter is explicable as consisting of small indivisible objects and their interactions, and the impressions these cause in the observer.

**dukha**    (Skr.) Suffering, misery, seen as an inevitable result of existential misconceptions about reality.

**dvaita, advaita**    (Skr.) double, not-double. States of mind in which (1) only I and That are experienced as real, (2) I becomes merged with That in an experience of a seamless plenum.

**eigenvalue**    One of the characteristic values expressed by a state function.

**epigenesis**    In individual development, epigenetic effects are those due to environmental influences rather than to built-in programming in the cell.

**epiphenomenon**    A phenomenon which results from the behavior and organization of a complex system, but is not displayed by the isolated parts of that system.

**Everett worlds**    Separate world-lines generated in Hugh Everett's model (p. 16), in which time bifurcates at each quantum choice.

**Fourier analysis**    Reduction of a function to a superposition of frequencies.

**Grassmann algebra**    Algebra based on complex-plane rotations of a function, similar to Hamilton's quaternions, q.v.

**guṇa**    (Skr.) Quality, property.

**Hilbert space**    Technically an inner-product space where for a vector j (j.j.) = $|j|^2$. A multidimensional mathematical space over which subatomic particles can be represented by vectors (arrows).

**hyper-**    (space, cube, solid, etc.). One of higher dimensions than "ordinary" Euclidean space; thus a hypercube has four spatial dimensions, not three, and cannot be visualized.

**hypercomplex number**    see *quaternion*.

**hyperloop**    Problem of circularity if matter composes brain, brain generates mind, and matter is definable only with reference to mind. See p. 191.

**hypertime**    Time considered as having more than one dimension, e.g. breadth as well as length.

**iterant**    A way of presenting a superposition by showing its states as an alternation. A rough physical model is a bar-magnet, i.e. a single object with two opposite poles. However often we bisect it, each part will have a N and a S pole. If we shrink the magnet to a point (by viewing it end-on) what we see is a superposition of N & S. See p. 68 and appendix 254.

**jatismara** (Skr.). One who professes to recall past lives.

**jñāna** (Skr.) Knowledge. jnana-yoga is the discipline of knowledge as against devotion, gnosis etc.

**Kālī** (Skr.) The Dark Lady. In Hinduism the Goddess of Time, consort of Śiva, seen as the generator of what we experience as middle-order reality.

**karma** (Skr.) Deed, action. Real-time actions and attributes which influence our nature and future behavior.

**Kruskal-Szekeres black hole** Also Schwartzchild black hole, one with a static (nonrotating) massive center.

**Lamarckian** Derived from the inheritance of acquired characters, as opposed to the result of selection among pre-existent genes.

**Laplacian transformation** One which, roughly, turns a process into a field or contour map.

**māya** (Skr.) Phenomenal (measurable) reality—often rendered "illusion": the apparent world.

**mantra** (Skr.) A phrase or syllable repeated as a means of inducing a mental effect or state of mind. "Hail Mary" and "Om mani padme hum" are mantras.

**nairātmya** (Skr.) A state in which the ātman ceases to be experienced (see ātman).

**nāma-rūpa** (Skr.) Name and form. The attributes of "things" in common experience.

**negentropic** Tending to increasing order: the reverse of entropic.

**Pauli exclusion principle** This states that no two protons etc. can occupy the same quantum state at the same time (applies to class of particles called fermions).

**plasmagene** A gene present in the protoplasm, not in the nuclear DNA.

**quantum** One of the indivisible "packets" or steps by which transitions in particle energy etc. take place—a unit of fundamental discontinuity in subatomic processes.

**quantum logic** Non-Boolean non-distributive logic developed originally by Von Neumann and Birkhoff in which $a \cap {\sim}a \neq \emptyset$

**quaternions** Hypercomplex numbers invented by Hamilton, which involve rotations in one real and three complex dimensions. See p. 170.

**recursive** Operating on itself. Escher's picture of two hands, each of which draws the other, is a model of recursion.

**sādhana** (Skr.) Askesis, practice, trip, exercise: any discipline undertaken to achieve a particular mental or mystical experience.

**samādhi** (Skr. making even, equalization). A nairātmya (q.v.) state in which Reality is experienced as seamless and without-distinctions; aim of Hindu yogas.

**saṃsara** (Skr.) "Wandering." The Buddhist designation of the Hindu term "māya"—insightless real-world experience.

**siddhī** (Skr. success, achievement). Ability to induce singularities as a result of successful sādhana.

**state function** an expression which contains enough information about the condition and past history of a system to allow its future behavior to be computed.

**śunya** (Skr.) The Empty Plenum, the ground of reality postulated by Buddhism.

**superposition** Addition of two states to make a single "whole" or function. Sound-waves are physically additive; alternative quantum states are both present in the wave-function even though only one is observable. A superposition in logic is the condition where a and not-a are both "true."

**toroidal** Shaped like a donut.

**transformation** An algorithm (q.v.) for expressing a system in different mathematical terms. A photograph and a hologram of the same scene represent different transformations.

**transluminal** depending on faster-than-light propagation.

**Turing machine** An imaginary calculating robot, used as a model system to estimate computability.

**vectors and scalars** A scalar has quantity but not orientation; a vector has quantity and orientation. If we describe the author as age 63, 170 lb., 5.9 feet tall, 63 and 170 are scalars and 5.9 is a vector.

**virion** A virus particle, an independent self-replicating "piece of information" which can take over the machinery of a cell.

**wave function** A state function using wave-mechanics which gives the average result for every conceivable experiment on a system. Usually written $\Psi$.

# REFERENCES

Abbott, E.A. 1952. *Flatland*. New York, Dover reprint.

Agassi, J. 1964. In *The critical approach to science and philosophy*, edited by M. Bunge. London: Collier-Macmillan.

Aspect, A., Grangier P. & Rogier G. 1982 *Phys. Rev. Lett.* 49: 91. See also Quantum Mechanics passes another test. *Science* 1982 217: 435–6.

Beloff, J. 1962. *The existence of mind*. London: McGibbon & Kee.

Bergson, H. 1908. *Matière et mémoire*. Paris: Félix Alcan.

Bergson, H. 1911. *Creative evolution*. London: Macmillan.

Bergson, H. 1913. Presidential address. *Proc. Soc. Psych. Res.* 26: 462–479 1913.

Blanco, I.M. 1975. *The unconscious as infinite sets*. London: Duckworth.

Bohm, D., 1957. *Causality and chance in modern physics*. Philadelphia: Temple University Press.

———. 1971. Quantum theory as an indication of a new order in physics. Part A. The development of new orders as shown through the history of physics. *Foundations of Physics* 1:359–381.

———. 1973. Quantum theory as an indication of a new order in physics. Part B. Implicate and explicate order in physical law. *Foundations of Physics* 3: 139–160.

———. 1980. *Wholeness and the implicate order*. London: Routledge Kegan Paul.

———, and B. Hiley. 1975. On the intuitive understanding of nonlocality as implied by quantum theory. *Foundations of Physics* 5: 93–103.

———. 1982. in Wilber, K. (ed) *The holographic paradigm and other paradoxes.* Boulder: Shambhala.

Broad, W.J. 1981. Fraud and the structure of science. *Science.* 212:137–141.

de Broglie, L. 1959. In *Albert Einstein: philosopher-scientist.* Edited by P.A. Schilpp. Evanston, Ill.: Library of Living Philosophers.

Campbell, K. 1970. *Body and mind.* New York: Anchor Press.

Capra, F. 1975. *The Tao of physics.* New York: Random House.

———. 1978. Quark physics without quarks: a review of recent developments in S-matrix theory. Lawrence Berkeley Laboratory USDE LBL-7596 (preprint).

Clark, R. W. 1980. *Freud: the man and the cause.* New York: Random House.

Comfort, A. 1960. Darwin and Freud. *Lancet:* 107–111.

———. 1969. On originality and ecstasy. *Hum. Context* 1: 243–258.

———. 1979A. *I and That: notes on the biology of religion.* New York: Crown.

———. 1979B. The Cartesian observer revisited: ontological implications of the homuncular illusion. *J. Soc. Biol. Struct.* 2: 211–223.

———. 1980. Demonic models and historical in biology. *J. Soc. Biol. Struct.* 207:216.

Cooper, L.N., and D. van Vechten. In *The many-worlds interpretation of quantum mechanics.* Edited by B.S. De Witt and N. Graham. Princeton: Princeton University Press.

David-Neel, A. 1971. *Magic and mystery in Tibet.* Baltimore: Penguin Books.

Davies, R.C.W. 1974. *The physics of asymmetry.* London: Surrey University Press.

Dewdney, A. K. 1979. Exploring the planiverse. *J. recreat. Math.* 12: 16–20.

———. 1980A. *Two-dimensional science and technology.* London, Ontario: University of Western Ontario.

———. 1980B. See also [column by] M. Gardner *Sci Amer.* 6:18–31.

Dobbs, H.A.C. 1971. The dimensions of the sensible present. *Stud. Gen.* 24: 108–126.

Driesch, H. 1921. *Philosophie des Organischen.* Leipzig: Georg Thieme.

Edelman, G.M., and V. Mountcastle. 1979. *The mindful brain.* Cambridge, Massachusetts: MIT Press.

Ehrenwald, J. 1948. *Telepathy and medical psychology.* New York: Norton.

———. 1954. *New dimensions of deep analysis.* London: Allen and Unwin.

———. 1972. A neurophysiological model of psi phenomena. *J. Nerv. Ment. Dis.* 154: 406–416.

———. 1975. Cerebral localization and the psi syndrome. *J. Nerv. Ment. Dis.* 161: 393–398.

Erlich, P.R., and P.H. Raven. 1962. *Science* 137:652.

Everett, H. 1957. "Relative state" formulation of quantum mechanics. *Rev. Mod. Physics* 29: 454–462.

———. 1973. The theory of universal wave-function. In *The many-worlds interpretation of quantum mechanics.* Edited by B.S. De Witt and N. Graham. Princeton: Princeton University Press.

Farges, A. 1926. *Mystical phenomena.* London: Burns, Oates.

Feigl, H. 1967. *The mental and the physical.* University of Minnesota Press.

Fodor, J.A. 1980. The mind-body problem. *Sci. Amer.* 244: 114–123.

Fraser, J. T. 1978. Temporal levels: sociobiological aspects of a fundamental synthesis. *J. Soc. Biol. Struct.* 1: 339–356.

Frescura, F.A. M., and B. J. Hiley. 1980 The implicate order, algebras and the spinor. *Foundations of Physics* 10: 7–31.

Gardner, M. 1979. Quantum theory and quack theory. May 17, *New York Review of Books.*

Geroch, R., and G.T. Horowitz. 1979. In *General relativity: an Einstein centenary survey.* Edited by S. W. Hawking and W. Israel. Cambridge: Cambridge University Press.

Globus, G. G. 1973. Unexplained symmetries in the 'world-knot'. *Science* 180: 1129–1136.

Goedel, K. 1959. In *Albert Einstein: philosopher-scientist.* Edited by P.A. Schilpp. Evanston, Ill.: Library of Living Philosophers.

Goodwin, B. 1976. *Analytical physiology of cells and developing organisms.* London, New York: Academic Press.

———. 1978. *Theoria to Theory* 11: 247.

Gottfried, K. 1966. *Quantum Mechanics.* New York: Benjamin.

Grof, S. 1970. LSD psychotherapy and human culture. *J. Stud. Consciousness* 3: 100–187.

Halstead, B. 1980. Karl Popper—good philosophy, bad science? *New Scientist* 87, 215–217.

Hansel, C.E.M. 1966. *ESP—a scientific evaluation.* New York: Scribners.

Hawking S.W., and W. Israel 1979. *General relativity: an Einstein centenary survey.* Cambridge: Cambridge University Press.

Heisenberg, W. 1958. The representation of nature in contemporary physics. *Daedalus* 87: 95–108.

Heywood, R. 1974. *Beyond the reach of sense.* New York: E.P. Dutton.

Hiley, B.J. 1980. Towards an algebraic description of reality. *Ann. Fond. Louis de Broglie* 5:(2).

Hilgard, E. R. 1977. *Divided consciousness.* New York: John Wiley.

Hinton, C.H. 1904. *The fourth dimension.* London: Sonnenschein.

Hofstadter, D. R. 1979. *Goedel, Escher, Bach.* New York: Basic Books.

Humphreys, Christmas. 1968. in Stryk L. *The World of the Buddha.* New York: Doubleday.

Jaynes, J. 1977. *The origin of consciousness in the breakdown of the bicameral mind.* Boston: Houghton Mifflin.

Jung, C. G. 1959. *Collected Works.* Vol. 9, Part I, *The archetypes and the collective Unconscious.* New York: Pantheon.

———, and W. Pauli. 1955. *The interpretation of nature and the psyche.* New York: Pantheon.

Kammerer, P. 1919. *Das Gesetz der Serie.* Stuttgart and Berlin.

Kauffman, L.H., and F.J. Videla. 1980. Form dynamics. *J. Soc. Biol. Struct.* 3: 171–206.

Koestler, A. 1972. *The roots of coincidence.* London: Hutchinson.

———. 1974. *The heel of Achilles: Essays 1968–1973.* London: Hutchinson.

Leibniz, G.W. (1914). Monadologie *in* Opera philosophica 19 vols. 1843–90. Leipzig: Pertz & Gerhardt.

LeShan, L. 1969. Physicists and mystics: similarities in world view. *J. Transpers. Psychol.* 1: 1–20.

Lindley, J. 1846. *The vegetable kingdom.* London: Bradbury and Evans.

Mach, E. 1976. In *The world of mathematics*, edited by J.R. Newman. New York: Simon and Schuster.

*Majjhimanikāya.* In Stryk L. 1968. *The world of the Buddha.* New York: Doubleday.

Maynard Smith, J. 1970. *J. Stud. Gen.* 23: 266.

Medawar, P.B. 1942. Discussion of growth and new growth. *Proc. Roy. Soc. Med. 35:* 500.

———. 1967. *The art of the soluble.* London: Methuen.

Meredith, P. 1972. The psychophysical structure of temporal information. In *The study of time.* Edited by J.T. Fraser, F.C. Haber and G.H. Muller. Berlin: Springer Verlag.

Misner, C.W., K.S. Thorne and J.A. Wheeler. 1973. *Gravitation.* San Francisco: Freeman.

Morowitz, H. J. 1980. Rediscovering the mind. *Psychology Today* 14; 12–17.

Nāgasena, 1963. *The Questions of the mind.* Translated by Rhys Davids. London: Dodle Books.

Nash, C. 1978. *Relativistic quantum fields.* London: Academic Press.

Needham, J. 1956. *Science and civilization in China.* Cambridge: Cambridge University Press.

Ouspensky, P. D. 1931. *The new model of universe.* New York: Knopf.

Pahnke, W.N. 1969. The psychedelic mystical experience in human encounter with death. *Harvard Theol. Rev.* 62: 1.

———, and W.A. Richards. 1966. Implications of LSD and experimental mysticism. *J. Relig. Hlth.* 5: 175–208.

Park, D. 1972. The myth of the passage of time. In *The study of time.* Edited by J.T. Fraser, F.C. Haber and G.H. Muller. Berlin: Springer Verlag.

Pattee, H.H. 1978. The complementarity principles in biological and social structures. *J. Soc. Biol. Struct.* 1: 191–200.

———. 1979. In *A question of physics.* Edited by P. Buckley and F.D. Peat. London: Routledge Kegan Paul.

Penrose, R. 1978. In *An encyclopedia of ignorance.* Edited by R. Duncan and M. Weston-Smith. New York: Wallaby Books (Pocket Books).

———. 1979. In *General relativity: an Einstein centenary survey.* Edited by S.W. Hawking and W. Israel. Cambridge: Cambridge University Press.

Popper, K. R. 1934. *Logik der Forschung.* Vienna: Julius Springer.

———. 1959. *The logic of scientific discovery.* London: Hutchinson.

———. 1974. *Unended quest.* Evanston, Ill.: Library of Living Philosophers.

Post, H. 1963. Individuality and physics. *Listener*, 10 November 1963.

Pribram, K.H. 1979. Behaviorism, phenomenology and holism in psychology: a scientific analysis. *J. Soc. Biol. Struct.* 2: 65–71.

———, M. Nuwer and R. Baron. 1974. The holographic hypothesis of memory structure in brain function and perception. In *Contemporary developments in mathematical psychology.* Edited by R.C. Atkinson, et. al., San Francisco: Freeman.

Progoff, I. 1973. *Jung, synchronicity and human destiny.* New York: Julian Press.

Rao, K. R. 1966. *Experimental parapsychology.* Springfield: Thomas.

Reichenbach M. and R.A. Mathers. 1959. In J.E. Birren, *Handbook of aging and the individual.* Chicago: University of Chicago Press.

Rucker, R. 1977. *Geometry, relativity and the fourth dimension.* New York: Dover.

Ryle, G. 1962. *The concept of mind.* New York: Barnes and Noble.

Schmeidler, G. R. and R.A. McConnell. 1958. *ESP and personality patterns.* London: Oxford University Press.

Schroedinger, E. 1964. *My view of the world.* Cambridge: Cambridge University Press.

Sheldrake, R. 1981. *A new science of life: The hypothesis of formative causation.* London: Blow & Briggs.

Sidgwick H. 1894. Report on the census of hallucinations. *Proc. Soc. Psychic Res.* 10: 25–426.

Spencer Brown, G. 1957. *Probability and scientific inference.* London.

———. 1972. *Laws of Form.* New York: Julian Press.

Spinelli, D.N. 1970. In *The biology of memory.* Edited by K.H. Pribram and D. Broadbent. New York: Academic Press.

Spurway, H. 1954. In *Proc. 11th Ornithol. Congress,* Basel: 340.

Stapp, H.P. 1971. S-matrix interpretation of quantum theory. *Phys. Rev.* D3: 1303.

———. 1977. Are superluminal connections necessary? *Nuovo Cimento* 40B: 191.

Stevenson, I. 1972. *Twenty cases suggestive of reincarnation.* Charlottesville: University of Virginia Press.

Symons, D. 1979. *The evolution of human sexuality.* Oxford: Oxford University Press.

Tarthang T. 1980. *Time, space and knowledge.* Berkeley: Dharma Publishing.

Tipler, F. 1974. *Phys. Rev.* D 9: 2203–2219.

Ullmann, M. 1966. An experimental approach to dreams and telepathy. *Arch. Gen. Psychiat.* 14: 605–613.

———. 1975. In *Comprehensive Textbook of Psychiatry.* Edited by A.M. Freedman, H.I. Kaplan, and B.J. Sadock. Baltimore: Williams and Wilkins.

von Weiszäcker, C.F. 1979. In *A question of physics.* Edited by P. Buckley and F.D. Peat. London: Routledge.

Waddington, C.H. 1957. *The strategy of the genes.* London: Allen and Unwin.

West, D.J. 1948. A mass-observation questionnaire on hallucinations. *J. Soc. Psychic Res.* 34: 187–196.

Wheeler, J. A. and R. P. Feynman. 1945. *Rev. Mod. Phys.* 17: 157.

Whewell, W. 1840. *The philosophy of the inductive sciences.* London.

Wigner, E. P. 1979. *Symmetries and reflections.* Woodbridge: Ox Bow Press.

Wilber, Ken, ed. 1982. *The holographic paradigm and other paradoxes.* Boulder: Shambhala.

Yalom, I. D. 1980. *Existential psychiatry.* New York: Basic Books.

Yates, F.A. 1972. *The Rosicrucian enlightenment.* Boulder: Shambhala.

Zimmer, H. 1946. Bollingen Series. Vol. 6. *Myths and symbols in Indian art and civilization.* Princeton: Princeton University Press.

Zukav, G. 1979. *The dancing Wu Li masters.* New York: Morrow.

# INDEX

0 0 4 6 5 2 2

REALITY    AND  EMPATHY
PHYSICS      MIND

COMFORT